THE  TIMES

good university guide 1999

About the authors

John O'Leary is Education Editor of *The Times*. He joined the paper in 1990 as Higher Education Correspondent and assumed responsibility for the whole range of education coverage in 1992. Previously the deputy editor of *The Times Higher Education Supplement*, he has been writing on the subject for more than a decade. He has a degree in politics from Sheffield University.

Most of the statistical material for this guide derives from information originally provided by the institutions themselves. It has been compiled by a team of university experts: Andrew Hindmarsh (admissions and academic planning), Bernard Kingston (graduate careers and international affairs) and Robert Loynes (statistics).

THE TIMES

good university guide 1999

edited by John O'Leary

TIMES BOOKS
London

Published in 1999 by Times Books
HarperCollins*Publishers*
77-85 Fulham Palace Road
Hammersmith
London W6 8JB
The HarperCollins website address is www.**fire**and**water**.com

First published in 1993 by Times Books
Second edition 1994
Third edition 1995
Fourth edition 1996
Fifth edition 1997
Sixth edition 1998
Seventh edition 1999
Copyright © Times Newspapers 1993, 1994, 1995, 1996, 1997, 1998, 1999

Cover illustration: Nick Barker

University rankings data:
The data for entry standards, staff/student ratios, library and computer spending, facilities spending, firsts and upper seconds, graduate destinations and international student
enrolments were provided by the Higher Education Statistics Agency (HESA). Teaching
and research assessments are based on the Teaching Quality Assessments and Research
Assessment Exercise carried out by the funding councils, QAA and OFSTED. In a few
cases the source data were not available and were obtained directly from the individual
universities. The data providers do not necessarily agree with data aggregations or manipulations appearing in this book and are not responsible for any inferences or conclusions
thereby derived. Every effort has been made to ensure accuracy, but no responsibility can
be taken for errors or omissions. All universities were provided with complete sets of their
own HESA date well in advance of publication and where anomalous figures were identified
in the 1996/7 HESA data institutions were also requested to provide a check. Direct comparison with earlier years is not always possible because of the gradual refinement of the process.

Typeset by Times Books

Printed and bound in Great Britain by Caledonian

British Library Cataloguing in Publication Data
A catalogue record for this book is available from the British Library.

ISBN 0-7230-1020-X

CONTENTS

INTRODUCTION

T he impact of major changes in society can take years to assess accurately. Politicians and commentators, including academics, may think they know how people will react, but only time will tell. So it is with the introduction of tuition fees for full-time undergraduates – a major change, by any standards, for the growing section of British society which aspires to higher education. The collapse in demand for university places predicted by some experts did not materialise in the first year of the scheme, but fees have deterred many mature students and even school-leavers appear to be questioning the value of some degrees.

Prospective students are becoming more discriminating about their choice of university and the subject they study. This book attempts to help applicants make a more informed choice for, unlike other guides, its emphasis is on the quality of courses. The original university rankings, which now have their imitators, are supplemented by more than 40 separate subject tables providing the detailed comparisons needed to identify the top degree programmes.

The rankings reflect the state of flux which characterises British higher education at the end of the 20th century. For the first time since *The Times Good University Guide* appeared in 1993, Oxford University has slipped out of the top two places. Its eclipse by Imperial College London demonstrates the value of specialisation, as well as the enduring strength of the University of London, which has four colleges in the national top ten. Further down the overall table, Oxford Brookes University continues to show that it is possible for the former polytechnics to overhaul some of their longer-established counterparts. Other new universities, such as Napier and Brighton are poised to make the same breakthrough.

Mindful of the competition for graduate jobs, applicants are looking as never before for quality and are also gravitating towards the more vocational subjects. The pattern established in Australia, which began charging for higher education more than a decade ago, is being repeated in Britain. Business courses, computing and some branches of engineering are seeing a significant rise in applications, while teacher training and some arts subjects are struggling. The indications are that there will be a place somewhere in the higher education for most of those hoping to start a course in 2001, but competition for the top degrees will be as fierce as ever. To give yourself the best possible chance of coming out ahead of the field requires careful consideration of the options, as well as hard academic work.

This book offers a starting point in the increasingly complex search for the right course. No guide can cater for individual tastes, but a wealth of information is available to narrow the possibilities. *The Times Good University Guide* distils some of this information into a more manageable form, with profiles of each institution, rankings and advice on the applications process.

The university explosion

At first sight, choosing a university appears to have become simpler as the decade has worn on. The distinction between universities and polytechnics was swept away in 1992 and the number of places expanded to the point where far more young (and not so young) people could benefit from higher education. A consensus has grown among politicians and business leaders that, quite apart from the benefits to the individual, a modern economy needs mass higher education. Countries such as the United States and Japan reached the same conclusion long ago but a combination of factors - - not all of them planned - has seen Britain making up for lost time at a rate that has prompted concerns about the quality of some courses.

Almost a third of 18-year-olds are now going on to higher education, compared with one in seven in 1980, while at least twice that proportion will take a higher education course at some point in their life. The Labour government has promised to raise that number still further. Yet, paradoxically, by ridding Britain of its 'elite' university system, the last government sowed the seeds of a different form of elitism. The very process of opening up higher education ensured the creation of a new hierarchy of institutions. The old myth that all degrees were equal could not survive in a nation of almost 100 diverse universities and a growing number of degree-providing colleges.

The new hierarchy

Of course, there always was a pecking order of sorts. Oxford and Cambridge were world leaders long before most British universities were established, and parts of London University have always enjoyed a high status in particular fields. But few could or would discriminate between Aberdeen and Exeter, for example. Employers, careers advisers, even academics, had their own ideas of which were the leading universities, but there was little hard evidence to back their conclusions. Often they were based on outdated, inaccurate impressions of distant institutions.

The expanded higher education system has made such judgments more scientific as well as more necessary. Prospective employers want to know not only what a graduate studied, but where. Those who are committing their money to student sponsorship or funding research are comparing institutions department by department. This has become possible because of a new transparency in what a former higher-education minister described as the 'secret garden of academe'. Official demands for more and more published information may have taxed the patience of university administrators, but they have also given outsiders the opportunity to make more meaningful comparisons.

Many see the beginnings of a British Ivy League in the competitive culture that has ensued. Even before the recent upheavals, the lion's share of research cash went to fewer than 20 traditional universities, enabling them to upgrade their facilities and attract many of the top academics. As student numbers have gone through the roof, however, general higher-education budgets have been squeezed and the funding gap has widened. Beneath the veneer of a unified higher-education system, three types of university are emerging: the research-based elite; a large group dedicated primarily to teaching; and an indeterminate number of mixed-economy institutions in the middle struggling to maintain a research base.

Whatever the intentions of ministers following the publication in summer 1997 of Sir Ron Dearing's review of higher education, it is hard to imagine that pattern changing in the short or medium term. There is no need for formalised divisions because the market is already taking the university system in the direction that both main political parties probably favour.

Why university?

Doubtless some will be tempted, once the cost of living has been added to the new fees burdens and the attractions of university life balanced against loss of potential earnings, to write off higher education. There are plenty of self-made millionaires who still swear by the University of Life as the only training ground for success. Yet even by narrow financial criteria it would be rash to dismiss higher education. The graduate labour market is still recovering from the recession and, with so many more competing for jobs, a degree will never again be an automatic passport to a fast-track career. But graduates' financial prospects still compare favourably with school leavers'.

Even for those who cannot or do not wish to afford three or more years of full-time education after leaving school, university remains a possibility. The modular courses adopted by most universities enable students to work through a degree at their own pace, dropping out for a time if necessary, or switching to part-time attendance. Distance learning is another option, and advances in information technology now mean that some nominally full-time courses are delivered mainly via computers.

For many – perhaps most – students, therefore, the university experience is not what it was in their parents' day. There is more assessment, more crowding, more pressure to get the best possible degree while also finding gainful employment for at least part of the year. The proportion of students achieving first-class degrees has risen significantly, while an upper-second (rather than the ubiquitous 2:2) has become the norm. Research shows that the classification has a real impact in the labour market: a quarter of those taking a third-class degree in 1992 were unemployed six months later, compared with a mere 4.5 per cent of those with a first.

Toward the future

There will be no slackening in the pace of change. In future, it is likely that more students will begin their degrees at further education colleges, more will opt initially for two-year courses and the range both of subjects and teaching methods will grow still further. Some predict the rise of the 'virtual university' or the demise of the conventional higher-education institution, as companies customise their own courses. However, universities have demonstrated enduring popularity and show every sign of weathering the current turbulence.

The demand for degree places this year will follow a familiar pattern. Especially in traditional universities, arts and social science degrees remain oversubscribed and some science subjects also have high entrance requirements. Places will again be plentiful, however, in engineering, technology and the 'hard' sciences, such as physics, for those with the right qualifications.

Other sources of information

This book should provide some food for thought in the process of choosing a university, but it cannot provide all the answers. Among the many other sources of information are the universities' increasingly glossy prospectuses – often on CD Rom and computer disk as well as paper – the vice-chancellors' annual reports and the subject-by-subject assessments published by the higher education funding councils. For further information on the universities' departments, which will eventually all be graded, contact the addresses below:

Higher Education Funding Council for England,
Northavon House, Coldharbour Lane, Bristol BS16 1QD. Tel: 0117-931 7493. Also for reports on the two universities in Northern Ireland.
Scottish Higher Education Funding Council,
Donaldson House, 97 Haymarket Terrace, Edinburgh EH12 5HD. Tel: 0131-313 6500
Higher Education Funding Council for Wales,
Lambourne House, Cardiff Business Park, Llanishen, Cardiff CF4 5GL. Tel: 01222-761861

Part I

WHICH UNIVERSITY?

1
UNIVERSITY RANKINGS

The league table in this chapter is a distinctive method of measuring the performance of British universities. Since its first appearance in *The Times* in October 1992, it has been the subject of continued and heated debate among academics.

There are those who believe that all attempts to measure the performance both of individual institutions and of the system as a whole are wrong in principle. Institutions are unique and autonomous. They serve distinct communities and have diverse missions. In the eyes of critics, any attempt to rank universities can be misleading, may be spurious and might be dangerous. This is despite the success and the contribution of comparable guides elsewhere. Since the early 1980s, for example, *US News and World Report* have produced similar rankings of American colleges and universities every year, and more countries have followed suit since *The Times* rankings appeared. Increasingly, analyses of this type have come to be seen as legitimate aids to students, staff and institutions alike.

There have been only minor changes this year to the methodology behind the rankings, but the addition of the School of Oriental and African Studies, in London, means that the universities' positions in the table are not directly comparable to 1998. It is hoped that completion rates and a calculation of value added, both of which were dropped because of concerns about accuracy, will be restored when suitable data is available.

There have been a number of changes over the years in which the tables has been published, both to the indicators used and the way in which they are calculated. Accommodation, for example, is no longer included, both because of concerns about the quality of the data and because growing numbers of universities felt it was no longer generally relevant to those looking for a higher education place. Although essential to those leaving home to study, more and more students are not in this position. The indicator has been replaced by one measuring the amount spent on more general student facilities. This year's table retains the 1997 weighting for two of the indicators. As the official benchmarks of quality in British higher education, the funding councils' assessments of teaching and research deserve pride of place. The research ranking, which was revised in 1996, has been given a weighting of 1.5 (compared to 1 for other indicators). That for teaching – the prime concern for an undergraduate – carries 2.5.

The teaching assessments, which are still controversial in academic circles, were omitted from *The Times* table until 1996, when they covered 50 per cent of students for the first time. Another tranche of subjects has since been added, so the indicator now gives the best available guide to standards of teaching across whole universities, and has been weighted accordingly.

The weightings have the effect of excluding one university – Buckingham – from the table. As Britain's only private university, Buckingham does not fall under the aegis of the Higher Education Funding Council for England, and therefore does not have the quality of its teaching and research assessed. Buckingham has fared well in previous tables and is included in the university profiles in chapter 9. However, with additional weight being given to the official quality assessments, any overall figure for the university would be meaningless.

Other changes, such as the inclusion of spending on information technology in the libraries measure, are detailed below. Raw data from published sources were used for all the calculations. The information came from a number of sources, including the Higher Education Statistics Agency (HESA), the Universities and Colleges Admissions Service (UCAS) and the higher education funding councils.

HESA, which provided the majority of the statistics, does not necessarily concur with data aggregations or manipulations, and is not responsible for inferences or conclusions drawn from exercises such as this. Figures were drawn mainly from 1996-97. Every effort has been made to ensure the accuracy of all the statistics used, and universities were contacted individually where there were obvious gaps or anomalies in the national figures, but no responsibility can be taken for errors or omissions.

How the table works

The table measures eight key aspects of university life, using the most recent figures available at the time of going to press. Each has been chosen to highlight the performance of individual universities and to allow potential students to make their own judgments. In each area, the top-rated university is awarded 100 points and the remainder a proportion of this based on their unadjusted scores. The spread of points between indicators varies according to the actual range in each category. Where universities have scored the same number of points, they are graded equally and their position in the table determined solely by alphabetical order.

1 Teaching assessment This indicator uses the average score for each university in the cycle of funding council assessments completed in 1998. Not all subjects have yet been assessed, but those covering a majority of students now have. Early ratings, produced by expert assessors, varied between England and Northern Ireland, Scotland and Wales. All scores are now out of 24, and the original categories of excellent, satisfactory and (in Scotland) highly satisfactory, have been given expressed numerically. Education, which is included for the first time, makes use of Ofsted scores.

2 Research assessment This measure is based on the average score for each university in the 1997 Research Assessment Exercise carried out by the three funding councils, again using panels of expert assessors. The averages are calculated for all university academic staff, rather than only those entered for assessment.

3 Entry standards This is probably the indicator most familiar to university applicants.The indicator is based on the average entry qualifications across each university of students commencing courses in 19999. For an explanation of how these are calculated, *see* chapter 8.

Inevitably, universities committed to 'access' initiatives designed to widen participation in higher education will find their scores on this measure depressed. Scottish Highers tend to be undervalued in the conversion to A-level points, with the result that some Scottish universities' positions may be understated. No accepted formula yet exists to take account of vocational qualifications.

4 Staff/student ratios Staffing levels are central to the nature of a student's learning experience. These figures are based on the average staffing level across the university, using full-time equivalent student numbers on non-franchised courses and total teaching and teaching/research staff in 1996-97. Data is from HESA.

5 Library and computer spending Libraries have been described as the 'heart and soul' of a university, and their quality is of vital importance to the student. The spending measured here includes books, periodicals and library staff, but excludes buildings and equipment. The figure is for 1996-97, and is calculated as an average per full-time equivalent student.

For the first time, HESA data has been used in order to take account of the growing importance of IT spending in libraries.

6 Facilities spending Based on HESA data. This ranking is derived from the amount spent on social and recreational, including sporting, facilities per full-time student in 1996-97.

7 Degree classifications This measure covers both firsts and upper seconds in order to iron out differences in universities' awarding policies. The indicator is based on the proportion of first degree qualifiers in the top two classes in 1996-97.

Students following four-year degree programmes at Scottish universities are entitled to receive an Ordinary degree after three years of study and, as such, many first degrees awarded in Scotland are unclassified. Where Ordinary degrees have been identified, these have been removed from the grand total prior to calculating the proportion of qualifiers with firsts and upper seconds.

The inclusion of degree classifications as an indicator of excellence has been criticised on the grounds that it is controlled by universities themselves. However, they remain the primary measure of individual success in British higher education and, as such, cannot be ignored by applicants.

8 Graduate destinations The method of compiling this indicator has changed this year because HESA was unable to release data on numbers of graduates whose destination was unknown. The ranking is based on the proportion of UK-domiciled graduates taking up employment or further study/training in 1996-97.

Conclusions

Universities' positions in *The Times* table inevitably reflect more than their performances over a single year. Many of those at the top have built their reputations and developed their expertise over many decades or even centuries, while some of those at the bottom are still carving out a niche in the unified higher education system. British universities now offer a range and level of diversity to meet most needs.

Perhaps the least surprising conclusions to be drawn from the table are that Oxbridge and the University of London remain the dominant forces in British higher education and that, on the measures adopted here, the new universities still have ground to make up on the old. The former polytechnics have different priorities from those of many of their more established counterparts, however, and can demonstrate strengths in other areas.

Even on the traditional measures adopted here, the table belies the system's reputation for rigidity. For example, a former polytechnic (Oxford Brookes) continues to outperform several traditional universities. No doubt others will follow before long. The remarkable rise of universities such as Warwick and York, both founded less than 40 years ago, show what can be achieved in a relatively short space of time. Specialist institutions such as Imperial College London and the London School of Economics are doing even better, the former having now overtaken Oxford.

In an exercise such as this, some distortions are inevitable. Small universities and those specialising in the arts and social sciences tend to be at a disadvantage; those with medical schools the reverse. An institution in an economically-deprived area will find it more difficult to raise the private funding which enables its rivals to thrive. The use of a variety of indicators is intended to diminish such factors, but they should be borne in mind when making comparisons.

The abbreviations below are used in the following table, and in the tables in chapters 5, 6 and 7:

Glasgow Cal	Glasgow Caledonian University
Goldsmiths'	Goldsmiths' College
Guildhall	London Guildhall University
Imperial	Imperial College of Science and Technology
King's	King's College London
Lampeter	St David's University College
Lincs & Humber	University of Lincolnshire and Humberside
Liverpool JMU	Liverpool John Moores University
LSE	London School of Economics
Queen Mary	Queen Mary and Westfield College
Royal Holloway	Royal Holloway and Bedford New College
SOAS	School of Oriental and African Studies
UCL	University College London
UMIST	University of Manchester Institute of Science and Technology

		Teaching assessment	Research assessment	Entry standards	Staff/student ratios	Library/computing spending	Facilities spending	Firsts and upper seconds	Graduate destinations	TOTAL
WEIGHTING		250	150	100	100	100	100	100	100	1000
1	Cambridge	100	100	100	79	85	69	100	95	929
2	Imperial	100	85	92	100	82	100	71	91	914
3	Oxford	95	96	97	70	97	65	91	93	893
4	LSE	93	96	92	77	100	82	77	87	892
5	UCL	91	84	79	95	80	75	80	83	845
6	SOAS	95	72	66	93	100	77	78	81	841
7	Warwick	96	85	85	60	72	75	79	94	832
8	Bristol	88	72	86	64	69	93	86	96	823
8	Edinburgh	90	79	87	57	76	80	86	93	823
10	St Andrews	94	72	81	51	68	74	92	98	807
11	Nottingham	90	69	88	61	69	75	85	96	802
12	York	98	79	80	54	69	79	72	84	800
13	Sheffield	92	70	84	59	65	75	72	92	782
14	Lancaster	89	79	74	47	69	80	76	91	780
15	Bath	79	78	77	49	78	85	77	93	774
16	Birmingham	88	69	81	58	66	75	75	95	773
17	King's	81	69	77	87	76	70	69	86	771
18	Durham	89	72	84	49	66	74	72	92	768
19	Newcastle	85	64	74	70	76	77	71	84	762
20	Manchester	84	74	80	55	74	69	75	89	761
21	Glasgow	91	58	77	51	67	69	80	88	747
22	Southampton	85	68	73	58	69	72	68	92	748
23	Leeds	84	70	77	53	69	72	74	87	746
24	Reading	86	67	67	60	66	74	71	91	743
24	UMIST	81	76	71	56	65	75	65	94	743
26	Loughborough	88	63	69	40	63	77	80	94	740

		Teaching assessment	Research assessment	Entry standards	Staff/student ratios	Library/computing spending	Facilities spending	Firsts and upper seconds	Graduate destinations	TOTAL
WEIGHTING		250	150	100	100	100	100	100	100	1000
26	Royal Holloway	83	68	71	49	65	77	79	90	740
28	Queen Mary	89	60	60	68	68	72	70	89	739
29	Essex	87	76	57	53	68	81	63	78	731
30	Surrey	78	61	62	67	68	77	66	100	729
31	Dundee	84	55	63	68	66	75	69	94	728
31	Leicester	81	66	71	59	67	71	68	89	728
33	Hull	86	56	65	64	68	63	72	96	727
33	Stirling	88	56	66	50	70	74	76	87	727
35	Cardiff	82	71	75	43	63	72	70	92	726
36	Aberdeen	88	61	64	45	64	72	77	92	723
37	East Anglia	82	69	69	40	63	74	73	90	719
38	Liverpool	82	61	73	57	65	71	61	92	715
38	Sussex	77	74	68	47	69	70	67	91	715
40	Exeter	82	58	74	52	66	68	74	85	710
41	Keele	78	61	69	60	62	68	72	90	707
42	Heriot-Watt	82	52	59	50	69	82	67	92	703
43	Queen's (Belfast)	84	52	55	46	68	81	69	93	701
44	City	76	39	64	73	73	81	59	90	690
45	Strathclyde	90	53	52	51	63	71	66	83	689
46	Swansea	83	53	62	56	64	70	68	79	685
47	Kent	80	56	67	45	67	69	59	91	683
48	Aberystwyth	81	55	64	41	66	74	66	88	682
49	Aston	78	52	73	32	65	73	73	89	679
50	Goldsmiths'	72	64	63	51	65	66	67	85	673
51	Bangor	81	46	52	56	70	69	61	83	661
52	Bradford	69	62	57	42	64	81	56	87	651

		Teaching assessment	Research assessment	Entry standards	Staff/student ratios	Library/computing spending	Facilities spending	Firsts and upper seconds	Graduate destinations	TOTAL
WEIGHTING		250	150	100	100	100	100	100	100	1000
53	Oxford Brookes	85	22	47	49	62	76	65	94	641
54	Brunel	81	51	53	34	63	64	58	83	633
54	Ulster	78	36	68	44	65	58	71	79	633
56	Napier	76	8	43	75	65	72	59	91	608
57	Salford	70	51	49	46	64	63	53	77	605
58	Lampeter	72	52	48	39	62	63	52	78	602
59	Robert Gordon	78	14	48	49	65	63	61	98	601
60	Brighton	78	21	43	42	65	68	64	88	596
61	Westminster	77	15	44	58	69	67	63	79	595
62	Northumbria	86	11	53	50	64	58	56	81	594
63	West of England	86	13	49	43	60	65	55	89	594
64	Plymouth	79	22	51	47	61	61	59	84	593
65	Kingston	86	13	44	39	62	66	55	89	591
65	Sheffield Hallam	77	15	53	40	63	72	56	92	591
67	Anglia Polytechnic	76	8	42	49	61	68	67	87	576
68	Portsmouth	73	22	46	41	60	68	58	87	575
69	Nottingham Trent	71	16	52	32	59	67	62	95	569
70	De Montfort	71	22	43	38	60	64	62	91	568
71	Glasgow Cal	80	13	50	42	56	56	60	78	561
71	Manchester Metro	81	16	45	38	60	59	52	82	561
73	Coventry	78	13	41	37	62	65	51	87	560
74	Liverpool JMU	71	16	48	45	63	61	51	88	559
75	Greenwich	74	13	40	41	67	72	46	84	556
75	Paisley	77	7	37	54	67	57	59	80	556
77	Wolverhampton	72	8	43	41	59	75	61	83	554
78	Huddersfield	65	18	45	43	62	65	62	88	553

		Teaching assessment	Research assessment	Entry standards	Staff/student ratios	Library/computing spending	Facilities spending	Firsts and upper seconds	Graduate destinations	TOTAL
WEIGHTING		**250**	**150**	**100**	**100**	**100**	**100**	**100**	**100**	**1000**
79	South Bank	72	11	35	54	67	74	51	71	549
80	Glamorgan	78	8	40	42	63	69	45	81	548
81	Central Lancashire	75	9	48	42	61	58	54	82	547
82	Abertay Dundee	76	11	32	43	68	59	51	85	545
83	Hertfordshire	65	14	44	41	66	64	57	90	543
83	Staffordshire	72	13	43	35	60	63	58	84	543
85	Middlesex	73	18	42	29	63	64	57	77	542
86	Leeds Metro	69	9	51	38	60	62	56	87	541
87	Central England	73	11	47	46	58	65	51	69	536
87	Teesside	70	9	40	49	62	65	47	85	536
89	East London	67	16	39	39	64	67	56	72	526
90	North London	75	16	29	31	63	66	51	73	525
91	Sunderland	69	13	39	28	58	66	52	88	524
92	Derby	68	9	42	32	61	63	53	83	518
93	Luton	75	8	41	38	60	59	42	78	516
94	Thames Valley	69	4	38	50	67	71	46	64	513
95	London Guildhall	69	12	40	31	65	63	44	77	512
96	Bournemouth	60	6	52	33	60	62	57	82	507
97	Lincs & Humber	64	8	40	27	61	57	56	78	494

2 CHOOSING A UNIVERSITY

For those who decide that higher education is for them, choosing a university is one of life's great steps. Not only will it determine where you spend three or more formative years, but the choice will set your career path and probably be the major influence in your social life.

With more courses available than ever before and conflicting pressures at every turn, it will not be an easy choice. You will need all the advice you can get – from school or college, parents and friends, books such as this and the universities' own prospectuses. Eventually, you will have to settle for six applications through the Universities and Colleges Admissions Service (UCAS) before whittling them down to two final choices.

Obviously, selecting a subject and selecting a university are different sides of the same coin; they will have to come together in the end. But they should be approached separately at the start of the process. No matter how outstanding the department, you must consider whether the university as a whole has what you are looking for. Is it in the right place? Does it have the facilities you value? And will its reputation appeal to future employers or other academic establishments? If the answer to any of these questions is 'no', you might be better looking elsewhere.

Lists are in fashion at the moment, so try writing down your objectives in applying to university and narrowing down the possibilities accordingly. Your objectives can be seen as:

Long term Commonly referred to as life goals, these might cover the kind of career you hope to follow, how mobile you want to be, or issues about security or risk. Both the choice of university and subject will be affected.

Medium term Usually related to life goals, these might be staging posts along the way. If, for example, your long-term goal is to be a barrister, a good law degree is an important first step. It might also determine whether or not you consider a university in Scotland, where the legal system is different.

Short term These are about how you want to spend the next few months or years, a consideration which you should not underestimate. Not only may they affect how you progress towards your longer-term objectives, but they are the least likely to change or be overtaken by events.

Circumstances are bound to alter at least some of your objectives, so try to build flexibility into your approach. Your goals should be a spur to action and an aid to decision-making, not a straitjacket. Consider, for example, what you will do if your results are much better (or worse) than you expect. In the end, instinct may be your best guide. Think, too, about when you want to start your course. Many people favour a year off between school and university, but can you afford it? Will the university allow it? Do you have something worthwhile to do?

All these questions have to be faced if you are not to put yourself at a disadvantage before you even start a university career. A gap year can be a richly rewarding experience, but it must come second to the real business that follows. If you satisfy yourself that the risks are not too great, however, there are plenty of sources of information on gap years. Among the main ones are:

The Gap Year Guidebook 1999/2000, Peridot Press, 2 Blenheim Crescent, London W11 1NN (£8.95 plus 50p p&p)
Taking a Year Off, Butcher, V, Trotman & Co., Richmond, Surrey (£8.99 plus £1.60 p&p)
A Year Off, A Year On? Hobsons, Bateman Street, Cambridge CB2 1BR (£8.99 including p&p from Biblios, Star Road, Partridge Green, West Sussex RH13 8LD)
How To Spend A Year Abroad, Vandome, N, How To Books (£8.99)
Summer Jobs Abroad (£7.99); *Teaching English Abroad* (£9.99); *Summer Jobs in Britain* (£7.99), all published by Vacation Work Publications and available from most bookshops

Once you have decided whether and when to go to university, the decisions come thick and fast. Try to take them in order of priority, which inevitably means thinking clearly about what matters to you. The overall ranking in the previous chapter should highlight some of the issues. Its presentation as a poll of polls is designed to enable the reader to examine the areas of most personal interest.

There are many other important questions to address, most of which will be a matter of personal taste. Many will be answered through close scrutiny of the prospectus; others may need a phone call or, better still, a visit. Universities are as anxious to get the best students as you are to find the best course, and all are geared up to answering queries by phone or arranging a visit. Among the topics you may wish to pursue are:

- The availability of subjects and possible combinations
- Course options and freedom of choice
- Teaching systems (including the size of seminars or tutorials)
- Type of assessment
- Flexibility (the ability to change subjects)
- Access to technology

- Location
- Sports and leisure facilities
- Transport and communications (both while studying and between home and university)
- Desired special facilities (e.g. for the disabled)
- Availability of access courses

Which type of university?

Perhaps the first question should be whether you have a strong preference for a particular type of university. The 97 institutions can be split any number of ways: new and traditional, collegiate, technological, city or campus. And some will fall into more than one category. Bath, for example, is a campus university but also primarily technological. Coventry is a new university but also city-based. The profiles in Part 2 of this book give a more detailed description of type and location, but the following gives an idea of the main terms you will encounter:

Ancients As the name implies, the oldest universities in England and Scotland. As well as Oxford and Cambridge, they include Aberdeen, Edinburgh, Glasgow and St Andrews.

Civics and redbricks These are the city-based traditional universities, many dating from the last century and established as municipal institutions. They include Birmingham, Bristol, Hull, Leeds, Leicester, Liverpool, Manchester, Newcastle, Nottingham, Queen's Belfast, Sheffield and Southampton.

Campus Normally used to describe the 1960s universities built on greenfield sites. These were East Anglia, Essex, Exeter, Keele, Kent, Lancaster, Reading, Stirling, Sussex, Warwick and York.

Collegiate Oxford and Cambridge are the prime examples, but Durham, York and Kent all use the pattern of wheels within wheels.

Federal London and Wales, where the larger colleges are recognised as universities in their own right.

New The post-1992 universities, mainly former polytechnics. They are too recent a phenomenon to have divided further, but perhaps the main subgroup consists of the metropolitan universities, where the majority of students is home-based and part-time courses predominate. These include West of England, Central England, Coventry, Huddersfield, Leeds and Manchester Metropolitan, Liverpool John Moores, Napier, Northumbria, Nottingham Trent, Plymouth, Portsmouth, Robert Gordon, Sheffield Hallam, Sunderland, Teesside, Wolverhampton and the former inner-London polytechnics.

Split-site Most universities have more than one site, but a growing number have complete campuses in more than one town. They include Anglia, De Montfort, Hertfordshire, Lincolnshire and Humberside, Staffordshire, Thames Valley and Ulster.

Technological A number of the new universities would claim to be primarily technological, but the term is generally applied to a group of traditional universities, most of which date from the 1960s. They include Aston, Bath, Bradford, Brunel, City, Dundee, Loughborough, Heriot-Watt, UMIST, Salford, Strathclyde and Surrey.

The remainder, mainly new universities, defy pigeon-holing. Most are based in large towns or cities, like Brighton or Oxford, but have their own campuses, like Middlesex or Central Lancashire. Try to visit a selection to see what the various categories have to offer. Some students like the bustle of city life, others prefer the intimacy of college life or the particular atmosphere of a self-contained campus.

Location

Some students are tied by family circumstances to a local university, and more may become so as the cost of higher education rises. Others are restricted by the choice of an obscure subject to an institution at the other end of the country. Most students, however, choose a university within 100 miles of home, far enough away to avoid too regular parental contact but close enough to make a visit manageable when funds are particularly low or the washing is piling up.

Geography, the cost of living and pure fashion have all contributed to the popularity of universities in the big cities of the midlands and north of England. The section on university cities, at the back of this book, examines the competing claims of the main student centres. But there is no doubt that the large civic and metropolitan universities, which are within easy reach of the majority of the population, offering lively cultural and leisure opportunities without the extra costs associated with life in London and the Home Counties, have enjoyed lasting popularity.

Naturally, London remains a magnet for many prospective students, and others would not hear of studying outside Scotland, Wales or Northern Ireland. Every applicant has his or her particular preferences, but it is important to remember your priorities and not to be influenced too heavily by attractive but ultimately marginal features. Legendary nightclubs or a successful football team might be a bonus, but they are as nothing for the impecunious student compared to the availability of part-time work or the length and cost of a journey home.

Accommodation

For those who are leaving home to study, the availability of accommodation could be the clinching factor in choosing a university. On the other hand, those who run universities with a high proportion of home-based students argue, reasonably enough, that they would be wasting taxpayers' money if they provided the same amount of accommodation as those in rural locations.

Especially in the first year, it is essential to have somewhere comfortable and convenient to live. After that, you may sacrifice some home comforts for the sake of cash or friendship; you may be prepared to travel that bit further once you know the area. But the first year is when you are going to make most of your friends and, if you are away from home for the first time, when you may still be picking up lifeskills like cooking. The advantages of living in a university flat or hall of residence are not to be underestimated.

Several universities have added substantially to their residential stock in recent years. Most give priority to first-year students in the allocation of residential places and a growing number offer the guarantee of accommodation with the acceptance of a place.

Facilities

Library facilities   One way or another, you will spend a lot of of time in the library. Four aspects are especially important: 1) expenditure on books or periodicals; 2) staff support; 3) study space; 4) access. Often absolute expenditure on books can be less important than the quality of support given by library staff. Similarly, restrictions on the capital expenditure of universities over the last few years has placed a massive premium on study space, especially during the periods just before examinations.

Leisure facilities   Going to university is not just about getting a degree. It is about learning to live, work and enjoy yourself with others. Campus universities and those in small communities have often invested in excellent arts and leisure facilities while urban universities have built powerful links with their local communities.

Safety and Security   One of the saddest features of university life is the increased risk to students and their property from both within and outside the university. Find out the care and security arrangements, especially the guidance and help given by university authorities.

Facilities for groups with special needs

The increasingly heterogeneous nature of today's student population has highlighted the importance of providing special facilities for those who need them: the blind, the deaf, those with impaired sight or hearing, those in wheelchairs and student mothers or fathers who need child-care support. Some of the newer foundations were able to plan for the needs of these groups from the start. Others have invested heavily in alterations to existing buildings. In these latter cases there can be a significant lag between agreeing building plans and executing them. For example, if a university has bought existing buildings to accommodate new departments, they are unlikely to be designed for effective wheelchair access. Whatever its final intentions, the university in question may well find it takes some time before such access can be provided.

Many aspects of a university's response to special needs are reflected in investment in areas other than building and facilities.

Disabled students support offered by some universities includes: readers for the blind and partially sighted; interpreters for the deaf; and counselling for those suffering from specific learning or personal difficulties.

Mature students often find that their needs change significantly at different stages in their university career. Before admission, the institution's commitment to their needs may be reflected in the nature of and support for its access courses. Immediately on admission, concerns often centre on likely changes in financial circumstances, lifestyle and domestic arrangements. Good quality financial advice backed by proper counselling may be crucial in tackling the 'entry' or 're-entry' problems.

Women students Women students in particular face a range of distinct problems. These range from sexual harassment to pregnancy advice. Alternative prospectuses are among the best sources of information and guidance on a university's response to these questions. A high-profile court-case involving students at King's College London prompted the Committee of Vice-Chancellors in late 1993 to set up a Task Force to review procedures.

Sexual orientation The last few years have seen signs of increasing intolerance in this area at some universities and among some communities. If tolerance is important to you, check out the university's policies in advance, preferably through the institution's gay society – if there is one.

Ethnicity All universities have a formal commitment to equal opportunity. This will be codified in either their Charter or Articles of Association. In some cases, this commitment may go no further. National student organisations are pressing institutions to develop more clear-cut policies to tackle discrimination, harassment or abuse and to introduce programmes of affirmative action.

The universities with the clearest commitments in this area can generally be identified by the resources they devote to it and the identifiable programmes of action they have introduced.

Overseas students It is useful to sub-divide this group into those from within the European Union (EU) and those from outside the EU. For all institutional purposes, EU students are treated as 'home' students. This does not eliminate special needs or avoid tensions, for instance over accommodation, but it does provide a framework for producing policy responses.

Students from outside the EU have become increasingly important to the financing of many UK universities. This has had positive and negative effects. It has encouraged many institutions to recruit actively and thus to introduce greater cultural and social diversity. Unfortunately, some have not backed this up with investment in appropriate facilities, for example, in accommodation, support for spouses, help with transitional arrangements or finance. It is vital to be fully informed on these issues before choosing a university. For more specific information for overseas students, see chapter 6.

Other sources of information

The National Union of Students, 461 Holloway Road, London N5. Tel: 0171-272 8900
The British Council, 10 Spring Gardens, London SW1X 0DU. Tel: 0171-930 8466 (for overseas students and studying abroad)
Skill: National Bureau for Students with Disabilities, 336 Brixton Road, London SW9 7AA. Tel: 0171-274 0565
UKCOSA (UK Council for Overseas Student Affairs), 9-17 St Albans Place, London N1 0NX. Tel: 0171-354 5210

In addition to this book and the universities' own prospectuses, a variety of guides are published which give valuable information on different aspects of student life. They include:

How to Choose Your Degree Course, Heap, B, Trotman & Co., Richmond, Surrey (£13.95)
Degree Course Offers, Heap, B, Trotman & Co. (£16.99)
Getting into Oxford and Cambridge, Trotman & Co. (£6.95)
How to Complete Your UCAS Form, Higgins, T (£6.95)
Student Grants and Loans, Department for Education and Employment (free if you call 0171-510 0150)
Access to Higher Education Courses Directory, ECCTIS, Fulton House, Jessop Avenue, Cheltenham, Glos GL50 3SA

Costs and how to cope

Alongside the decisions of what, where and even when to study, come the financial implications of your choice. While your degree may hold the key to future riches, university life does not come cheap, although help does exist, especially if you know where to look.

Costs for students come in all shapes and sizes, from the newly instigated burden of fees to more pleasurable expenses. While an element of prioritising is undoubtably important, you will be unable to afford everything and this will involve a word that strikes fear into the heart of the student: budgeting.

Firstly the, what are the costs involved?
1) your contribution towards **tuition fees**
2) your various **living costs** such as:
🎓 accommodation
🎓 food
🎓 travel
🎓 study materials, from books to stationery
🎓 social and leisure activities

Tuition fees

Amid inevitable controversy the 1998 academic year saw the introduction of tuition fees. Fears that they are but the thin end of the wedge are yet to be tested. They rise to a maximum of £1,025 per year for full-time students in the 1999/2000 academic year, though the increase merely reflects inflation.

Tuition fee support will be available through your Local Education Authority (LEA) and this will be means-tested in the same way that the old grants were. Your LEA handles everything to do with fees and loans and as soon as you have received an offer of a place at university, even a conditional offer, you should contact your LEA to discover whether you are entitled to any help. It will be up to your university to decide when exactly these fees will be payable each year.

Living costs

Your cost of living will vary immensely depending principally on where you choose to study. Financially crippling London is thus acknowledged with a larger student loan available to the capital's students, but many other southern cities are also notoriously expensive and do not receive any such weighting. Day-to-day living is an important consideration to bear in mind. But equally, if you live in the south, you will have to ask yourself whether the cheaper price of a pint in the north may not be outweighed by the likes of travel expenses and telephone calls to loved ones left behind. On the other hand the cost of rent as well as living in general should be significantly lower. So how can you fiance all of this? Various systems of support are available.

Student loans

These are government-funded loans intended to cover your living costs. Apply through your LEA. These loans will replace the existing system of maintenance grants but will provide the same level of support, both by increasing the amount of loan available each year and with supplementary grants.

Student loans are intended as a cheap way to borrow money to finance yourself through university so interest on these loans is only linked to inflation. Repayment starts the April after you have finished your course, provided that you are earning above a threshold currently set at £10,000.

The size of each repayment will vary depending on exactly how much you are earning and will be deducted at source along with your income tax and national insurance contributions. Payments may be deferred should your income fall below this level.

Prospective students must apply to their LEA for a loan at the same time as they apply for support towards tuition fees. Your LEA will assess the exact amount of the loan to which you are entitled. You must then tell the Student Loans Company this sum and they will pay it to you in three installments throughout the year, the first one arriving before term starts in September.

All students on eligible courses who are under 50, or those now between 50 and 54 who plan to return to work after studying, will be entitled to around three-quarters of the maximum loan available. Your eligibility for the remaining quarter of the loan will be means-tested and whether you receive this or not will depend on your income or, if applicable, that of your family. For the academic year 1999/2000 the **maximum loan** available will be:

	full year	final year
For students living away from their parents' home and studying		
in London	£4,480	£3,885
elsewhere	£3,635	£3,150
Students living at their parents' home		
	£2,875	£2,510

Thus **three-quarters** of this amount will be:

	full year	final year
For students living away from their parents' home and studying		
in London	£3,360	£2,913
elsewhere	£2,727	£2,346
Students living at their parents' home		
	£2,167	£1,882

Supplementary grants

Intended, where necessary, to top up the loans to the previous level of the maintenance grants, supplementary grants may be available for the following students:

- disabled students;
- those with dependents;
- those incurring travel costs in certain circumstances;
- those leaving care to enter higher education.

Exact details of who will qualify are available from your LEA, or from the Department for Education and Employment (DfEE) leaflet *Financial Support for Students in 1999/2000*, available by ringing 0800 731 9133. These grants are not normally repayable. Again your LEA will handle applications for these allowances. All of these grants are means-tested except those for disabled students.

Career development loans

These cover a wide variety of vocational courses for up to two years, plus one year of practical experience if it is part of the course. Up to £8000 may be available to cover 80% of course fees plus the full cost of books, materials and other expenses. The downside is that repayments of the loan plus interest start immediately you have finished the course, although you can delay for up to 18 months if you are unemployed. Further information is available on 0800 585 505. They are not available in Northern Ireland.

Social security benefits

Although full-time students are not normally entitled to receive benefits, exceptions may be made for single parents or disabled students. Your local Benefits Agency will be able to advise you further.

Hardship loans and access funds

If you can convince your university or college of your need, you may be entitled to a further hardship loan of £250 a year, which will be repayable in the same way as the student loan. Similarly, you may apply to your university or college for a limited amount of help from their Access Fund.

Part-time jobs

An invaluable part of the student experience is undoubtably the score of part-time jobs you will need to take in order to provide yourself with those essential extras the government seems to think you can live without. With care, these can provide you with essential work experience to pad out your CV once you have left university and so may prove lucrative in more ways than one.

Banks

In addition to the excitement of making new lifelong friends, there is one further relationship at university that is vital to cultivate: that of your bank manager. Your choice of bank may well be the most important choice you make after you have chosen your course and university. Not all are lenient in their attitudes towards students.

Considerations you may like to bear in mind when signing on, aside from who offers the most record vouchers, include the following:

🐦 Where the bank is situated. It is often better to opt for a bank based in a university town as they will be more experienced at dealing with students then your home bank, who may often be unable to understand the expense involved in gaining a degree.

🐦 Past experiences older students may have had with certain banks.

🐦 Where cash points are situated relative to where you will be based.

🐦 The ease with which you are able to set up an overdraft and whether you will incur charges for using this facility. Many banks are flexible in this respect for which you may be very grateful.

🐦 General approachability of the bank staff and the quality of their customer-support services. This includes accessibility of the bank, does it prove 24-hour banking and is it considering moving onto the Net?

🐦 You may even like to look into the service they will continue to provide you with as a graduate. Some offer fantastic interest free loans for up to three years after you have graduated and these will be indispensable should your job search take longer than anticipated.

Other sources of information

Contact your local **Local Education Authority** (LEA). They can tell you if you are likely to qualify for support and how much this may be.

Non-UK EU students should contact the **Department for Education and Employment's** (DfEE) European team at Mowden Hall, Staindrop Road, Darlington, Co. Durham DL3 9BG.

Student Loans Company Limited at: 100 Bothwell Street, Glasgow G2 7JD

Department for Education and Employment (DfEE), DfEE Publications Centre, PO Box 2193, London E15 2EU.

Educational Grants Advisory Service (EGAS), 501-505 Kingsland Road, Dalston, London E8 4AU.

National Union of Students (NUS), The Welfare Unit, NUS, 461 Holloway Road, London N7 6LJ.

Student Awards Agency for Scotland, Gyleview House, 3 Redheughs Rigg, South Gyle, Edinburgh EH12 9HH.

Department of Education for Northern Ireland, Rathgael House, Balloo Road, Bangor, Co Down BT19 7PR.

Welsh Office Education Department, FHE1 Division, 4th Floor, Cathays Park, Cardiff CF1 3NQ.

Disabled Students Allowances – a DfEE leaflet, Bridging the Gap, is available from your LEA.

Sponsorship for Students 1999 – published and distributed by CRAC/Hobsobs (£8.99).

The Grants Register 1999 – published by Macmillan Reference Limited (£99.00).

Higher Education and Disability: The guide to higher education for people with disabilities – available from SKILL at 336 Brixton Road, London SW9 7AA priced £2.

Student Life – A Survival Guide – published by Hobsons Publishing plc (£8.99).

A Guide to University Scholarships and Awards by Brian Heap – published by Trotman and Company.

3
CHOOSING A COURSE

Britain's universities offer a massive array of courses, programmes, combinations and options. *The Official Guide to University Entrance*, published by UCAS, lists more than 30,000 courses from accountancy to zoology. Many of these are non-degree courses.

The organisation and structure of the course can make an enormous difference to the satisfaction obtained. For some, a sandwich course or a year abroad is an important part of the value of the degree, while others want the opportunity to concentrate uninterrupted with their studies. Some courses place a major emphasis on project work, sometimes on a group basis. Remember that courses can vary greatly between institutions, reflecting the approach of a given university and/or the interests of faculties. Always check the way a programme is organised at the university you are considering.

It is worth adapting the following check-list to fit your needs:

- Is it a single honours programme (if that is your preference)?
- Will I get a chance to spend a year abroad?
- Is continuous assessment used for more than 50 per cent of grades?
- Will I be able to do project work of my own choosing?
- Will I be expected to present my work to fellow students?
- Can I see my tutors frequently?
- Are practicals held frequently?
- Are the laboratories well equipped?
- Will I be expected to pay lab fees?
- Does the department have its own library or specialist material?
- Is free study time available? (and how much?)

Degree courses

Some courses are single honours, that is they concentrate on one subject. Others are joint honours, built around two subjects. Many are combined honours linking disciplines. It is also possible to study some subjects to general (rather than honours) degree level. There are advantages to each model.

Single honours courses allow students to look into subjects in depth. Variety comes from within the subject. Combined honours are frequently designed to link cognate, or related, subjects. For example, English and history may be especially relevant to those interested in the fit between culture and history. There has also been a trend in recent years for universities to provide a vocational dimension to combined honours, for example chemistry and business studies, while the nature of some areas effectively means that they are 'combined' subjects, for example manufacturing engineering. In Scotland the 'general degree' tradition is much stronger than in the rest of the UK. The increased flexibility stemming from modularisation, credit transfer and other initiatives has also added greatly to the diversity of university offerings.

Non-degree courses

The range of courses on offer in universities has widened significantly over the last few years. In part, this is because the pioneers and providers of these programmes became today's new universities. These courses include:

- BTEC and ScotVec Higher National Certificate or Diploma, General National Vocational Qualifications (GNVQs)
- Professional studies, e.g. Institute of Chartered Secretaries & Administrators
- Special studies, such as Certificate in Industrial Relations and Trades Union Studies

For many, non-degree courses are as valuable an educational experience as a conventional degree. Some are a route into a degree course.

New and unconventional course structures

Credits, transfers and exemptions Some non-degree courses offer credits towards a final degree, meaning that a course or its equivalent which is part of a degree programme need not be taken again. Credit accumulation and transfer has emerged as an increasingly important feature of university education and means that a course credit obtained at one university can be transferred to a programme at another.

The Credit Accumulation and Transfer Scheme (CATS) works by universities agreeing to recognise studies successfully completed elsewhere as equivalent to those undertaken at their university. A student who is forced to move will, therefore, be able to graduate. More and more companies are taking advantage of this type of scheme to link their in-company courses to university programmes by establishing a course equivalence. The qualifications of some professional bodies are being treated in much the same way. It also means that students who are obliged to break off their studies can return later with a minimum degree of disruption.

Modules The entire process of change toward credit accumulation and transfer is made easier by the increased modularisation of degree courses: the breaking-down of courses into relatively free-standing units or modules. These can then be combined in ways which give far greater freedom and flexibility to institutions in course design and to students in programme choice. It is based on the system used extensively in the USA. Typically, new students are expected to identify their main area of study,

English, say. In the first three terms, they will be expected to complete a course in English by completing three modules: English 1, English 2 and English 3. This is a 'major'. They might also be required to complete an associated subsidiary of two or more linked courses and several electives or minors.

Some institutions have experimented with a virtual free choice in course combinations, the so-called supermarket system. Most, however, are stricter and insist on more tightly defined structures to courses. For example, you can't take English 3 until English 2 is successfully completed.

Semesters The move to modules is closely associated with the reorganisation of the academic year at many universities into semesters. In some, this is largely a cosmetic change. Others have followed the example of pioneers such as the University of Stirling and introduced sweeping changes. At Stirling there are two 15-week semesters instead of the traditional three terms. The academic year starts in late August with the first semester, which lasts until Christmas. The second semester starts in mid-February and goes straight through until June.

Distance, open and flexible learning The Open University was a pioneer of many of the above changes. It is, however, best known for its development of distance and open learning for degrees. This means that students do not follow their studies within the physical confines of the institution. They often work at a distance, supported by a system of course materials, local tuition and various forms of assessment and counselling. Many other institutions have introduced distance learning into their portfolios.

Flexible learning has also grown in importance. Flexible learning programmes are designed around the needs and circumstances of particular groups of students. In one form, a consortium of companies works with a university to develop a range of courses for their employees. In some cases, Ford for example, there is no need or expectation that this will lead to a formal qualification. In other cases, such as the flexible learning courses in information technology, a new degree programme may be developed.

Which course?

Your choice from the bewildering variety of courses will largely be determined by the interaction of four different pressures. In brief, they are:

1 **Opportunity** Mix ambition with realism to eliminate those subjects you cannot follow. If in doubt, talk to a careers advisor.
2 **School studies** Recognise your strengths and weaknesses. Use this self-assessment to guide your choice.
3 **Career aspirations** Think long and hard about the type of career you hope to follow. Ask parents, friends and careers staff about the links between courses and the career you hope to have.
4 **Personal/life interest** Build interest, enjoyment and stimulation into your course. Taking a degree is rarely plain sailing and you will need self-motivation and commitment to get through your studies.

Opportunity In the UK, applications for courses generally exceed the number of places available. Choice is therefore immediately restricted by your realistic chances of getting an offer and meeting its requirements. The six universities to which you can apply rapidly change from being too many choices to too few – especially if options are used up in unrealistic choices. The first step in the selection process is to eliminate those options for which you either do not have or are unlikely to obtain the entry requirements. (See chapter 7 for broad indications of likely requirements.)

Many courses, for example economics, require A-level or Higher maths or a minimum grade at GCSE, O-level or HNC. Others demand A-levels or Highers in a related, cognate subject: for example, English for American studies, biology for medicine, and Greek for archaeology. There are subjects, too, that you will be able to take at university only if you have studied them for A-level or Highers.

These requirements may be waived for mature students, especially those entering through an access course. Other directly relevant experiences, especially work experience, may also be taken into account when you apply.

School studies There will probably be a strong link between what you study at school and what you study at university. But while an aptitude or liking for a particular subject at school can often be continued successfully at university, it is important to recognise that the nature of a subject and your response to it can change significantly between school and university. It may be rare to find someone who disliked a subject at school but enjoyed it at university, but the reverse is all too common. Consider too the many subjects not offered in schools.

Career aspirations These play an important role in the choice of university degree for many entrants. There are three important aspects of this issue to bear in mind in selecting a course:
1   Your views, attitudes and aspirations are very likely to change as you follow your studies. There are risks in making a firm choice too early and considering only a vocational degree.
2   Examine the reality of the course and its genuine link with the career in question. Names can be deceptive, especially in fashionable areas. Environmental Science courses, for example, often pay far more attention to geology and soil science than to Friends of the Earth.
3   The dynamics of the graduate job market have become increasingly volatile. A degree might get you an interview but getting the job probably depends on a host of other factors.

Personal/life interest Because many subjects offered at university are not part of the school curriculum, the scope for extending your interests and your personal development at university is immense. So don't limit your choice of subject to what you already know. Be imaginative – but be realistic, too.

To take an example at random, psychology provides new and exciting views of human behaviour. It is a powerful and well-structured body of knowledge and can lead to a wide range of career opportunities. Furthermore, it is a subject that requires careful attention to detail if it is to be most rewarding. Much of this detail may only be accessible through painstaking laboratory work. Sometimes the analysis of nervous systems requires dissection and other skills.

A sound choice depends on a proper understanding of:

🎓 the subject
🎓 the differences between courses at various institutions
🎓 the style, strength and character of the departments offering the programme

Staying with the example of psychology, the experience offered by a department with a dominant commitment to research and a specialist interest in primatology will be different to that provided by a teaching-oriented unit with a major preoccupation with child psychology.

The facilities on offer vary considerably between institutions. Resource shortages have hit laboratory subjects especially hard, with the traditional notion of the well-founded laboratory under particular threat.

Other sources of information

Which Subject? Which Career?, edited by Jamieson, A, CRAC Publications, Cambridge
How to Choose Your Degree Course, Heap, B, Trotman & Co., Richmond, Surrey
The NatWest Student Book 2000, Boehm, K and Lees-Spalding, J, Macmillan
Degree Course Offers, Heap, B, Trotman & Co., Richmond, Surrey

4
STUDYING ABROAD

University education has always been international. In the Middle Ages, the travelling scholar and his students moved from country to country to pursue their work. In the 17th, 18th and 19th centuries European academics moved between countries with a greater ease than virtually anyone else. It is now common for university staff to spend long periods working in institutions outside their home country, either with substantive appointments or on sabbaticals. Students, too, increasingly wish to spend part of their studies in a foreign university.

This pattern is especially well established in North America. Most US and Canadian universities have 'study abroad' programmes which enable their students to follow courses at an overseas institution and gain credits towards their degree. There are three basic approaches:

1 Study at another university, gaining credits by completing its courses.
2 Study at facilities owned by your university in Europe, Asia, etc.
3 Follow courses organised by your university in a foreign country and largely run by the university's own staff.

The opportunities created by the first of these methods has stimulated British universities to establish extensive exchange programmes with institutions in North America and Europe. In recent years some universities have extended these schemes and are able to include exchanges with universities in other parts of the world, especially in Asia and Australia.

How do I set about going on one of these programmes?

Not all universities offer exchange programmes. Where they operate, they might be linked to specific departments, schools or faculties. Anyone keen to undertake an exchange must choose an institution offering such a programme. You should establish the terms and conditions in advance. Most of the programmes are highly competitive and may, for example, be restricted to students with a minimum average grade. Some host universities impose their own conditions, for example they may restrict their exchanges to UK students.

The European Union sees student mobility and exchanges as an important element in building a 'community of learning' and a greater sense among students of European citizenship. This view influenced the creation of the EU action programme, Erasmus, or European Union Action Scheme for the Mobility of University Students. The scheme was named after the Swiss-born 16th-century humanist and philosopher Desiderius Erasmus who spent his working life as a professor in universities in the Netherlands, France, England, Italy and Switzerland. It has now been succeeded by a larger programme named after an even more eminent scholar, Socrates.

Students spend at least three months at a university (or equivalent) in another EU country. The success of the programme has since encouraged universities to develop fully integrated common courses involving staff and students from several EU countries. A key feature of the Socrates programme is the building up of a European system of credit transfer (ECTS). Initially, automatic credit transfer is being introduced in five subjects: mechanical engineering, chemistry, medicine, business studies and history.

Outside North America and Europe student exchanges are more patchy. Institutions such as London University's School of Oriental and African Studies that have direct links with other countries are the exception rather than the rule. The growing interest in Japan among UK academics has prompted some institutions to build up exchange and/or visit programmes. The main constraint on these and other international exchanges tends to be money.

The costs of these programmes vary a great deal. Formal exchanges with US universities will probably cost students next to nothing. The institutions concerned meet the bills, albeit only within strict guidelines. Under the Socrates programme specific grants are provided to meet such expenses as language preparation, cost-of-living differentials and travel. Elsewhere, the pattern tends to be determined by local circumstances.

Always consult fully with the university's international links or liaison staff – they are often attached to the registrar's department – and the relevant departmental or faculty staff. They are in the best position to advise on what is available and the likely effect on you and your prospects. The best route into study overseas lies through programmes linked to UK universities. The links already exist and there is a wealth of institutional support if things go wrong.

You may see advertisements for the UK campus of American colleges. Although some of these are linked to institutions of high standing, you should take a great deal of care in dealing with them. Their links with their parent institutions should be scrutinised closely to ensure full and proper accreditation. Without this, it is very hard to win any recognition for the qualifications provided.

Can I opt to go to university overseas?

In theory, the answer is yes. In practice, it is very difficult without either links with the country/university in question or some compelling reason such as the fact that no British university offers the programme you want to study.

That said, studying at a university in Europe has become easier with the introduction of the Single European Market in January 1993. Some barriers are already being dismantled, especially those linked to recognition of qualifications.

Others, however, will take much longer to change, especially those to do with language, degree structure and student support. In North America, some of these barriers do not exist but others, notably cost, can be equally daunting. In 1994 the average cost of attending one of the top ten US universities was over $70,000 pa, while the average across the top 100 US universities was over $25,000 pa.

Other sources of information

Information on Socrates programmes can be obtained from your university or from:

The Erasmus Bureau, rue Montoyer 70, B-1040 Bruxelles, Belgium or, for grant information:

UK Erasmus Students Grants Council, The University, Canterbury, CT2 7PD

General information on higher education in Europe, North America and elsewhere:

Higher Education in the European Community, Mohr, B, and Liebig, I, Kogan Page, London

How to Study Abroad, Tinsley, T, How To Books, Plymouth

America's Best Colleges, US News and World Report, Washington DC, USA

Barron's Guide to US Universities and Colleges (annual)

Guide to American Colleges and Universities, ARCO, Prentice Hall, New York (annual)

How to Apply to American Colleges and Universities, Brennan, M and Briggs, S, VGM Career Horizons, Illinois, USA.

The International Student's Guide to the American University, National Student Textbook Co., Illinois, USA

A Guide to the Admission of Foreign Student, National Association for Foreign Student Affairs, Washington DC, USA

5
THE TOP
UNIVERSITIES
BY SUBJECT

Knowing where a university stands in the pecking order of higher education is a vital piece of information for any prospective student, but the quality of the course is what matters most. The most modest institution may have a centre of specialist excellence and even famous universities have mediocre departments. This section offers some pointers to the leading universities in those subjects assessed by the higher education funding councils. Expert assessors have produced official ratings for research in every subject, but the judgments on teaching are still not complete. The tables in this chapter cover all the areas in which teaching has been assessed in England. The assessments have not been completed for all universities in Scotland and Wales, but all-UK rankings have been compiled wherever possible.

The method used to compare departments takes account of new information on entrance qualifications and to be consistent with the overall university rankings. Three elements are included: average A-level entry scores; the funding councils' ratings for teaching; the funding councils' ratings for research. The three indicators are combined using the same weightings as in the main university league table: 1 for entrance; 2.5 for teaching; 1.5 for research. Where only two measures were available, they were averaged to produce a third score. Differences in the gradings used by the Scottish and Welsh funding councils have been accommodated by calculating an equivalent on the English scale.

The tables confirm the dominance of the traditional universities in most areas of higher education. This is to be expected in research, where decades of differential funding have left the former polytechnics struggling to compete. Less predictably, however, the ratings for teaching have usually told the same story. This is partly because the academics who inspect departments take into account facilities such as library stock, while the traditional universities' generally smaller teaching groups also give them an advantage.

There are exceptions, however. In linguistics, for example, Thames Valley collected maximum ratings for both teaching and research, overtaking numerous universities with higher entrance requirements. Only the small proportion of academics assessed for research prevents its reaching top place. Overall, however, Cambridge is again by far the most successful university, with a 14 top placings and bettered in only a handful of the subjects in which it offers undergraduate courses. Oxford has the next highest number of top places with five.

The subject rankings demonstrate that there are 'horses for courses' in higher education. Thus LSE is more than a match for its rivals in social sciences while Imperial College London confirms its reputation in engineering. In their own fields, table-toppers such as East Anglia (environmental sciences) and Bath (mechanical engineering) are equally well-known.

AGRICULTURE

1 Nottingham
2 Newcastle
3 Edinburgh
4 Aberdeen
5 Reading
6 Cranfield
7 Leeds
8 Queen's, Belfast
9 Lincs & Humber
10 Bournemouth
11 Plymouth
12 Bangor
13 Aberystwyth
14 De Montfort

Total institutions: 14

AMERICAN STUDIES

1 Keele
2 Nottingham
3 Sussex
4 East Anglia
5 Reading
6 Hull
7 Birmingham
8 Kent
9 Central Lancashire
10 Middlesex
11 Brunel
12 Wolverhampton
13 Swansea

Total institutions:: 13

ANTHROPOLOGY

1 Cambridge
2 LSE
3 Manchester
4 Brunel
5 UCL
6 Oxford
7 Durham
8 SOAS
9 Sussex
10 Oxford Brookes
11 St Andrews
12 Kent
13 Edinburgh
14 Goldsmiths'
15 Hull
16 Queen's (Belfast)
17 Swansea

Total institutions: 17

ARCHITECTURE

1 Cambridge
2 Sheffield
3 UCL
4 Cardiff
5 Nottingham
6 Newcastle
7 York
8 Bath
9 Strathclyde
10 Edinburgh
11 Westminster
12 Liverpool
13 Greenwich
14 Lincs & Humber
15 Oxford Brookes
16 East London
17 Manchester
18 Robert Gordon
19 Queen's (Belfast)
20 Brighton

Total institutions: 33

BUILDING

1 Reading
2 Ulster
3 Loughborough
4 UCL
5 Westminster
6 UMIST
7 Kingston
8 Salford
9 Oxford Brookes
10 Heriot-Watt
11 Nottingham Trent
12 Northumbria
13 Liverpool JMU
14 Plymouth
15 Coventry
16 Greenwich
17 Luton
18 Hertfordshire
19 Liverpool
20 Teesside

Total institutions: 40

BUSINESS AND MANAGEMENT STUDIES

1 UMIST
2 Lancaster
3 Warwick
4 LSE
5 Bath
6 Nottingham
7 Manchester
8 City
9 Strathclyde
10 Edinburgh
11 Loughborough
12 Imperial
13 St Andrews
14 Cranfield
15 Cardiff
16 Reading
17 Southampton
18 Sheffield
19 Glasgow
20 Bradford

Total institutions: 86

CHEMICAL ENGINEERING

1 Imperial
2 Cambridge
3 UMIST
4 Sheffield
5 Loughborough
6 Bath
7 UCL
8 Birmingham
9 Swansea
10 Newcastle
11 Queen's (Belfast)
12 Nottingham
13 Edinburgh
14 Aston
15 Bradford
16 Surrey
17 Heriot-Watt
18 Leeds
19 Strathclyde
20 South Bank

Total institutions: 21

CHEMISTRY

1 Cambridge, Oxford
3 Imperial
4 Bristol
5 Durham
6 Edinburgh
7 Nottingham
8 Southampton
9 Leeds
10 St Andrews
11 Strathclyde
12 Leicester
13 Manchester
14 Glasgow
15 Hull
16 Cardiff
17 Birmingham
18 Sheffield
19 York
20 Bath

Total institutions: 73

CIVIL ENGINEERING

1 Bristol
2 Imperial
3 UCL
4 Cardiff
5 Nottingham
6 Swansea
7 Bath
8 Sheffield
9 Queen's (Belfast)
10 Edinburgh
11 Newcastle
12 Liverpool
13 Surrey
14 UMIST
15 Loughborough
16 Heriot-Watt
17 Birmingham
18 Dundee
19 Greenwich
20 Southampton

Total institutions: 50

COMPUTER SCIENCE

1 Cambridge
2 Warwick
3 York
4 Glasgow
5 Oxford
6 Imperial
7 Edinburgh
8 Manchester
9 Southampton
10 Exeter
11 Swansea
12 Kent
13 Bristol
14 Bath
15 Lancaster
16 Heriot-Watt
17 UCL
18 St Andrews
19 Durham
20 Dundee

Total institutions: 93

COMMUNICATION, CULTURAL AND MEDIA STUDIES

1 Warwick
2 East Anglia
3 Sussex
4 Westminster
5 West of England
6 Birmingham
7 Central Lancashire
8 Leeds
9 Goldsmiths'
10 Leicester
11 Stirling
12 Napier
13 Ulster
14 Brunel
15 Nottingham Trent
16 South Bank
17 Liverpool JMU
18 Glasgow Cal
19 Sunderland
20 Sheffield Hallam

Total Institutions: 35

DRAMA, DANCE AND CINEMATICS

1 Warwick
2 Royal Holloway
3 Lancaster
4 Hull
5 Bristol
6 Kent
7 Brunel
8 Reading
9 Exeter
10 Glamorgan
11 Manchester
12 Queen Mary
13 Loughborough
14 Birmingham
15 Goldsmiths'
16 North London
17 Manchester Metropolitan
18 East Anglia
19 Surrey
20 Ulster

Total institutions: 34

EAST AND SOUTH ASIAN STUDIES

1 Cambridge
2 Oxford
3 Leeds
4 SOAS
5 Hull
6 Durham
7 Edinburgh
8 Sheffield
9 Westminster
10 Stirling

Total institutions: 10

EDUCATION

1 Oxford
2 East Anglia
3 Birmingham
4 Sheffield
5 Cambridge
6 Cardiff
7 Durham
8 Manchester
9 Warwick
10 Newcastle
11 Stirling
12 York
13 Leeds
14 Exeter
15 Bristol
16 Brighton
17 Sussex
18 King's
19 Ulster
20 Reading

Total institutions: 59

ELECTRICAL AND ELECTRONIC ENGINEERING

1 Sheffield
2 Southampton
3 Edinburgh
4 UCL
5 Imperial
6 Bristol
7 Surrey
8 York
9 Birmingham
10 Queen's (Belfast)
11 Strathclyde
12 Essex
13 Cardiff
14 Nottingham
15 Leeds
16 UMIST
17 Heriot-Watt
18 Hull
19 Loughborough
20 King's

Total institutions: 75

ENGLISH

1 Oxford
2 UCL
3 Cambridge
4 Leeds
5 Birmingham
6 Nottingham
7 Sussex
8 York
9 Warwick
10 Durham
11 Leicester
12 Queen Mary
13 Southampton
14 Bristol
15 Sheffield
16 Liverpool
17 Lancaster
18 Edinburgh
19 Dundee
20 Newcastle

Total institutions: 70

ENVIRONMENTAL SCIENCE

1 East Anglia
2 Reading
3 Lancaster
4 Southampton
5 Aberystwyth
6 Queen Mary
7 Liverpool
8 Sheffield
9 Plymouth
10 Ulster
11 Stirling
12 Hertfordshire
13 Sussex
14 Bangor
15 Huddersfield
16 Northumbria
17 Salford
18 West of England
19 Coventry
20 Teesside

Total institutions: 41

GENERAL ENGINEERING

1 Cambridge
2 Oxford
3 Imperial
4 Durham
5 Southampton
6 Warwick
7 Lancaster
8 Brunel
9 Ulster
10 Leicester
11 Liverpool
12 Liverpool JMU
13 Hertfordshire
14 Exeter
15 Central Lancashire
16 Queen Mary
17 Bradford
18 Cranfield
19 Sussex
20 Aberdeen

Total institutions: 34

FRENCH

1 Cambridge
2 Oxford
3 UCL
4 Oxford Brookes
5 Aberdeen
6 Durham
7 Aston
8 Portsmouth
9 Warwick
10 Leeds
11 Exeter
12 Sussex
13 St Andrews
14 Queen Mary
15 Glasgow
16 Sheffield
17 Royal Holloway
18 Strathclyde
19 Newcastle
20 Bristol

Total institutions: 55

GEOGRAPHY

1 Cambridge
2 Bristol
3 Durham
4 UCL
5 Leeds
6 Sheffield
7 Southampton
8 Edinburgh
9 Oxford
10 Nottingham
11 East Anglia
12 Birmingham
13 Exeter
14 Manchester
15 Lancaster
16 Swansea
17 St Andrews
18 Aberystwyth
19 Reading
20 King's

Total institutions: 63

GEOLOGY

1   Cambridge, Oxford
3   Newcastle
4   Edinburgh
5   Leeds
6   Liverpool
7   Reading
8   Durham
9   Manchester
10 Plymouth
11 Imperial
12 Glasgow
13 UCL
14 Royal Holloway
15 Bristol
16 Southampton
17 Birmingham
18 Cardiff
19 Queen's (Belfast)
20 Leicester

Total institutions: 34

GERMAN

1   Nottingham
2   Cambridge
3   Oxford
4   Warwick
5   Exeter
6   UCL
7   Aston
8   Queen Mary
9   Swansea
10 King's
11 St Andrews
12 Manchester
13 Edinburgh
14 Birmingham
15 Bristol
16 Leeds
17 Leicester
18 Bristol
19 Sheffield
20 Newcastle

Total institutions: 47

HISTORY

1   Cambridge
2   Warwick
3   King's
4   Oxford
5   UCL
6   Durham
7   LSE
8   Sheffield
9   Birmingham
10 St Andrews
11 Lancaster
12 Liverpool
13 Royal Holloway
14 Edinburgh
15 Hull
16 York
17 Leicester
18 Queen's (Belfast)
19 Swansea
20 Bristol

Total institutions: 77

HISTORY OF ART

1   UCL
2   Cambridge
3   SOAS
4   Nottingham
5   Leeds
6   Reading
7   Essex
8   East Anglia
9   Warwick
10 Sussex
11 Edinburgh
12 York
13 Manchester
14 St Andrew's
15 Birmingham
16 Kent
17 Oxford Brookes
18 Leicester
19 Middlesex
20 Staffordshire

Total institutions: 37

IBERIAN LANGUAGES

1 Cambridge
2 Queen Mary
3 Birmingham
4 Aberdeen
5 St Andrews
6 Hull
7 King's
8 Bristol
9 Liverpool
10 Leeds
11 Sheffield
12 Oxford
13 Swansea
14 Glasgow
15 Edinburgh
16 Queen's (Belfast)
17 Newcastle
18 Exeter
19 Manchester
20 Stirling

Total institutions: 32

ITALIAN

1 Cambridge
2 Exeter
3 Royal Holloway
4 Oxford
5 Birmingham
6 UCL
7 Bristol
8 Edinburgh
9 Reading
10 Glasgow
11 Lancaster
12 Strathclyde
13 Swansea
14 Kent
15 Oxford Brookes
16 Leeds
17 Hull
18 Warwick
19 Cardiff
20 Leicester

Total institutions: 24

LAND AND PROPERTY MANAGEMENT

1 Kingston
2 Reading
3 Cambridge, Liverpool JMU
5 Greenwich
6 Oxford Brookes
7 City
8 De Montford
9 Portsmouth
10 Leeds Metropolitan
11 West of England
12 Sheffield Hallam
13 Westminster
14 Anglia
15 Staffordshire
16 South Bank
17 Central England

Total institutions: 17

LAW

1 Cambridge
2 Oxford
3 Manchester
4 King's
5 LSE
6 UCL
7 Nottingham
8 Sheffield
9 Warwick
10 Leicester
11 Durham
12 Oxford Brookes
13 Bristol
14 Liverpool
15 Essex
16 Aberdeen
17 Edinburgh
18 SOAS
19 East Anglia
20 Queen's (Belfast)

Total institutions: 73

LINGUISTICS

1 Cambridge, Thames Valley
3 Lancaster, Queen Mary
5 UCL
6 Oxford
7 Newcastle
8 Manchester
9 York
10 Sheffield
11 Durham
12 Sussex
13 Edinburgh
14 Essex
15 SOAS
16 Reading
17 Bangor
18 Hertfordshire
19 East Anglia
20 UMIST

Total institutions: 26

MANUFACTURING, MECHANICAL AND AERO-NAUTICAL ENGINEERING

1 Imperial
2 Bath
3 Nottingham
4 UMIST
5 Loughborough
6 UCL
7 Bristol
8 Southampton
9 Cardiff
10 Cranfield
11 Queen's (Belfast)
12 Liverpool
13 Manchester
14 Birmingham
15 Kingston
16 Brunel
17 Central England
18 King's
19 Queen Mary
20 Anglia

Total institutions: 43

MECHANICAL ENGINEERING

1 Bath
2 Sheffield
3 Cardiff
4 Nottingham
5 Bristol
6 Cranfield
7 Imperial
8 Heriot-Watt
9 Manchester
10 Leeds
11 Stratchclyde
12 UMIST
13 Aberdeen
14 Southampton
15 UCL
16 Reading
17 Queen's (Belfast)
18 Robert Gordon
19 Liverpool
20 Loughborough

Total institutions: 62

METALLURGY AND MATERIALS

1 Oxford
2 Cambridge
3 Imperial
4 Sheffield
5 Swansea
6 Liverpool
7 Manchester
8 UMIST
9 Birmingham
10 Nottingham
11 Loughborough
12 Bath
13 Surrey
14 Exeter
15 Queen Mary
16 Leeds
17 Sheffield Hallam
18 Guildhall
19 Manchester Metropolitan
20 Brunel

Total institutions: 26

MIDDLE EASTERN AND AFRICAN STUDIES

1 Cambridge
2 Birmingham
3 Oxford
4 Durham
5 SOAS
6 Edinburgh
7 Manchester
8 Exeter
9 Leeds

Total institutions: 9

MUSIC

1 SOAS
2 King's
3 Cambridge
4 Birmingham
5 Nottingham
6 York
7 Sheffield
8 Leeds
9 Keele, Lancaster
11 Manchester
12 Southampton
13 Surrey
14 Queen's (Belfast)
15 City
16 Goldsmiths'
17 Oxford
18 Edinburgh
19 Sussex
20 Liverpool

Total institutions: 44

NUTRITION AND FOOD SCIENCE

1 Nottingham
2 Reading
3 Leeds
4 Queen's (Belfast)
5 Oxford Brookes
6 North London
7 Huddersfield
8 Teesside
9 Bournemouth
10 Lincs & Humber
11 Manchester Metropolitan
12 South Bank

Total institutions: 12

PLANNING

1   Kingston
2   Cardiff
3   Sheffield
4   Liverpool
5   Reading
6   Oxford Brookes
7   Salford
8   Nottingham
9   Newcastle
10 Aberdeen
11 Queen's (Belfast)
12 Manchester
13 West of England
14 South Bank
15 Leeds Metropolitan
16 Sheffield Hallam
17 Dundee
18 Strathclyde
19 Coventry
20 De Montfort

Total institutions: 25

RUSSIAN, SLAVONIC AND EAST EUROPEAN LANGUAGES

1   Sheffield
2   Cambridge
3   SEES
4   St Andrews
5   Bristol
6   Birmingham
7   Oxford
8   Bangor
9   Strathclyde
10 Nottingham
11 Queen Mary
12 Glasgow
13 Keele
14 Edinburgh
15 Leeds
16 Wolverhampton
17 Durham
18 Exeter
19 Manchester
20 Sussex

Total institutions: 22

SOCIAL POLICY AND ADMINISTRATION

1   LSE
2   Loughborough
3   Warwick
4   Kent
5   Nottingham
6   York
7   Bath
8   Edinburgh
9   Manchester
10 Brunel
11 Southampton
12 Hull
13 Sheffield
14 Ulster
15 Newcastle
16 Leeds
17 Glasgow
18 Royal Holloway
19 Bristol
20 Birmingham

Total institutions: 42

SOCIAL WORK

1 Lancaster, York
3 Edinburgh
4 East Anglia
5 Keele
6 Southampton
7 Bristol
8 Hull
9 Queen's (Belfast)
10 Huddersfield
11 Stirling
12 Robert Gordon
13 Warwick
14 Dundee
15 Leicester
16 Durham
17 Anglia
18 Swansea
19 Bradford
20 Birmingham

Total institutions: 46

SOCIOLOGY

1 Warwick
2 Edinburgh
3 Sussex
4 Loughborough
5 Essex
6 Sheffield
7 Lancaster
8 York
9 Manchester
10 Sheffield Hallam
11 Stirling
12 Brunel
13 Glasgow
14 LSE
15 Surrey
16 Aberdeen
17 Southampton
18 Goldsmiths'
19 Bristol
20 Leeds

Total institutions: 72

6
FOR OVERSEAS STUDENTS

T his chapter has been introduced for the first time in this year's edition to assist students from other countries planning to come to a university in the United Kingdom. If it is difficult enough for individuals living here, faced with the bewildering choice among the 100 or so universities, to decide which university to apply to, then it is all the more so if you are on the other side of the world where, in addition, you will want to consider the significant costs of living and studying in another country. Nonetheless, though you should certainly supplement the information in this chapter with that from other sources, it will give you a good start and point you in the right direction.

Britain's universities have long had a global outlook. It's a trend that shows no signs of slowing. More than one in ten of the country's student population comes from overseas and in many universities you will find yourself rubbing shoulders with students from more than 100 countries. That said, the economic difficulties that have beset some Asian countries since the mid-1990s have seen a reduction in demand for university places in Britain from those countries. On the other hand, there has been a growth in student numbers from Latin America, particularly Argentina, Brazil and Mexico, and from the Indian sub-continent.

Support for international students is more comprehensive than in most other countries and begins long before you arrive in the UK. Most universities have advisers, even offices, in other countries on whom you can call and they are likely to put you in touch with current students or graduates from your own school or country. Then there may well be pre-departure receptions for you and your family. There will certainly be full pre-arrival information on all aspects of living and studying in Britain.

Having come here, there are generally facilities in place to meet and greet you when you arrive; a guarantee of warm and comfortable university accommodation; an orientation programme – often lasting several days – to meet friends and to help you adjust to your new surroundings; and, for those who need them, courses in English. Each university has a Students Union which organises social, cultural, religious and sporting clubs and events, including many specifically for overseas students. Both the university and its Student Unions are likely to have full-time staff whose sole purpose is to look after your welfare. You will have free medical treatment under the National Health Service, full access to a professional Counselling Service and a University Careers Service network – with an enviable reputation throughout the world – to help you decide what to do on completion of your studies.

Sources of information

Advice and information on the UK universities are available through the British Council and its Educational Counselling Service. The Council maintains a comprehensive network of information centres in cities throughout the world and organises more than 50 University Exhibitions in some 25 key countries every year. Its 'Virtual Campus' is a good guide to studying and living in Britain. It contains profiles of all UK universities as well as further details of support services for overseas students and information of course fees, living costs and English language requirements. Visit it on: **www.britcoun.org/eis/**

UKCOSA, The Council for International Education, is another useful source of advice and information to international students. Its web site can be viewed at: **www.ukcosa.org.uk**

The tables

Much of the information in these tables reflects no more than the numbers of overseas students at any given university, not that institution's quality. It is important, therefore, that you cross refer to the main ranking of British universities in chapter 1 and the individual subject tables in chapter 5, both of which are concerned with quality.

The data are based on international students enrolling on first degree courses at UK universities in 1996–97 and are the latest figures available. They exclude those students whose complete study programmes were outside the UK.

The first two tables give a broad overview of international students in Britain, breaking down students as EU and non-EU, and highlighting the most popular courses and where they are studied. Most students, regardless of their country of origin, pursue courses of study which are strongly vocational in that they lead to careers in business and the professions.

Our 'Where Do They Study' table on page 56 lists those universities with large numbers of international students. Ulster owes much of its popularity to its close proximity to the Republic of Ireland while big numbers at Middlesex and Glamorgan, particularly in Business and Administrative Studies, include large exchange programmes. EU students are well represented in the new universities whereas students from other countries gravitate to all parts of the sector. This pattern of distribution largely reflects chosen fields of study and the universities where these subjects are available. As emphasised earlier, you must satisfy yourself about quality by going back to chapters 1 and 5.

Probably the most useful information is to be found in the tables listing numbers of overseas students in any one subject group in any one university.

Again, use these tables in conjunction with the tables of quality measures in earlier chapters. We have given details for nine of the 19 subject groups summarised in the 'What Do They Study' table on this page.

For the record, 'Subjects Allied to Medicine' includes nursing; 'Business and Administrative Studies' includes financial management and accountancy; and 'Creative Arts and Design' includes music and drama.

WHAT DO THEY STUDY?

	EU	Non-EU	Total
Engineering and Technology	7426	10331	17757
Business and Administrative Studies	7207	8210	15417
Social, Economic and Political Studies	3507	2784	6291
Law	1272	3949	5221
Languages	2974	911	3885
Biological Sciences	2614	1220	3834
Subjects Allied to Medicine	1844	1943	3787
Computer Studies	1642	1923	3565
Architecture, Building and Planning	1480	1940	3420
Creative Arts and Design	1296	1404	2700
Physical Sciences	1935	643	2578
Medicine and Dentistry	328	1618	1946
Mathematical Sciences	565	529	1094
Education	337	707	1044
Humanities	681	353	1034
Librarianship and Information Science	468	254	722
Agriculture and Related Subjects	308	130	438
Veterinary Science	40	165	205
Combined	4253	3298	7551

WHERE DO THEY STUDY?: THE TOP 20 UNIVERSITIES

EU students	Total	Non-EU students	Total
1 Ulster	1998	1 Middlesex	1171
2 Middlesex	1293	2 Portsmouth	1051
3 Glamorgan	1267	3 Sheffield	1004
4 Coventry	1221	4 Leeds	922
5 Portsmouth	810	4 UMIST	922
6 Essex	781	6 LSE	912
7 Queen's (Belfast)	769	7 East London	910
8 Brighton	739	8 Nottingham	905
9 Kent	676	9 Imperial	903
10 Sunderland	671	10 UCL	898
11 Hertfordshire	644	11 Manchester	863
12 Anglia	638	12 Coventry	819
13 Thames Valley	629	13 Birmingham	784
14 Wolverhampton	627	14 Thames Valley	763
15 Sussex	622	15 Hertfordshire	744
16 Manchester Metro	621	16 Cardiff	739
17 Lincs and Humber	619	16 Northumbria	739
18 Luton	598	18 Wolverhampton	708
19 Westminster	572	19 Warwick	680
20 Kingston	543	20 Oxford Brookes	673

THE TOP 15 UNIVERSITIES BY SUBJECT
ENGINEERING AND TECHNOLOGY

	EU	Non-EU	Total
1 Coventry	543	300	843
2 UMIST	136	642	778
3 Imperial	175	543	718
4 Leeds	126	458	584
5 Birmingham	63	477	540
6 Portsmouth	214	285	499
7 Hertfordshire	187	298	485
8 Surrey	177	281	458
9 Glasgow	143	293	436
10 Sheffield	54	353	407
11 Glamorgan	257	135	392
12 Bradford	137	230	367
13 UCL	78	274	352
14 Newcastle	130	213	343
15 Loughborough	37	301	338

BUSINESS AND ADMINISTRATIVE STUDIES

	EU	Non-EU	Total
1 Middlesex	523	618	1141
2 Glamorgan	702	211	913
3 Coventry	279	262	541
4 Lincs and Humber	382	119	501
5 Thames Valley	125	306	431
6 Brighton	291	131	422
7 Portsmouth	140	265	405
8 Wolverhampton	238	143	381
9 South Bank	152	228	380
10 Northumbria	143	220	363
11 LSE	86	275	361
12 Oxford Brookes	149	202	351
13 De Montfort	53	262	315
14 Ulster	297	3	300
14 Westminster	240	160	300

SOCIAL, ECONOMIC AND POLITICAL STUDIES

	EU	Non-EU	Total
1 LSE	201	485	686
2 Portsmouth	120	143	263
3 Sussex	169	73	242
4 Anglia	206	31	237
5 Kent	112	93	205
6 Essex	117	66	183
7 Cambridge	48	122	170
8 Warwick	55	108	163
9 East London	95	63	158
10 UCL	56	98	154
11 Middlesex	114	26	140
12 Queen Mary	62	72	134
13 Leicester	5	127	132
14 Bristol	27	93	120
15 City	48	65	113

LAW

	EU	Non-EU	Total
1 Thames Valley	97	173	270
2 King's	111	146	257
3 Wolverhampton	27	214	241
4 Sheffield	4	231	235
5 Cardiff	11	192	203
6 Essex	85	115	200
7 Kent	94	105	199
8 East London	34	144	178
9 Glamorgan	31	132	163
10 Bristol	6	150	156
11 Staffordshire	28	119	147
12 Leicester	8	130	138
13 Sussex	41	88	129
14 Oxford	17	103	120
15 Warwick	8	110	118

LANGUAGES

	EU	Non-EU	Total
1 Thames Valley	211	19	230
2 Essex	142	22	264
3 Wolverhampton	112	19	131
4 Portsmouth	109	21	130
5 UCL	90	39	129
6 Luton	109	8	117
7 Oxford	55	52	107
8 Kent	34	144	178
8 Queen Mary	81	14	95
10 Ulster	92	2	94
11 Salford	61	30	91
12 Royal Holloway	65	22	87
13 Manchester	71	15	86
14 Cambridge	48	34	82
15 South Bank	76	3	79

SUBJECTS ALLIED TO MEDICINE

	EU	Non-EU	Total
1 Ulster	370	38	408
2 King's	97	104	201
3 Robert Gordon	104	92	196
4 Strathclyde	30	159	189
5 Brighton	97	72	169
6 Sunderland	118	42	160
7 Bradford	50	80	130
8 East London	21	107	128
9 Liverpool JMU	22	97	119
10 Anglia	7	106	113
10 Luton	37	76	113
12 Portsmouth	43	67	110
13 Nottingham	6	97	103
14 Hertfordshire	79	14	93
15 Cardiff	19	56	75

ARCHITECTURE, BUILDING AND PLANNING

	EU	Non-EU	Total
1 Greenwich	102	173	275
2 Northumbria	35	169	204
3 South Bank	49	140	189
4 Westminster	96	51	147
5 Portsmouth	48	92	140
6 Oxford Brookes	77	57	134
7 Ulster	116	6	122
8 Nottingham	16	76	92
9 Glamorgan	61	28	89
10 Manchester Metro	27	61	88
11 Central England	40	46	86
11 Robert Gordon	24	62	86
13 Napier	73	11	84
14 Luton	51	30	81
15 East London	45	31	76

CREATIVE ARTS AND DESIGN

	EU	Non-EU	Total
1 Central England	54	146	200
2 Middlesex	75	117	192
3 Goldsmiths'	51	121	172
4 Westminster	68	68	136
5 Ulster	103	7	110
6 Kingston	35	64	99
7 De Montfort	53	30	83
8 Manchester Metro	35	46	81
9 Nottingham Trent	18	62	80
10 Brighton	31	45	76
11 Lincs and Humber	57	16	73
12 Salford	26	42	68
13 Wolverhampton	30	37	67
14 East London	35	31	66
15 Thames Valley	29	30	59

MEDICINE AND DENTISTRY

	EU	Non-EU	Total
1 Manchester	13	163	176
2 Sheffield	38	124	162
3 Nottingham	8	114	122
4 Leeds	13	93	106
5 Dundee	26	74	100
6 Bristol	21	78	99
7 Glasgow	13	85	98
8 Liverpool	17	78	95
8 Queen's (Belfast)	23	72	95
10 Newcastle	6	85	91
11 Edinburgh	17	64	81
11 Aberdeen	11	70	81
13 Queen Mary	11	67	78
14 Cambridge	16	61	77
15 Leicester	7	69	76

7
APPLYING TO UNIVERSITY

here has been a single applications system for all British universities since 1992. UCAS (Universities and Colleges Admissions Service) acts as a clearing house for more than 200 institutions. Candidates for entry in 2000 will be allowed six choices, which must be whittled down to two later in the process.

Finding out

The first step is to get a copy of the UCAS Handbook. All schools, colleges and libraries will have one. They are also available direct from UCAS, PO Box 28, Cheltenham, Gloucestershire GL50 3SA.

Other valuable sources of information include:

* *University and College Entrance 1999*, published by UCAS and available from Sheed and Ward, 14 Coopers Row, London EC3N 2BH
* *The Scottish Universities Entrance Guide*, available from the Scottish Universities Council on Entrance, 12 The Links, St Andrews, KY16 9JB
* The prospectuses of those universities you are interested in

Use them to draw up your shortlist of universities, programmes and courses. It is important to recognise that to gain entry you will need to:

* Meet the general requirements of the university
* Satisfy the specific demands of the course you choose
* Follow the correct admissions procedures

These are spelt out in the prospectuses of all universities.

The application process for 2000

The formal application process begins slightly more than one year before you want to go to university. In other words, if you're hoping to go to university in 2000, you need to apply in the autumn of 1999. On the other hand, you should begin doing your homework a few months earlier. This is the timetable.

* **Between May and September 1999:** Find out all you can about the universities and courses you are interested in attending. Complete the selection processes described in the earlier chapters.

🎓 **Between September 1 and October 15:** If you are hoping to go to Oxford or Cambridge, complete and submit separate applications (see chapter 8).

🎓 **Between September 1 and December 13:** Applicants for all other universities must complete and submit their applications.

There is no point submitting your application before September 1. All early applications will be held over until that date. Equally, there is no point delaying your application – a prompt application can work in your favour by allowing you more choice. Aim to have your application in by late October/early November. If for whatever reason you miss the December 13 deadline, UCAS will still process your application but universities have complete discretion over whether to take it.

Similarly, if you are applying for a grant, do so as early as possible. For most degree courses you will get a mandatory award from your local authority or from the Scottish Education Department (2 South Charlotte Street, Edinburgh EH2 4AP). If you are not eligible for a mandatory award – because of the course you are following or because you have already had a grant – you may get a discretionary award. These are available from the same sources.

The next steps are:

🎓 **From mid-September:** Applicants receive acknowledgments from UCAS that their applications have been received and are given a personal application number.

🎓 **Late September and early October:** Early applicants to Cambridge who have left school may be invited for interview.

🎓 **From mid-October:** Universities and colleges review applications, send out invitations for interview or advisory visits and inform UCAS of their decisions.

🎓 **From November:** UCAS informs candidates of the offers made to them – if any.

The application form

The application form lies at the heart of the entire process. For some, it is their only point of contact with the admissions tutor or selection staff at the universities of their choice. Making a mess of this can mean making a mess of the entire application. Put yourself in the shoes of the admissions staff. They may go through hundreds, even thousands, of application forms during a year. Make the application easy to read and understand by printing clearly in black ink. The main categories of information are:

🎓 **Name and address** Normally straightforward, but make sure you let UCAS and the university know – immediately – any change in address. Don't bank on the Post Office forwarding letters.

🎓 **Choice of course** This, too, should be straightforward form-filling if you have followed the advice given in chapter 3, Choosing a Course. But before you complete this part of the form, take the opportunity to review your choices – and think again about the offers you are likely to receive and your chances of meeting their conditions. Be absolutely sure you know what you want to put on the form before you fill it in. Make a rough copy first. Then fill in the form.

🖙 **Examinations you have passed** Honesty is the best policy here.

🖙 **Examinations to be taken** Put everything down, even if it does not seem directly relevant.

🖙 **Education and any employment** Be comprehensive but avoid minor details.

🖙 **Further information** This can be the most important section. An interesting and informative set of comments can get the admissions officer on your side. But be wary of making yourself a hostage to fortune. In other words, be sensible. If you get asked to an interview, it's quite likely that you will be asked about the comments you have made in this section. Check your form very carefully on completion. Make sure you have made clear if you want deferred entry. Ask someone you trust – a parent? – to look at it. Sign and date it. Hand it, with your fee and acknowledgement card, to your educational referee – in plenty of time.

The academic reference is crucial. Make sure that he/she knows why you are interested in the course or programme you have chosen. Encourage them to bring out your positive features, especially when the subject is new to you. Within a few days of submitting your application you will receive an acknowledgement card from UCAS. If this does not happen – after allowing for delays such as over Christmas – contact UCAS to make sure it has not gone astray. Some time after receiving the acknowledgement card you will receive a letter from UCAS giving your application number and details of your choices. Check this carefully and contact UCAS only if there are errors.

Mature students

Typically, these are defined as 21 years of age or older (23 in some cases). For those with conventional admissions qualifications, applications follow broadly the same route as for all other students. Candidates without these are still encouraged – some universities operate targets for the numbers or proportion of mature students. There is often a 'non-standard entry' route.

The University of Hertfordshire's prospectus, for example, comments 'Although [mature students] may not have standard entry requirements, we are happy to discuss and, whenever possible, accept alternative qualifications or work experience. We aim to give special support to mature students in several areas. For example, we run pre-entry workshops for those who need extra confidence and help in coping with a return to study.' These services are often backed by adult guidance services offered by the local authority or local TEC (Training and Enterprise Council) in England and Wales or LEC (Local Enterprise Company) in Scotland.

Overseas students

The best source of advice in most cases is the British Council. Virtually all universities have appointed overseas student officers with specific responsibility to help you. You should, however, note that:

🎓 You will probably need to provide evidence of the ability to speak and read good English.

🎓 UK universities are not well supplied with family accommodation or facilities.

🎓 You may need to meet strict requirements for passports, visa, medical insurance and certification and probably provide evidence of financial support.

🎓 You should NOT travel to the UK unless you have written confirmation from the university of your choice that you have been accepted for a course of study.

Some universities are better than others at providing hardship or other support for overseas students. Use your contacts, family or friends to find out about the institution before you apply. Don't turn up hoping things will easily and quickly fall into place if you have not made adequate preparations. All UK universities can be contacted by fax or telex. More information for international students is given in Chapter 6.

General entry requirements

The most common general requirements (that is, for all courses) are for GCSE or Scottish O grade passes in one or more of English, maths, a modern language or a science. Some universities specify a minimum grade, for instance C or above in GCSE.

Some institutions reserve the right to waive these. The University of Westminster, for example, notes only that, 'a GCSE pass or its equivalent in English language and mathematics are required for entry to most of the first degree or diploma courses'. Elsewhere, universities have decided to dispense with general entry requirements. Brunel University prospectus comments that 'there are no general requirements beyond the minimum course requirements stated in the details of individual courses'.

It is, however, increasingly common to see standard minimum entry requirements for a first degree course being spelt out in the type of detail given by Nottingham Trent University as:

a Passes in two subjects at GCE A-level with passes in three other subjects at GCSE or GCE O-level. You should note that General Studies is not always acceptable as an A-level pass

b Passes in three subjects at GCE A-level with passes in one other subject at GCSE or GCE O-level

c A Scottish Certificate of Education with five passes, of which three are at Higher grade

d A Scottish Certificate of Education with passes in four subjects,

all at Higher grade
e A Leaving Certificate of the Department of Education, Republic of Ireland, with grade C or better in five approved subjects, including English, at Higher level (obtained at one sitting)
f An Ordinary National Certificate or Diploma (ONC/OND) at a good standard
g Business and Technical Council (BTEC) National Certificate or Diploma at Level III with appropriate levels of passes
h Awards of the Scottish Vocational Education Council (SCOTVEC) with appropriate levels of passes
i International Baccalaureate
j European Baccalaureate

Normally, universities go on to point out that 'it is important to understand that possession of the minimum requirements does not, in itself, guarantee admission to the university'.

For BTEC HND courses you are likely to need some combination of:
- An appropriate BTEC National Certificate or Diploma
- An Ordinary National Certificate (ONC) or Ordinary National Diploma (OND)
- Passes at GCE A-level and GCSE or GCE O-levels in appropriate subjects

Other qualifications The simple rule is, if in doubt ask – in advance. Universities are increasingly willing to offer places on the basis of US Scholastic Aptitude Tests (SATs), Achievement and Advanced Placement Tests (APTs) and other internationally recognised entry qualifications.

The exceptions The above guidelines do not necessarily apply to Oxford and Cambridge (see chapter 8) and some Scottish universities.
Scottish universities are part of the UCAS system but have a number of distinct features, notably:

- The four-year degree structure. Some Scottish universities offer exemptions from the first year for candidates with A-levels or relevant technical qualifications.
- A more open degree structure. This is true especially in the first, foundation year where first-year classes are often open to students with a wide range of initial interests. Resource shortages in recent years have forced some institutions to restrict admission to the more popular subjects to those in closely related areas, usually in the same faculty.
- As far as possible, Scottish universities try to establish the same offer or 'going-rate' for the entire faculty or – in the case of Stirling University – the university. Again, this type of open and flexible approach is being adversely affected by resource shortages.
- Interviews are not normally required for entry, though several Scottish universities offer 'advisory interviews'. These are designed to give

a potential entrant an insight into the university and its way of life.

Meeting course entry requirements

The next necessity is to meet the requirements for the courses on offer. These vary enormously between universities and courses. Universities such as Cambridge, Oxford, LSE, Bristol, Bath, Manchester and Imperial College can ask for very high A-level entry requirements. Some other universities eschew this approach and put a far greater emphasis on local links, specific skills or needs. Glasgow and Strathclyde, for example, have a tradition of drawing a high proportion of students from the west of Scotland. Aston and Sussex look for specific skill mixes in their students. The University of Central England in Birmingham and the University of East London have pioneered affirmative action programmes to encourage applications from a wide range of social classes and ethnic groups.

Chapter 8 indicates how entry requirements for courses vary between institutions and across departments in the same university. Admission standards are one of the few ways institutions can regulate entry and balance their portfolio of activities. Typically, the department, faculty or university will set its admissions standards to ensure that it gets the number of new entrants to the programme that it needs to ensure a proper balance of activities. There is always an element of risk in this. A department with restrictive requirements may find that it has too few new students. On the other hand, too relaxed an approach can lead to a flood of students. There is a tendency to err on the side of caution – making restrictive offers and, if necessary, going into 'clearing' to make up any shortfall. Universities are reluctant to increase 'offer' levels over the year. The dynamics of this process mean that any predictions of likely offers must be treated with caution. This caveat must be applied to the information in chapter 8.

Universities' income for students consists of two basic elements: a fee per student, normally paid by the local authority; and a recurrent grant from the Funding Councils. The fee will be paid almost regardless of student numbers, but to obtain the recurrent grant universities have to adhere to strictly defined quotas. In the past, it was possible to compensate for over-shooting in one area with short-falls elsewhere. This is no longer acceptable and universities are being penalised if their numbers are significantly out.

Interviews

These take two forms: 1) advisory interviews; 2) selection interviews. Advisory interviews give candidates a chance to see the university and get a feel for its distinct features. Selection interviews give the university information about you, so they can decide what, if any, offer to make.

The ground-rules are fairly straightforward. Anyone invited should recognise that interviews cost the university time and money. They take place because the institution and the interviewers have decided that they matter and are worth the effort. Your approach should mirror this and be based on the five Ps:

🎓 **Participation** If you are invited, go.

🎓 **Preparation** Make clear that you have chosen the university and course for positive reasons.

🎓 **Practice** Get a teacher, friend or family member to take you through a mock interview.

🎓 **Presentation** Play safe: dress smartly. You can make personal statements about appearance once you have been accepted.

🎓 **Punctuality** Most interviews are tightly scheduled. Lateness without a good reason will work against you. If you are going to be late because of unavoidable delays, telephone and let the university know.

Offers

Offers usually take three forms:

1 **An unconditional offer**. This means that your existing qualifications are good enough to win you admission.

2 **A conditional offer**. You will be given a place if you meet certain specified conditions, generally particular grades at A-level.

3 **A rejection**. The university is not willing to admit you.

After receiving offers, candidates must respond to UCAS and make clear whether they: 1) accept the offer; 2) accept the offer and one other as insurance, i.e. a university that will take you on the basis of significantly lower grades; 3) reject the offer.

There is no point replying to UCAS until all your offers are in: you gain nothing and risk missing out on an opportunity. Once you have heard from all the universities to which you applied, UCAS will anyway send you a further statement outlining all their decisions. You should reply to this final statement within 14 days, though extensions may be granted if you are attending open days at any of the universities or simply hoping to visit them. Either way, however, you must respond to UCAS by May 13. Failure to inform UCAS of which offers you want to accept, either firmly or as insurance, is taken as a rejection by you. UCAS will then inform the universities of this rejection on your behalf. Blank spaces on your form are also taken as rejections. Note that you cannot change your mind once you have accepted an offer. UCAS is adamant on this point.

What will the offer look like?

As mentioned above, offers are usually unconditional or conditional. In the former case, you have already been accepted. In the latter case, you will be required to achieve either certain grades at A-level, GNVQ or Highers or a specified number of points in these exams.

A grade-based offer may be BBC, for example. In some cases, you will have to achieve these grades in specified subjects, for instance a B in maths, a B in chemistry and a C in physics. In others, the university will say only that you must get these grades without specifying in which subjects.

A points-based offer is similar and works by awarding points for particular grades on the following basis:

A-levels		AS-levels	
Grade	Points	Grade	Points
A	10	A	5
B	8	B	4
C	6	C	3
D	4	D	2
E	2	E	1

Offers based on vocational qualifications assume completion of the relevant national certificate or diploma. Offers may vary from successful completion to a requirement for merits or distinctions in some, all or specified units. For BTEC, GNVQ and Scotvec national certificates, consult the university prospectus very carefully.

Note that the Scottish system is very different. These figures should be used only as the roughest guide.

What should I do when my results come out?

There are several golden rules.

🎓 **Be at home** You may need to take action or make decisions quickly.

🎓 **If in doubt – ask** Universities are under a lot of pressure at this time of the year but they are normally willing to help if possible. The people who cannot be helped are those who do not ask.

🎓 **Don't fret – act** If you have met the offer you should hear from the university within three or four days. If you don't, telephone the admissions tutor to confirm arrangements.

If I do better than expected, what should I do?

Some applicants receive rejections from all the universities they applied to but then get higher grades than expected. They should contact UCAS about vacancies. At the same time get access to one of the electronic databases through your school, college, local library or careers office. They are constantly up-dated. Check with the media, especially those that list vacancies. Get in touch with the universities you are interested in. Persistence and flexibility pay off at this stage.

Other candidates who underestimate their A-level performance have offers but could have won a place on a better course. Although there are annual tales of 'poaching' by leading universities, the system does not allow trading up once two offers have been held. You cannot even take your insurance offer in preference to your top choice.

If you are determined to trade up, you can ask to be released from your offer and go into clearing, but it is risky. The top universities have very few places available after A-levels are over. You may have to withdraw altogether from the current entrance round and apply again for the year 2001.

If I do worse than expected, what should I do?

Some candidates fall short by one or two points. Most universities think long and hard about whether to take them. As a first step, telephone the university to make sure they know about you. This is especially worth doing if there are particular reasons to explain your exam results, for example illness. If you do telephone, a follow-up letter making the same points is always advisable. A call from your school or college may carry more weight, if staff are available to take up your case.

Assuming you have fallen short of the offer you most wanted but have met the conditions of your insurance offer and that, after getting in touch with them, your first-choice university will not take you, this is the moment to take up your insurance offer. If you have also fallen short of your insurance offer by three or more points, don't despair. Though you will almost certainly receive a rejection letter from your second-choice university, there are still options open to you.

One option is through 'clearing', when UCAS attempts to match students in your position with surplus places at other universities. UCAS will automatically send a Clearing Entry Form to you; it comes with full instructions. At the same time, talk to your school. It may well be able to help. And follow up any leads for vacancies such as those in the papers and on electronic databases.

Don't be afraid to contact universities direct. They are as keen to fill their places as you are to go to university. Universities adjust their numbers as late as the second week of term when students do not turn up or change their minds.

If you are determined to find a place, you almost certainly will.

Other sources of information

Besides those listed earlier try:

CRAC Degree Courses Guide, Hobsons Press, Cambridge

Getting into Oxford and Cambridge, Heap, B, Trotman & Co., Richmond

Getting into University, Heap, B and Lamely, S, Trotman & Co., Richmond

Grants to Students, Department for Education, London

Access to Higher Education Courses Directory, ECCTIS, Fulton House, Jessop Avenue, Cheltenham, Glos GL50 3SH

UCAS Handbook, Universities and Colleges Admissions Service, PO Box 28, Cheltenham, Glos GL50 35A

8
ENTRY REQUIREMENTS

The high standing of British higher education in the world reflects, in part, the competitive nature of the admissions process. Despite the recent expansion of the university system, less than one-in-three of those eligible to apply can gain admission in any one year and it is important – but difficult – to understand the entry requirements. You must understand this because there is little point in applying to institutions or departments which are unlikely to accept you because of the level or nature of your qualifications. That said, for a number of important reasons stated below, it is difficult to specify entry requirements in advance.

🎓 The entry requirements imposed by universities, faculties or departments largely reflect supply and demand for places. Demand patterns can shift rapidly from year to year. This might produce significant changes in entry requirements.

Media studies, for example, saw a surge in popularity in the 1980s. Pioneering institutions like Stirling had very large numbers of applicants for a relatively small number of places. Entry requirements were very high. As other institutions have started offering similar courses and demand has levelled off, entry requirements have changed to reflect the new situation.

🎓 Universities – especially the older institutions – are moving from their traditional dependence on school-based qualifications. They are increasingly keen to offer places to students with qualifications such as BTEC National, ScotVEC National, GNVQ or International Baccalaureate besides noting the applicant's post-16 Records of Achievement.

🎓 The nature of the admissions policy varies significantly between institutions. In some, admission is to the university with little variation between faculties or departments. Elsewhere, departments vary their offers considerably.

🎓 In the past many universities tried to interview virtually every promising candidate. This allowed them to tailor their offer to their view of the individual. Resource constraints have forced many universities to drop this approach and rely more on written references and qualifications.

🎓 Universities are widening the search for those who can benefit from higher education. Many of these new groups do not have traditional school-based qualifications. Access courses and other approaches are used extensively to make it easier for talented individuals to gain admission to university.

🎓 The last few years have seen some institutions build formal links with local colleges. The innovative link, for example, between Salford University and colleges in the northwest allows students to study initially at their local college. This changes the form of the necessary entry requirements.

These and other factors make it important to treat any predictions about entry requirements with considerable caution.

The Tables

The following tables merely indicate the broad pattern of requirements. **The only authoritative statement of entry requirements is the formal offer from the university**. In using the tables, you must note that for the reasons above, there may be sharp differences within a subject cluster at a university. For example, though environmental management and civil engineering may be listed together as requiring 20 points at a specific university, a higher level of demand for the former nearer the date could prompt the university to increase requirements to 22 points.

Although, for simplicity, all offers are given here in terms of points, many universities refuse to adopt this approach. They will frame their offer in terms of specific grades or courses, e.g. BCC at A-level, not 20 points which could be gained from ACD. This allows them to set a standard for all courses being taken and reduces their risk from students who shine in a narrow area but struggle elsewhere. In some cases, offers are changed in the course of a year as universities get a more accurate picture of demand for courses. For BTEC, Scotvec and GNVQ requirements in all subjects you should check the university prospectus. It is also important to note that universities offer a much wider array of courses than outlined here. The most comprehensive picture is supplied by *The UCAS Official Guide.*

The entry requirements outlined below are constructed from a host of sources. These range from interviews and information gathered directly from careers, admissions and information offices across the country and a host of secondary sources. Applicants should **always** refer to *The UCAS Official Guide to University and College Entrance* for more detailed information and to the university prospectus before applying.

Each subject area encompasses a wider array of specific programmes and courses. Those listed in the special requirements table give an indication of the scope but individual institutions may offer other variations.

In the second table, showing points requirements, a number of abbreviations have been used:

Acc.	Accounting	Euro.	European
Acc'y	Acountancy	Exerc.	Exercise
A&D	Art & Design	Ext.	Extended
Admin.	Administration	Fin.	Finance
Aero.	Aeronautical	Geog.	Geography
Agri.	Agricultural	Gov.	Government
Anal.	Analytical	Hist.	History
Anthrop.	Anthropology	Info.	Information
Appl.	Applied	Inst.	Instrumentation
Arch.	Architecture	Int.	International
Archaeol.	Archaeology	Intg'd	Integrated
Biochem.	Biochemistry	Lan.	Language(s)
Biol.	Biology/Biological	Lit.	Literature
Build.	Building	M'ment	Management
Bus.	Business	Manuf.	Manufacturing
Chem.	Chemical/Chemistry	Math'l	Mathematical
Comms.	Communication(s)	Mech.	Mechanical
Comp.	Computer/Computing	Mod.	Modern
Comp'l	Computational	Molec.	Molecular
Cont.	Contemporary	Perf.	Performing/Performance
Des.	Design	Pharma.	Pharmacology
D'ment	Development	Philos.	Philosophy
E.	Electrical	Phys'y	Physiology
Ecol.	Ecological	Psychol.	Psychology
Econ.	Economics	Sc.	Science
Educ.	Education	St.	Studies
E&E	Electrical and Electronic	Stat.	Statistical
Eng.	Engineering	Sys.	Systems
Env.	Environmental	Tech.	Technology
E'tronic	Electronic	Vet.	Veterinary

+ Several programmes or combinations of degrees may be offered
(t) Teaching focus in education

Times Health Warning: **The points requirements table is purely indicative and must be checked against other sources such as *The UCAS Official Guide* and – most important – the admissions officers of the university or college. Failure to do so could harm your chances of choosing the right course.**

Special Entry Requirements by Subject

BUSINESS AND FINANCE

Business & Management (industrial, commerce, transport, tourism, marketing, international business, European business, estate management, hotel management, human resources management, operational research)

Maths and English at GCSE often required

Accountancy & Finance (banking, insurance, investment, finance, actuarial science)

Maths at A-level or Highers often preferred

ENGINEERING

General (computer aided, design, automotive, systems, technology, energy, industrial systems)

Maths at A-level or Highers often required

Civil (environmental, architectural, quality surveying, structural, earth resources)

Maths at A-level or Highers often required

Mechanical & Production (manufacturing, production, off-shore, naval, food, material, robotics, automated)

Maths and Physics at A-level or Highers often required

Aeronautical (avionics, airframe)

Maths and Physics at A-level or Highers often required

Electrical & Electronic (micro-electronic, telecommunications, instrumentation, communications, electrical power, mechatronics, very large scale, optoelectronics, laser, systems, bio-electronics)

Maths at A-level or Highers often required

Chemical (process, fuel, energy, biochemical)

Maths and Chemistry at A-level or Highers often required

HUMANITIES

History (Welsh, Scottish, European, world, ancient, medieval, modern, contemporary, maritime, British, Jewish, art, ideas)

History A-level or equivalent often required

Archaeology (archaeological conservation, archaeological science, classical, industrial)

No special requirements

Philosophy (ethics, ethnology, history of ideas, history and philosophy of science)

Maths at GCSE often required

LANGUAGES

English (language, literature, American studies, Commonwealth studies, African and Caribbean studies)

A-level English or equivalent often required

French (modern languages, European studies, interpretation, translation) required

A-level French or equivalent often

German (modern languages, European studies, interpretation, translation)

A-level German or equivalent often required

MEDICINE AND RELATED SUBJECTS

Anatomy & Physiology (cellular, pathology, human biology, neuroscience, experimental)	Chemistry at A-level or Highers often required
Dentistry	Science A-levels, including Chemistry, or equivalents often required
Medicine	Science A-levels, including Chemistry, or equivalents often required
Veterinary Medicine	Science A-levels, including Chemistry, or equivalents often required

PHYSICAL AND MATHEMATICAL SCIENCES

Chemistry (industrial, environmental, biological, medical, materialism analytic, polymer, pharmaceutical, environmental, ecological, applied, biomedical)	Science A-levels including Chemistry, or equivalents often required
Physics (chemical, astrophysics, applied, theoretical, computational, measurement & instrumentation, molecular, linear, technological) often required	Science A-levels, including Maths and Physics, or equivalents
Geography (human, physical, marine, geographical information studies, topography, environmental, cartography)	Geography A-level or equivalent often required
Maths (pure, applied, business, computational, modelling, engineering)	Maths A-level or equivalent often required
Computer Studies (software technology, software engineering, business information studies, information technology, artificial intelligence, digital electronics, information systems engineering, computational mathematics)	Maths A-level or equivalent often required

BIOLOGICAL SCIENCES

Biology (zoology, environmental, marine, applied, aquatic, medical, animal, plant, biological imaging, aquaculture)	Science A-levels, including Chemistry, or equivalents often required
Biochemistry (cell, molecular, medicinal, medical, applied, exotoxicology, micro-biochemistry)	Science A-levels, including Chemistry, or equivalents often required
Psychology (behavioural science, cognitive science, human, animalf, primatology)	Maths at GCSE often required

Social sciences

Economics (business, mathematical, agricultural, land, applied, financial, econometrics, political, industrial, development, statistical)	Maths at A-level or Highers often preferred
Sociology (social research, social work, social policy, social anthropology)	Maths at GCSE often preferred
Law (English, European, international, comparative)	No special requirements
Politics (international, international relations, political development, public administrations, theory, government)	Maths at GCSE often preferred

Visual and performing arts

Art & Design (graphics, visualisation, illustration, ceramics, textiles, photography, design technology, interior design, printing)	A-level Art or equivalent plus portfolio often required
Music & Performing Arts (script writing, tv and broadcast studies, movement, media production)	A-level Music or equivalent often required
Architecture (building conservation, building engineering, landscape architecture, environmental planning, urban planning, construction engineering, town planning)	Maths at A-level or Highers often preferred

Education

Education (primary, secondary, teaching, early years, languages, physical)	Maths and English at GCSE required

Points Required by Subject and University

BUSINESS, MANAGEMENT, ACCOUNTANCY AND FINANCE

Business/Management

	COURSES	POINTS		COURSES	POINTS
Aberdeen	M'ment+	22	King's	M'ment+	18-26
Abertay Dundee	Bus.+	8-12	LSE	M'ment Sc.+	24-26
Aberystwth	Bus.+	16-20	Queen Mary	Bus. St.+	18
Anglia	Bus.+	12-14	Royal Holloway	M'ment+	20-26
Aston	Bus.+	18-24	SOAS	M'ment	20-24
Bangor	M'ment+	18	UCL	M'ment+	20-24
Bath	Bus.+	24-26	Wye	Bus.+	14
Birmingham	Bus.+	22-24	London Guildhall	Bus.+	12-14
Bournemouth	Bus.+	14-18	Loughborough	M'ment+	20-22
Bradford	Bus.+	20	Luton	Bus.+	12-16
Brighton	Bus.+	14-18	Manchester	Bus.+	18-24
Bristol (W. of E.)	Bus.+	14-22	Manchester Met	Bus.+	12-20
Brunel	M'ment+	18-24	Middlesex	Bus.+	10-16
Buckingham	Bus.+	12-14	Napier	Bus.+	8-12
Cardiff	Bus.+	22-24	Newcastle	Bus. M'ment	20-24
Central England	Bus.+	12-14	North London	Bus.+	12-14
Central Lancs	Bus.+	12-16	Northumbria	Bus.+	12-18
City	Bus.+	24	Nottingham	M'ment+	24
Coventry	Bus.+	12-16	Nott'ham Trent	Bus.+	12-18
Cranfield	M'ment+	12-18	Oxford	M'ment+	28
De Montfort	Bus.+	12-18	Oxford Brookes	Bus. Admin. &	
Derby	Bus.+	12-14		M'ment+	10-22
Dundee	M'ment+	12-20	Paisley	Bus. & M'ment	12-18
Durham	M'ment+	22	Plymouth	Bus.+	10-18
East Anglia	Bus.+	18-24	Portsmouth	Bus.+	16-18
East London	Bus.+	12-14	Queen's, Belfast	M'ment.	20-26
Edinburgh	Bus.+	24	Reading	M'ment+	20-24
Essex	M'ment	20	Robert Gordon	Bus.+	18
Exeter	M'ment+	20-24	Salford	Bus.+	18-24
Glamorgan	Bus.+	12-18	Sheffield	Bus.+	22-26
Glasgow	M'ment+	22	Sheffield Hallam	M'ment+	12-18
Glasgow Cal	M'ment+	10-20	Southampton	Bus.+	22-24
Greenwich	Bus.+	12-16	South Bank	Bus.+	12-18
Heriot-Watt	Int. Bus.	18-22	St Andrews	M'ment Sc.+	18-24
Hertfordshire	Bus.+	12-18	Staffordshire	Bus.+	10-16
Huddersfield	Bus.+	14-18	Stirling	Bus.+	18-22
Hull	Bus.+	20-24	Strathclyde	Bus.+	18-24
Keele	Bus.+	20-22	Sunderland	Bus.+	8-18
Kent	M'ment Sc.+	18-22	Surrey	Bus.+	18-20
Kingston	Bus.+	10-18	Sussex	Bus. M'ment	18-20
Lampeter	M'ment +	14-18	Swansea	Bus.+	22-24
Lancaster	M'ment+	20-28	Teesside	Bus.+	10-16
Leeds	M'ment+	20-26	Thames Valley	Bus.+	8-12
Leeds Met	Bus.+	12-16	Ulster	Bus.+	18-22
Lincs & Humber	Bus.+	12-16	UMIST	M'ment Sc.+	18-26
Liverpool	M'ment+	18-22	Warwick	Bus.+	20-26
Liverpool JMU	Bus.+	14-16	Westminster	Bus.+	12-14
London			Wolverhampton	Bus.+	10-16
Imperial	M'ment+	20-24	York	Bus. M'ment+	20-28

Accountancy/Finance

	COURSES	POINTS		COURSES	POINTS
Aberdeen	Acc'y+	22	Leeds	Acc.+	22-24
Abertay Dundee	Acc.+	10	Leeds Met	Acc. & Fin.	16
Aberystwth	Acc.+	16-18	Lincs & Humber	Acc'y & Fin.	12
Anglia	Acc.+	12	Liverpool	Acc.+	18-20
Aston	Acc. for		Liverpool JMU	Acc. & Fin.	14-16
	M'ment	24	London		
Bangor	Acc.+	18	LSE	Acc. & Fin.	24-26
Birmingham	Acc.+	22-24	London Guildhall	Acc'y+	8-14
Bournemouth	Acc.	16	Loughborough	Acc.+	20-22
Brighton	Acc.+	18	Luton	Acc.+	12-16
Bristol	Econ. & Acc.	22	Manchester	Acc.+	22-24
Bristol (W. of E.)	Fin.+	16-22	Manchester Met	Acc. & Fin.	16-18
Brunel	Acc.+	16-20	Middlesex	Acc.+	12-16
Buckingham	Acc.+	16	Napier	Acc.+	12-16
Cardiff	Acc.+	22-24	Newcastle	Acc.+	20-24
Central England	Acc'y+	14	North London	Acc. & Fin.	12-14
Central Lancs	Acc.+	14	Northumbria	Acc'y+	12-18
City	Acc'y+	22-24	Nottingham	Acc.+	24
Coventry	Acc.+	12	Nott'ham Trent	Acc. & Fin.	16
De Montfort	Acc.+	14-18	Oxford Brookes	Acc.+	8-20
Derby	Acc.+	14	Paisley	Acc.+	12-18
Dundee	Acc'y+	14-18	Plymouth	Acc.+	14-16
Durham	Econ. & Acc.	18	Portsmouth	Acc.+	14-16
East Anglia	Acc'y+	22-24	Queen's, Belfast	Acc.+	24-26
East London	Acc. & Fin.	12-14	Reading	Acc.+	18-26
Edinburgh	Acc'y+	24	Robert Gordon	Acc. & Fin.	18
Essex	Acc.+	20	Salford	Acc.+	18-20
Exeter	Acc'y+	24	Sheffield	Acc.+	24
Glamorgan	Acc.+	12-14	Sheffield Hallam	Acc.+	14-18
Glasgow	Acc'y+	22-24	Southampton	Acc.+	22-24
Glasgow Cal	Acc'y+	14	South Bank	Acc.+	12-18
Greenwich	Acc'y & Fin.	12-16	Staffordshire	Acc.+	12-16
Heriot-Watt	Acc'y+	20	Stirling	Acc'y	18-20
Hertfordshir	Acc.+	18	Strathclyde	Acc.	22-24
Huddersfield	Acc'y+	12-16	Sunderland	Acc.+	10-16
Hull	Acc.+	18-20	Teesside	Acc. & Fin.	10-12
Keele	Fin.+	20-24	Thames Valley	Acc.+	8-12
Kent	Acc.+	20-22	Ulster	Acc.+	22
Kingston	Acc.+	18	Warwick	Acc.+	26
Lancaster	Acc.+	22-24	Wolverhampton	Acc. Fin.	16

ENGINEERING

Electrical & Electronic Engineering

	COURSES	POINTS		COURSES	POINTS
Aberdeen	E&E	22-24	Liverpool	E&E+	18-22
Abertay Dundee	E&E+	6-16	Liverpool JMU	E&E+	12
Anglia	E'tronics+	10-14	London		
Aston	E&E+	18-24	Imperial	E&E+	26-28
Bangor	E&E+	12-24	King's	E&E+	20-22
Bath	E&E+	20-24	Queen Mary	E&E+	20-28
Birmingham	E&E+	20-24	Royal Holloway	E'tronics+	22
Bournemouth	E'tronic Sys.	10	UCL	E&E+	24-28
Bradford	E&E+	12-26	Loughborough	E&E+	20-22
Brighton	E&E+	18	Luton	Comms. Eng.	12-16
Bristol	E&E+	24	Manchester	E&E+	20-26
Bristol (W. of E.)	E&E+	16	Manchester Met	E&E+	10-12
Brunel	E&E+	20	Middlesex	Scientific Inst.	10
Cardiff	E&E+	18-24	Napier	E&E+	8
Central England	E&E+	12	Newcastle	E&E+	18-26
Central Lancs	E&E+	8	North London	E. & Comms.	
City	E&E+	16-22		Eng.	12
Coventry	E&E+	10-18	Northumbria	E&E+	12-16
Cranfield	E. Sys. Eng.	14-18	Nottingham	E&E+	14-24
De Montfort	E&E+	16-18	Nott'ham Trent	E&E+	14-18
Derby	E&E+	10-14	Oxford	E. Eng.	28
Dundee	E&E+	12-14	Oxford Brookes	Micro E. Sys.	8-22
Durham	E&E+	22	Paisley	E&E+	4-8
East Anglia	E&E+	14-24	Plymouth	E&E+	10-18
East London	E&E+	12	Portsmouth	E&E+	14-18
Edinburgh	E&E+	18	Queen's, Belfast	E&E+	20-24
Essex	E&E+	18-24	Reading	E'tronic Eng.+	18-24
Exeter	E&E+	18-20	Robert Gordon	E&E+	8
Glamorgan	E&E+	8-12	Salford	E&E+	18-24
Glasgow	E&E+	16-20	Sheffield	E&E+	18-24
Glasgow Cal	E'tronic Eng.	10	Sheffield Hallam	E&E+	8
Greenwich	E&E+	10-14	Southampton	E&E+	24
Heriot-Watt	E&E+	14	South Bank	E. Eng.	8
Hertfordshire	E&E+	12-22	Staffordshire	E&E+	12
Huddersfield	E&E+	12-18	Strathclyde	E&E+	16-22
Hull	E'tronic Eng+	18-24	Sunderland	E&E+	12
Kent	Digital		Surrey	E&E+	18-24
	E'tronics	16-20	Sussex	E&E+	20
Kingston	E'tronics+	10-24	Swansea	E&E+	20-24
Lancaster	E. & Comms.	20-24	Teesside	E&E+	10-12
Leeds	E&E+	22	Ulster	E'tronic Sys.	16-18
Leeds Met	E&E+	8-12	UMIST	E&E+	20-22
Leicester	E&E+	18-24	Warwick	E&E+	18-24
Lincs & Humber	E. & Comms.		Westminster	E&E+	12
	Eng.+	8-18	York	E&E+	26

Chemical Engineering

	COURSES	POINTS		COURSES	POINTS
Aston	Chem. Eng.+	20-26	Newcastle	Chem. &	
Bath	Chem. Eng.+	22		Process+	18-24
Birmingham	Chem. Eng.+	22	Northumbria	Chem. Eng.+	10
Bradford	Chem. Eng.+	18-26	Nottingham	Chem. Eng.+	22
Cambridge	Chem. Eng.+	28-30	Oxford	Chem. Eng.+	28
Edinburgh	Chem. Eng.+	18	Paisley	Chem. Eng.+	4-18
Heriot-Watt	Chem. Eng.+	16	Queen's, Belfast	Chem. Eng.+	20-24
Huddersfield	Chem. Eng.+	10	Sheffield	Chem. Eng.+	20-22
Leeds	Chem. Eng.+	14-22	South Bank	Chem. Eng.+	8
London			Strathclyde	Chem. Eng.+	18-26
Imperial	Chem. Eng.+	24	Surrey	Chem. Eng.+	18-24
UCL	Chem. Eng.+	24-26	Swansea	Chem. Eng.+	20-24
Loughborough	Chem. Eng.+	22	Teeside	Chem. Eng.+	12-20
			UMIST	Chem. Eng.+	22

General Engineering

	COURSES	POINT		COURSES	POINTS
Aberdeen	Eng.+	22-24	London		
Abertay Dundee	Eng.+	6	Queen Mary	Eng.+	14-20
Birmingham	Math. Eng.+	24	UCL	Eng. Bus. Fin.	22-26
Bournemouth	Eng. Bus. D'ment	8	Loughborough	Eng. Sc.	18-22
Bradford	Manuf.		Luton	Comp.Aided	
	M'ment	16-18		Eng.+	12
Brighton	Eng.+	18	Manchester	Eng.+	18
Bristol	Eng. Maths	24	Manchester Met	Eng.	10
Brunel	Eng.+	18-20	Middlesex	Comp. Aided Eng.	10
Cambridge	Eng.	28-30	Napier	Eng.+	8-12
Cardiff	Intg'd Eng.	20-24	Northumbria	Comp. Aided	
Central England	Eng.Syst+	12		Eng.	12
Central Lancs	Comp. aided Eng.+	8	Nottingham	Eng.+	22
City	Eng. & Energy		Nott'ham Trent	Intg'd Eng.	14
	M'ment	16-24	Oxford	Eng.+	28
Coventry	Eng.+	10-18	Oxford Brookes	Eng.+	12
Durham	Eng.	22	Paisley	Eng.	10
East London	Eng.+	12	Portsmouth	Eng.+	18
Edinburgh	Eng.+	18	Reading	Intg'd Eng.	18-22
Exeter	Eng.+	18-20	Sheffield Hallam	Comp.Aided Eng.+	8
Glasgow Cal	Eng.+	12	South Bank	Eng.+	12-16
Greenwich	Eng.+	8-16	Staffordshire	Comp. Aided	
Hertfordshire	Eng. M'ment	14		Eng.	12
Huddersfield	Comp.Aided		Strathclyde	Eng.+	18-24
	Eng.+	8-18	Sunderland	Eng.+.	12
Hull	Comp.Aided Eng.	18	Surrey	Eng.+	18-22
Lancaster	Eng.+	20-24	Swansea	Eng.	12-16
Leeds Met.	Eng.	8	Teeside	Int. Eng.	10-12
Leicester	Eng.+	18-24	Ulster	Eng.+	18
Liverpool	Int. Eng.+	18-20	UMIST	Intg'd Eng.	20
Liverpool JMU	Eng.+	16-20	Warwick	Eng.+	18-24
			Wolverhampton	Comp. Aided Des.	8

Civil Engineering

	COURSES	POINTS		COURSES	POINTS
Aberdeen	Civil+	22-24	London		
Abertay Dundee	Civil+	8-14	Imperial	Civil+	26
Aston	Civil+	18-24	Queen Mary	Civil+	16-24
Bath	Civil+	18-24	UCL	Civil+	20-24
Birmingham	Civil+	18-22	Loughborough	Civil+	20-24
Bradford	Civil+	16-20	Manchester	Civil+	20
Brighton	Civil+	18	Napier	Civil+	8-12
Bristol	Civil+	22	Newcastle	Civil+	18-24
Cardiff	Civil+	18-24	Nottingham	Civil+	20-24
City	Civil+	18-24	Nott'ham Trent	Civil+	12-14
Coventry	Civil+	10-18	Oxford	Civil+	28
Cranfield	Civil+	12	Oxford Brookes	Civil+	12
Dundee	Civil+	12-24	Paisley	Civil+	8-18
Durham	Civil+	22	Plymouth	Civil+	14-18
East London	Civil+	12	Portsmouth	Civil+	16-18
Edinburgh	Civil+	18-26	Queen's, Belfast	Civil+	20-24
Exeter	Civil+	18-20	Salford	Civil+	12
Glamorgan	Civil+	6-12	Sheffield	Civil+	18-24
Glasgow	Civil+	16-24	Sheffield Hallam	Civil+	16-18
Glasgow Cal	Civil+	6	Southampton	Civil+	20-24
Greenwich	Civil+	12-20	South Bank	Civil+	8-14
Heriot-Watt	Civil+	18	Strathclyde	Civil+	18-24
Hertfordshire	Civil+	12-22	Surrey	Civil+	18-22
Kingston	Civil+	10-24	Swansea	Civil+	20-24
Leeds	Civil+	18	Ulster	Civil+	12-18
Leeds Met	Civil+	10	UMIST	Civil+	24-26
Liverpool	Civil+	18-24	Warwick	Civil+	18-24
Liverpool JMU	Civil+	12-18	Westminster	Civil+	4-12
			Wolverhampton	Civil+	14

Aeronautical Engineering

COURSES		POINTS	COURSES		POINTS
Bath	Aero.+	26	Linc & Humber	Aircraft	
Brighton	Aero.	18		Structures	18
Bristol	Aero.+	24-28	Liverpool	Aerospace+	24
Bristol (W. of E.)	Aero. Manuf.		London		
	Eng.	14	Imperial	Aero.	28
Brunel	Aeronautics+	20	Queen Mary	Aero.+	16-24
City	Aero.+	20-26	Loughborough	Aero.+	22-26
Coventry	Aero. Systems		Manchester	Aero.+	24
	Eng.	10-18	Queen's, Belfast	Aero.+	22-26
Cranfield	Aero. Mech.		Salford	Aero.+	18-20
	Sys. Eng.	20	Sheffield	Aerospace	24
Glasgow	Aero.+	24	Southampton	Aero.+	28
Hertfordshire	Aerospace+	18-22	Strathclyde	Aerodynamics+	24
Kingston	Aerospace	10-24	UMIST	Aerospace	24

Mechanical & Production Engineering

	COURSES	POINTS		COURSES	POINTS
Aberdeen	Mech.+	24	Liverpool JMU	Mech.+	10-20
Abertay Dundee	Mech.+	16	London		
Anglia	Product Des.+	10	Imperial	Mech.+	28
Aston	Mech.+	18-22	King's	Manuf.	20
Bath	Mech.+	26	Queen Mary	Mech.+	16-24
Birmingham	Mech.+	20-22	UCL	Mech.+	18-24
Bournemouth	Product Des.	14	Loughborough	Mech.+	18-20
Bradford	Mech.+	14-20	Manchester	Mech.+	18-24
Brighton	Mech.	18	Manchester Met	Mech.+	10-12
Bristol	Mech.+	24-28	Middlesex	Mech.+	10
Bristol (W. of E.)	Mech.	16	Napier	Industrial Des.	8-10
Brunel	Mech.	20-22	Newcastle	Mech.+	20-24
Cardiff	Mech.+	22-24	Northumbria	Mech.+	12
Central England	Mech.+	12	Nottingham	Mech.+	18-24
Central Lancs	Mech.+	16	Nottingham Trent	Mech.+	14
City	Mech.+	16-26	Oxford	Mech.+	28
Coventry	Mech.+	10-18	Oxford Brookes	Mech.+	12
Cranfield	Mech.+	20	Paisley	Mech.+	8-18
De Montfort	Mech.	16	Plymouth	Mech.+	6-16
Derby	Mech.+	12-18	Portsmouth	Mech.+	12-18
Dundee	Mech.+	12-16	Queen's, Belfast	Mech.+	20-24
Durham	Mech.+	22	Reading	Mech.+	18-22
East London	Product Des.+	12	Robert Gordon	Mech.+	4-8
Edinburgh	Mech.+	18	Salford	Mech.+	18
Exeter	Mech.+	18-20	Sheffield	Mech.+	24
Glamorgan	Mech.+	8	Sheffield Hallam	Mech.+	8
Glasgow	Mech.+	16-24	Southampton	Mech.+	24-26
Glasgow Cal	Manuf.	10	South Bank	Mech.+	8
Greenwich	Mech.+	10-14	Staffordshire	Mech.+	12
Heriot-Watt	Mech.+	14	Strathclyde	Mech.+	24
Hertfordshire	Mech.+	12-22	Sunderland	Mech.+	12
Huddersfield	Mech.+	10-18	Surrey	Mech.+	18-22
Hull	Mech.+	18	Sussex	Mech.+	20
Kingston	Mech.+	10-24	Swansea	Mech.+	20-24
Lancaster	Mech.+	20-24	Teesside	Mech.+	12
Leeds	Mech.+	22	Ulster	Manuf.+	12-18
Leicester	Mech.+	18	UMIST	Mech.+	20-24
Lincs & Humber	Manuf.+	8-18	Warwick	-Mech.+	18-24
Liverpool	Manuf.+	18-24	Westminster	Mech.+	12
			Wolverhampton	Manuf.	8

HUMANITIES

History

Courses	Points	Courses	Points
Aberdeen	Hist.+	22	King's	Hist.+	22-26
Aberystwyth	Hist.+	18-22	LSE	Hist.+	26
Anglia	Hist.+	12-14	Queen Mary	Hist.+	20
Bangor	Hist.+	16-18	Royal Holloway	Hist.+	20-24
Birmingham	Hist.+	22-26	SOAS	Hist.+	20-24
Bradford	Hist.+	16-18	SSEES	Hist.+	20
Bristol	Hist.+	20-26	UCL	Hist.+	20-26
Bristol (W. of E.)	Hist.+	16-22	London Guildhall	Mod. Hist.+	8-14
Brunel	Mod. Hist.+	16-20	Luton	Hist.	14
Buckingham	Mod. Hist.+	10-12	Manchester	Hist.+	20-24
Cambridge	Hist.+	28	Manchester Met	Hist.+	12-14
Cardiff	Hist.+	20-26	Middlesex	Hist.+	12-16
Central Lancs	Hist.+	16	Newcastle	Hist.+	24-26
Coventry	Hist.+	10	North London	Hist.+	12
De Montfort	Hist..+	8-16	Northumbria	Hist.+	16-22
Derby	Hist. +	14	Nottingham	Hist.+	20-28
Dundee	Mod. Hist.+	20	Nott'ham Trent	Hist.+	12-18
Durham	Hist.+	22-26	Oxford	Mod. Hist.	26-28
East Anglia	Hist.+	20-26	Oxford Brookes	Hist.+	10-20
East London	Hist.+	12-14	Plymouth	Hist.+	14-18
Edinburgh	Hist.+	24-28	Portsmouth	Econ. Hist.	10-16
Essex	Hist.+	20-22	Queen's, Belfast	Mod. Hist.+	20
Exeter	Hist.+	18-26	Reading	Hist.+	20-22
Glamorgan	Hist.+	12-14	Salford	Hist.+	18-22
Glasgow	Hist.+	22	Sheffield	Hist.+	24-26
Greenwich	Hist.+	10-16	Sheffield Hallam	Hist. St.	12-14
Hertfordshire	Hist.	14-16	Southampton	Hist.+	20-22
Huddersfield	Hist. +.	14-16	South Bank	Hist.+	12-18
Hull	Hist.+	20-24	St Andrews	Hist.+	24-28
Keele	Hist.+	20-24	Staffordshire	Hist.+	12-16
Kent	Hist.+	22-24	Stirling	Hist.+	18-22
Kingston	Hist.+	14-16	Sunderland	Hist.+	8-12
Lampeter	Hist.+	14-16	Sussex	Hist.+	24
Lancaster	Hist.+	20-24	Swansea	Hist.+	20-24
Leeds	Hist.+	20-24	Teesside	Hist.+	14-16
Leeds Met.	Hist. +	16-18	Thames Valley	Hist.+	8-12
Leicester	Hist.+	18-20	Ulster	Mod. & Cont.	
Liverpool	Hist.+	20-24		Hist.+	18
Liverpool JMU	Hist.+	8-14	Warwick	Hist.+	22-26
London			Westminster	Mod. Hist.	14
Goldsmiths'	Hist.+	18-20	Wolverhampton	Hist.+	14
			York	Hist.+	24-26

Archaeology

	COURSES	POINTS		COURSES	POINTS
Bangor	Archaeol.+	16-18	London		
Birmingham	Archaeol.+	22-24	King's	Classical Arch.+	20
Bournemouth	Archaeol.+	14-16	Royal Holloway	Archaeol.+	22-24
Bradford	Archaeol.+	20	SOAS	Archaeol.+	20-24
Bristol	Archaeol.+	20-22	UCL	Archaeol.+	20-24
Cambridge	Archaeol.+	28	Manchester	Archaeol.+	20-22
Cardiff	Archaeol.+	20-26	Newcastle	Archaeol.+	18-22
Durham	Archaeol.+	18-22	Nottingham	Archaeol.+	20-22
East London	Archaeol. Sc.+	12	Oxford	Archaeol.+	26-28
Edinburgh	Archaeol.+	24	Queen's, Belfast	Archaeol.+	20
Exeter	Archaeol.+	20-24	Reading	Archaeol.+	20
Glasgow	Archaeol.+	18-22	Sheffield	Archaeol. Sc.+	22-24
Lampeter	Archaeol.+	16-18	Southampton	Archaeol.+	18-20
Leicester	Archaeol.+	20	St Andrews	Archaeol.+	24
Liverpool	Archaeol.+	18-24	Warwick	Classical Arch.+	22
			York	Archaeol.+	22-24

Philosophy

	COURSES	POINTS		COURSES	POINTS
Aberdeen	Philos.+	22	London		
Anglia	Euro. Philos.		Heythrop	Philos.+	20-22
	& Lit.+	12-14	King's	Philos.+	20-24
Birmingham	Philos.+	24-26	LSE	Philos.+	24-26
Bradford	Philos.+	16-18	UCL	Philos.+	20-22
Bristol	Philos.+	22-28	Manchester	Philos.+	22-26
Cambridge	Philos.+	28	Manchester Met	Philos.+	12
Cardiff	Philos.+	20-26	Middlesex	Philos.+	12-16
Central Lancs	Philos.+	12	Newcastle	Phil. St.	24
Dundee	Philos.+	20	North London	Philos.+	10-12
Durham	Philos.+	22-24	Nottingham	Philos.+	22-28
East Anglia	Philos.+	20-24	Oxford	Philos.+	28
Edinburgh	Philos.+	24	Queen's, Belfast	Philos.+	20-22
Essex	Philos.+	20	Reading	Philos.+	20-22
Glamorgan	Philos.+	12	Sheffield	Philos.+	22-26
Glasgow	Philos.+	22-24	Southampton	Philos.+	20-22
Greenwich	Philos.+	10-16	St Andrews	Philos.+	24-26
Hertfordshire	Philos.	14	Staffordshire	Philos.+	12-16
Hull	Philos.+	20-24	Stirling	Philos.+	18-22
Keele	Philos.+	20-24	Sunderland	Philos.+	8-24
Kent	Philos.+	20-22	Sussex	Philos.+	24
Kingston	Hist. of Ideas	14-16	Swansea	Philos.+	20-22
Lampeter	Philos. St.	16	Ulster	Philos.+	18
Lancaster	Philos.+	20-22	Warwick	Philos.+	20-26
Leeds	Philos. of Sc.	20-26	Wolverhampton	Philos.+	10
Liverpool	Philos.+	20-24	York	Philos.+	20-26
Liverpool JMU	Philos.+	16-18			

LANGUAGES

English

COURSES	POINTS		COURSES	POINTS
Aberdeen	English+	22	King's	English+	22-24
Aberystwth	English+	20-22	Queen Mary	English+	20-26
Anglia	English+	12-16	Royal Holloway	English+	22-24
Bangor	English+	16-18	UCL	English+	26
Birmingham	English+	22-28	London Guildhall	English+	10-14
Bristol	English+	16-28	Loughborough	English+	20-24
Bristol (W. of E.)	Lit. Studies	16-22	Luton	English+	12-16
Brunel	English+	18-20	Manchester	English Lit.+	20-26
Buckingham	English+	10	Manchester Met	English+	10-14
Cambridge	English+	28-30	Middlesex	English+	12-16
Cardiff	English Lit.+	26	Newcastle	English+	22-24
Central England	English Lan. & Lit.	16-18	North London	English+	14
			Northumbria	English Lit.+	20-22
Central Lancashire	English Lit. Studs.	18	Nottingham	English Lit.+	22-24
De Montfort	English	10-18	Nott'ham Trent	English+	22
Dundee	English+	20	Oxford	English	28
Durham	English+	24-28	Oxford Brookes	English St.	8-20
East Anglia	English+	24-26	Plymouth	English+	16-18
East London	Lit.+	12-14	Portsmouth	English+	18
Edinburgh	English+	24-28	Queen's, Belfast	English Lit.+	20
Essex	English+	20-22	Reading	English Lit.+	20-24
Exeter	English+	24	Salford	English+	22
Glamorgan	English+	12-16	Sheffield	English Lit.+	24-26
Glasgow	English+	22	Sheffield Hallam	English St.	22
Greenwich	English	10-12	Southampton	English+	22-24
Hertfordshire	English+	14-18	South Bank	English St.	14-18
Huddersfield	English+	14-18	St Andrews	English+	24-26
Hull	English Lit.+	18-24	Staffordshire	English Lit.	12-16
Keele	English Lit.+	20-26	Stirling	English St.	18-22
Kent	English Lit.+	20-26	Sunderland	English Lit.+	10-12
Kingston	English+	14-18	Sussex	English Lit.+	24
Lampeter	English Lit.+	16-18	Swansea	English Lit.+	20-24
Lancaster	English Lit.+	22-24	Teesside	English+	14-16
Leeds	English+	22-28	Thames Valley	English+	8-12
Leicester	English+	24	Ulster	English+	20
Liverpool	English+	22-26	Warwick	English Lit.+	22-28
Liverpool JMU	Lit. Life & Thought+	12-20	Westminster	English+	12-16
			Wolverhampton	English+	16
London Goldsmiths'	English+	20-22	York	English+	22-26

French

	COURSES	POINTS		COURSES	POINTS
Aberdeen	French+	16-22	London		
Aberystwth	French+	18-24	Goldsmiths'	French+	18
Anglia	French+	12-14	King's	French+	22-24
Aston	French+	18-22	LSE	French+	24
Bangor	French+	16-20	Queen Mary	French+	18-20
Bath	French+	22	Royal Holloway	French+	20-24
Birmingham	French St.+	22-28	SSEES	French+	22
Bradford	French+	18-20	UCL	French+	20-24
Bristol	French+	22-26	London Guildhall	French+	8-14
Bristol (W. of E.)	French+	14-24	Loughborough	French+	20
Brunel	French+	18-24	Manchester	French+	20-26
Buckingham	French+	12-16	Manchester Met	French+	12-22
Cambridge	Mod. Lans.	28	Middlesex	French St.	12-16
Cardiff	French+	22-26	Newcastle	French+	20-24
Central England	French+	14	North London	French+	10-12
Central Lancs	French+	10	Northumbria	French+	12-16
Coventry	French+	10-16	Nottingham	French+	20-28
De Montfort	French+	10-16	Nottingham Trent	French+	12-16
Derby	French+	10	Oxford	Mod. Lans.	28
Dundee	French+	18-20	Oxford Brookes	French Lan.	
Durham	French+	18-24		& Lit.+	8-22
East Anglia	French+	18-24	Plymouth	French	12-18
East London	French+	12-14	Portsmouth	French+	12-14
Edinburgh	French+	24-28	Queen's, Belfast	French+	20-26
Essex	French+	20	Reading	French+	20-22
Exeter	French+	22-24	Salford	French+	18-30
Glamorgan	French+	12	Sheffield	French+	22-28
Glasgow	French+	22	Southampton	French+	22-24
Greenwich	French+	8-16	South Bank	French+	12-18
Heriot-Watt	French+	16-22	St Andrews	French+	20-28
Huddersfield	French+	14	Staffordshire	French+	12-18
Hull	French+	18-24	Stirling	French Lan.+	18-20
Keele	French+	20-24	Sunderland	French+	8-10
Kent	French+	20-22	Surrey	French+	20-22
Kingston	French+	12-16	Sussex	French+	18-22
Lampeter	French+	16	Swansea	French+	18-24
Lancaster	French St.+	20-22	Thames Valley	French+	8-12
Leeds	French+	22-26	Ulster	French+	18
Leicester	French+	18-20	UMIST	French+	18-24
Lincolnshire &			Warwick	French+	20-24
Humberside	French+	12	Westminster	French+	12
Liverpool	French+	20-22	Wolverhampton	French+	18
Liverpool JMU	French+	14-20	York	French+	22-26

German

COURSES	POINTS		COURSES	POINTS
Aberdeen	German+	16-22	Queen Mary	German Lan.+	18-26
Aberystwth	German+	18-24	Royal Holloway	German+	20-26
Anglia	German+	12-14	SSEES	German & Russian	22
Aston	German+	18-22	UCL	German+	20-22
Bangor	German+	16-20	London Guildhall	German+	8-12
Bath	German+	22	Loughborough	German+	20
Birmingham	German St.+	22-28	Manchester	German+	22-24
Bradford	German+	18-22	Manchester Met	German+	12-18
Bristol	German+	20-26	Middlesex	German+	12-16
Bristol (W. of E.)	German+	14-24	Newcastle	German+	20-22
Brunel	German+	18-24	North London	German+	10-12
Cambridge	Mod. Lans.	28	Northumbria	German+	12-14
Cardiff	German+	20-26	Nottingham	German+	20-26
Central England	German+	14	Nottingham Trent	German+	12-16
Central Lancs	German+	10	Oxford	Mod. Lans.	28
Coventry	German+	10-20		German Lan.	
De Montfort	German+	8-16	Oxford Brookes	& Lit.	8-24
Derby	German+	10	Plymouth	German+	14-22
Dundee	German+	18-20	Portsmouth	German+	12
Durham	German+	18-26	Queen's, Belfast	German+	20-26
East Anglia	German+	18-24	Reading	German+	20-22
East London	German+	12-14	Salford	German+	18-30
Edinburgh	German+	24	Sheffield	German+	22-24
Essex	German+	20	Sheffield Hallam	Int. Bus. (German)	16
Exeter	German+	20-24	Southampton	German+	22
Glamorgan	German+	10-12	South Bank	German+	12-18
Glasgow	German+	22-24	St Andrews	German+	20-28
Greenwich	German+	8-16	Staffordshire	German+	12-18
Heriot-Watt	German+	16-22	Stirling	German Lan.+	16-20
Huddersfield	German+	14	Strathclyde	German+	18
Hull	German+	16-24	Sunderland	German+	8-24
Keele	German+	20-24	Surrey	German+	20-22
Kent	German+	20-22	Sussex	German+	20
Kingston	German+	14-16	Swansea	German+	20-24
Lampeter	German+	14-18	Thames Valley	German+	8-12
Lancaster	German+	18-22	Ulster	German+	18
Leeds	German+	20-22	UMIST	German+	18-24
Leicester	German+	18	Warwick	German+	20-22
Lincolnshire &			Westminster	German+	12
Humberside	German+	12	Wolverhampton	German+	18
Liverpool	German+	20-22	York	German+	22
Liverpool JMU	German+	14-16			
London					
Goldsmiths'	German+	18			
King's	German.+	20-26			

MEDICINE AND RELATED SUBJECTS

Anatomy & Physiology

	COURSES	POINTS		COURSES	POINTS
Aberdeen	Phys'y	16	Royal Holloway	Phys'y+	20
Birmingham	Sport & Exerc. Sc.	24	UCL	Anatomy, Phys'y	18-22
Bradford	Cellular Pathology	16	Loughborough	Human Biol.	18
Bristol, W of			Luton	Human Biol.	12
England	App. Physical+	14	Manchester	Anatomy, Phys'y	20
Bristol	Anatomy, Phys'y	20	Middlesex	Human Biol.	12-16
Cambridge	Anatomy, Phys'y	28-30	Newcastle	Phys'y	20
Cardiff	Anatomy, Phys'y	18-20	North London	Human Biol.	10
Central Lancs	Neuroscience	8	Nottingham	Neuroscience.	26
Dundee	Anatomy, Phys'y	16	Nott'ham Trent	Phys'y/Pharma.	10
East Anglia	Zoology & Phys'y	18	Oxford	Phys'y	28
East London	Human Phys'y	12	Oxford Brookes	Human Biol. +	12-18
Edinburgh	Anatomy, Phys'y	22	Queen's, Belfast	Anatomy, Phys'y	18
Glasgow	Anatomy, Phys'y	18-22	Reading	Phys'y	18-24
Greenwich	Phys'y+	8-12	Salford	Phys'y+	16-20
Hertfordshire	Phys'y	14-16	Sheffield	Anatomy, Phys'y	22
Huddersfield	Human Biol.	10	Southampton	Phys'y	20-22
Keele	Neuroscience+	18-20	South Bank	Human Biol.+	12-18
Leeds	Phys'y	18-20	St Andrews	Phys'y	20
Leeds Met	Human Biol.	14	Staffordshire	Biochem. & Phys'y	12
Leicester	Animal Phys'y	20	Strathclyde	Phys'y	8
Liverpool	Anatomy, Phys'y	18	Sunderland	Phys'y	8-24
London			Sussex	Neuroscience	20
King's	Phys'y	20	Westminster	Phys'y	12

Medicine

	COURSES	POINTS		COURSES	POINTS
Aberdeen	Medicine	26	Royal Free	Medicine	26
Birmingham	Medicine	28	St George's	Medicine	26-30
Bristol	Medicine	28	UCL	Medicine	26-28
Cambridge	Medicine	30	UMDS Guys &		
Dundee	Medicine	26-28	St Thomas's	Medicine	26
Edinburgh	Medicine	28	Manchester	Medicine	26
Glasgow	Medicine	28	Newcastle	Medicine	28
Leeds	Medicine	24-28	Nottingham	Medicine	26
Leicester	Medicine	28	Oxford	Medicine	28-30
Liverpool	Medicine	26	Queen's, Belfast	Medicine	28
London			Sheffield	Medicine	26
Charing Cross	Medicine	24-28	Southampton	Medicine	26
Imperial	Medicine	26	St Andrews	Medical Sc.	26
King's	Medicine	26	UW College of		
Queen Mary	Medicine	26	Medicine	Medicine	28

Dentistry

	COURSES	POINTS		COURSES	POINTS
Birmingham	Dentistry	26	UMDS Guys &		
Bristol	Dentistry	26-28	St Thomas's	Dentistry	24
Dundee	Dentistry	24-26	Manchester	Dentistry	26
Glasgow	Dentistry	26	Newcastle	Dentistry	26
Leeds	Dentistry	26	Queen's, Belfast	Dentistry	28
Liverpool	Dentistry	26-28	Sheffield	Dentistry	26
London			UW College of		
King's	Dentistry	24	Medicine	Dentistry	26
Queen Mary	Dentistry	24			

Veterinary Medicine

	COURSES	POINTS		COURSES	POINTS
Bristol	Vet. Sc.	28	Liverpool	Vet. Sc.	28
Cambridge	Vet. Medicine	30	Royal Veterinary		
Edinburgh	Vet. Medicine.	28	College	Vet. Medicine	30
Glasgow	Vet. Sc.	28			

PHYSICAL AND MATHEMATICAL SCIENCES

Chemistry

	COURSES	POINTS		COURSES	POINTS
Aberdeen	Chem.+	16	London		
Abertay Dundee	Chem.+	8	Imperial	Chem.+	24
Anglia	Chem.+	10-12	King's	Chem.+	18-20
Aston	Chem.+	18-24	Queen Mary	Chem.+	18
Bangor	Chem.+	14-24	UCL	Chem.+	18-24
Bath	Chem.+	18-20	Loughborough	Chem.+	18
Birmingham	Chem.+	20-28	Manchester	Chem.+	18-20
Bradford	Chem.+	14-24	Manchester Met	Chem.+	10-14
Brighton	Chem.+	12	Napier	Appl. Chem.+	8
Bristol	Chem.+	18-22	Newcastle	Chem.+	18-20
Bristol (W. of E.)	Appl. Chem. Sc.	6-8	North London	Chem.+	8-12
Cambridge	Chem.+	28-30	Northumbria	Appl. Chem.+	10
Cardiff	Chem.+	16-20	Nottingham	Chem.+	18-24
Central Lancs	Chem.+	8-12	Nott'ham Trent	Chem.+	12-20
Coventry	Chem.+	10	Oxford	Chem.+	28
De Montfort	Chem.+	8-12	Oxford Brookes	Env. Chem. +	8-18
Derby	Chem.+	8-10	Paisley	Chem. +	4-18
Dundee	Chem.+	10-16	Plymouth	Chem.+	12-16
Durham	Chem.+	20	Portsmouth	Med. Chem.+	16
East Anglia	Chem.+	18-24	Queen's, Belfast	Chem.+	18-22
Edinburgh	Chem.+	16	Reading	Chem.+	18
Exeter	Chem.+	18-20	Robert Gordon	Appl. Chem.+	6
Glamorgan	Chem. Sc.+	8-12	Salford	Chem.+	16-22
Glasgow	Chem.+	18-22	Sheffield	Chem.+	20-26
Glasgow Cal	Chem.	6-8	Sheffield Hallam	Chem.+	14
Greenwich	Chem.+	8-18	Southampton	Chem.+	18-22
Heriot-Watt	Chem.+	12-16	St Andrews	Chem.+	18-20
Hertfordshire	Chem.+	8-18	Staffordshire	Chem.+	12-14
Huddersfield	Chem.+	10	Stirling	Chem.+	16-18
Hull	Chem.+	16-18	Strathclyde	Chem.+	18-26
Keele	Chem.+	16-24	Sunderland	Chem.+	8-16
Kent	Chem.+	16	Surrey	Chem.+	18-20
Kingston	Chem.+	10-14	Sussex	Chem.+	18-20
Lancaster	Chem. Sc.+	16-22	Swansea	Chem.+	20-22
Leeds	Chem.+	18-22	Teesside	Chem.+	6-12
Leicester	Chem.+	18-24	UMIST	Chem.+	18
Liverpool	Chem.+	16-20	Warwick	Chem.+	20
Liverpool JMU	Chem.+	8	Wolverhampton	Appl. Chem.+	8
			York	Chem.+	18

Physics

	COURSES	POINTS		COURSES	POINTS
Aberdeen	Physics+	16-22	Queen Mary	Physics+	18-24
Aberystwyth	Physics+	14-20	Royal Holloway	Physics+	20-22
Bangor	Appl. Physics+	12	UCL	Physics+	22-30
Bath	Physics+	18-22	Loughborough	Physics+	20
Birmingham	Physics+	20-22	Manchester	Physics+	20-22
Brighton	Physics+	12	Manchester Met	Appl. Physics+	12-18
Bristol	Physics+	20-24	Napier	Appl. Physics+	8-12
Cambridge	Physics+	28-30	Newcastle	Physics+	16-20
Cardiff	Physics+	18	Northumbria	Appl. Physics+	8
Central Lancs	Physics+	16	Nottingham	Physics+	16-24
Dundee	Physics+	10-14	Nott'ham Trent	Physics+	10-12
Durham	Physics+	18-24	Oxford	Physics+	28
East Anglia	Physics+	18-20	Paisley	Physics+	4-18
Edinburgh	Physics+	16-20	Portsmouth	Physics+	10-16
Exeter	Physics+	18-22	Queen's, Belfast	Physics+	18-22
Glasgow	Physics+	16-24	Reading	Physics+	18-20
Glasgow Cal	Appl. Physics+	6-8	Robert Gordon	Appl. Physics+	6
Heriot-Watt	Physics+	12-14	Salford	Physics+	4-20
Hertfordshire	Appl. Physics+	8-12	Sheffield	Physics+	20-24
Hull	Physics+	14-16	Sheffield Hallam	Physics+	10-16
Keele	Physics+	16-24	Southampton	Physics+	18-22
Kent	Physics+	16-18	St Andrews	Physics+	20-22
Kingston	Physics+	12-18	Staffordshire	Physics+	12
Lancaster	Physics+	14-22	Strathclyde	Physics+	10-24
Leeds	Physics+	18-24	Surrey	Physics+	12-24
Leicester	Physics+	16-20	Sussex	Physics+	18-20
Liverpool	Physics+	18-20	Swansea	Physics+	18-20
Liverpool JMU	Astrophysics	8	UMIST	Physics+	20
London			Warwick	Physics+	22-26
Imperial	Physics+	22-24	York	Physics+	20-22
King's	Physics+	18-20			

Geography

	COURSES	POINTS		COURSES	POINTS
Aberdeen	Geog.+	16-22	LSE	Geog.+	22-24
Aberystwyth	Geog.+	20-22	Queen Mary	Geog.+	18-20
Anglia	Geog.+	10-14	Royal Holloway	Geog.+	18-24
Birmingham	Geog.+	20-24	SOAS	Geog.+	20-24
Bradford	Geog.+	16-18	UCL	Geog.+	22-24
Brighton	Geog.+	12-16	Loughborough	Geog.+	20
Bristol	Geog.+	24-26	Luton	Geog.+	12
Bristol (W. of E.)	Geog.+	14-22	Manchester	Geog.+	20-24
Brunel	Geog.+	18-20	Manchester Met	Geog.+	12-18
Cambridge	Geog.+	28	Middlesex	Geog.+	12-16
Cardiff	Marine Geog.	18-20	Newcastle	Geog.+	18-22
Central Lancs	Geog.+	12-14	North London	Geog.+	12-14
Coventry	Geog.+	10-12	Northumbria	Geog.+	14
Cranfield	Phys. Geog.	18	Nottingham	Geog.+	22-26
De Montfort	Human Geog.	8-14	Nott'ham Trent	Env. Studies	12-16
Derby	Geog.+	8-10	Oxford	Geog.+	26-28
Dundee	Geog.+	20	Oxford Brookes	Geog.+	12-22
Durham	Geog.+	22-24	Plymouth	Geog.+	16-18
Edinburgh	Geog.+	18-26	Portsmouth	Geog. Sc.	10-18
Exeter	Geog.+	22-26	Queen's, Belfast	Geog.+	20-22
Glamorgan	Geog.+	10-12	Reading	Geog.+	22
Glasgow	Geog.+	18-22	Salford	Geog.+	16-20
Greenwich	Geog.+	12	Sheffield	Geog.+	22-26
Huddersfield	Geog.+	10-16	Sheffield Hallam	Urban Geog.	16
Hull	Geog.+	20-22	Southampton	Geog.+	20-24
Keele	Geog.+	20-24	South Bank	Human Geog.+	12-18
Kingston	Geog.+	14-18	St Andrews	Geog.+	22-26
Lampeter	Geog.+	16-18	Staffordshire	Geog.+	12-16
Lancaster	Geog.+	20-22	Strathclyde	Geog.+	18
Leeds	Geog.+	20-26	Sunderland	Geog.+	8-24
Leicester	Geog.+	18-22	Sussex	Geog.+	22
Liverpool	Geog.+	20-24	Swansea	Geog.+	20-22
Liverpool JMU	Geog.+	10-14	Ulster	Geog.+	14-18
London			Westminster	Human Geog.	14
King's	Geog.+	22	Wolverhampton	Geog.+	8-10

Maths

	COURSES	POINTS		COURSES	POINTS
Aberdeen	Maths+	16-22	King's	Maths+	20-24
Abertay Dundee	Maths+	10	LSE	Maths+	24-28
Aberystwth	Maths+	12-22	Queen Mary	Maths+	18-20
Anglia	Maths+	10-14	Royal Holloway	Maths+	20-26
Aston	Maths+	20	UCL	Maths+	20-30
Bangor	Maths+	14-24	London Guildhall	Maths+	8-12
Bath	Maths+	22-24	Loughborough	Maths+	20
Birmingham	Maths+	22-26	Luton	Maths+	12-16
Brighton	Maths+	12-14	Manchester	Maths+	22-24
Bristol	Maths+	22-28	Manchester Met	Maths+	12-18
Bristol (W. of E.)	Maths+	16-22	Middlesex	Math'l Sc.+	8-10
Brunel	Maths+	20-22	Napier	Maths+	12
Cambridge	Maths+	28-30	Newcastle	Maths+	18-24
Cardiff	Maths+	20-22	North London	Maths+	4-12
Central Lancs	Maths+	16	Northumbria	Maths+	8-14
City	Maths Sc.+	14-24	Nottingham	Maths+	22-28
Coventry	Maths+	10-20	Nottingham Trent	Maths+	12
De Montfort	Maths+	10-18	Oxford	Maths+	28
Derby	Maths+	8	Oxford Brookes	Maths+	8-24
Dundee	Maths+	10-20	Paisley	Math Sc.+	4-18
Durham	Maths+	24	Plymouth	Maths+	12-15
East Anglia	Maths+	14-20	Portsmouth	Maths+	14-20
East London	Maths+	12-14	Queen's, Belfast	Pure & Appl.	
Edinburgh	Maths+	20-24		Maths	18-22
Essex	Maths+	18-24	Reading	Maths+	20-24
Exeter	Maths+	20-22	Robert Gordon	Maths+	6
Glamorgan	Maths+	10-14	Salford	Maths+	20
Glasgow	Maths+	18-22	Sheffield	Maths+	24
Glasgow Cal	Maths for Bus.		Sheffield Hallam	Maths+	12-14
	Analysis	10	Southampton	Maths+	18-26
Greenwich	Maths+	8-16	St Andrews	Maths+	18-26
Heriot-Watt	Maths+	12-22	Staffordshire	Maths+	10-16
Hertfordshire	Maths+	12-18	Stirling	Maths+	16-18
Huddersfield	Maths+	20	Strathclyde	Maths+	10-22
Hull	Maths+	10-20	Sunderland	Maths+	8-10
Keele	Maths+	16-24	Surrey	Maths+	18-20
Kent	Maths+	20-22	Sussex	Maths+	20
Kingston	Maths+	12-16	Swansea	Maths+	20-24
Lancaster	Maths+	20-24	Teesside	Maths+	10-14
Leeds	Math'l Eng.	20-24	Ulster	Maths+	14-20
Leicester	Maths+	20	UMIST	Maths+	20-22
Liverpool	Maths+	20-22	Warwick	Maths+	26-30
Liverpool JMU	Maths+	10	Westminster	Maths+	10
London			Wolverhampton	Math'l Analysis	10
Goldsmiths'	Maths+	8	York	Maths+	20-28
Imperial	Maths+	26			

Computer Studies

	COURSES	POINTS		COURSES	POINTS
Aberdeen	Comp.+	16-22	Imperial	Comp.+	26-28
Abertay Dundee	Comp.+	10	King's	Comp. Sc.+	18-22
Aberystwyth	Comp. Sc.+	20	Queen Mary	Comp. &	
Anglia	Comp. Sc.+	10-14		Comp. Sc.	18-22
Aston	Comp. Sc.+	18-20	Royal Holloway	Comp. Sc.+	20-24
Bath	Comp.+	22-24	UCL	Comp. Sc.+	18-28
Birmingham	Comp. Sc.+	24-28	London Guildhall	Comp.+	24-30
Bournemouth	Comp. +	12	Loughborough	Comp.+	20-22
Bradford	Comp. Sc.+	18-22	Luton	Comp. &	
Brighton	Comp+	12-18		Comp. Sc.	12-16
Bristol	Comp. Sc.+	24-26	Manchester	Comp. &	
Bristol (W. of E.)	Comp. Sc.+	14-22		Comp. Sc.	22
Brunel	Comp. Sc.+	16-24	Manchester Met	Comp. Sc.+	12-18
Cambridge	Comp. Sc.+	28-30	Middlesex	Appl. Comp.+	12-16
Cardiff	Comp. Sc.+	18-20	Napier	Bus. Info. M'ment+	8-12
Central England	Comp. Sc+	12	Newcastle	Comp. &	
Central Lancs	Bus. Comp.+	12		Comp. Sc.	18-20
City	Comp.+	16-20	North London	Comp. Sc.+	10-12
Coventry	Comp. Sc.+	10-12	Northumbria	Bus. Info. Tech	12-14
Cranfield	Info. Sys.+	14-18		Comp. Sc.+	20-28
De Montfort	Comp.+	12-18	Nottingham	Comp.+	12-18
Derby	Comp.+	8-14	Nottingham Trent	Comp. &	
Dundee	Comp. Sc.+	10-14	Oxford	Comp. Sc.	28
Durham	Comp. Sc.+	22	Oxford Brookes	Comp.+	8-22
East Anglia	Comp. &		Paisley	Comp. &	
	Comp. Sc.	18-24		Comp. Sc.	12-18
East London	Comp.+	12-14	Plymouth	Comp.+	12-20
Edinburgh	Comp. Sc.+	18-24	Portsmouth	Comp.+	14-20
Essex	Comp. Sc.+	20-24	Queen's, Belfast	Comp. Sc.+	20-24
Exeter	Comp. Sc+	20	Reading	Comp. Sc.+	18-24
Glamorgan	Comp'l Sc.+	10-12	Robert Gordon	Comp. &	
Glasgow	Comp. Sc.+	18-22		Comp. Sc.	4-8
Glasgow Cal	Comp. Info.		Salford	Comp. Sc.+	16-20
	Sys.	12-14	Sheffield	Comp. Sc.+	22-26
Greenwich	Comp. &		Sheffield Hallam	Info. Tech.	
	Comp. Sc.	8-10		& Sys.+	12-14
Heriot-Watt	Comp. Sc.+	12-14	Southampton	Comp. Sc.+	20-22
Hertfordshire	Comp. &.		South Bank	Comp.+	12-18
	Comp. Sc.+	12-18	St Andrews	Comp'l Sc.+	18-20
Huddersfield	Comp.+	12-20	Staffordshire	Comp. &	
Hull	Comp. Sc.+	10-18		Comp. Sc.	10-18
Keele	Comp. Sc.+	18-24	Stirling	Comp. Sc.+	16-20
Kent	Comp.+	20-24	Strathclyde	Comp. Sc.+	14-18
Kingston	Comp.+	12-24	Sunderland	Comp.+	8-24
Lampeter	Infomatics+	14-16	Surrey	Comp. Sc.+	18-24
Lancaster	Comp. &		Sussex	Comp. Sc.+	20-24
	Comp. Sc.+	20-22	Swansea	Comp. Sc.+	20-24
Leeds	Comp. &		Teesside	Comp. Sc.+	8-18
	Comp. Sc.+	20-22	Thames Valley	Info. Sys. &	
Leeds Met	Comp.+	12-16		M'ment	8-12
Leicester	Comp. Sc.+	18-24	Ulster	Comp.+	14-20
Lincs & Humber	Comp.+	12-16	UMIST	Computation+	18-22
Liverpool	Comp. Sc.+	8-22	Warwick	Comp. &	
Liverpool JMU	Comp. &			Comp. Sc.	24-28
	Comp. Sc.+	12	Westminster	Comp.+	10-12
London			Wolverhampton	Comp.+	10
Goldsmiths'	Comp. Sc.+	8-18	York	Comp. Sc.+	26-28

BIOLOGICAL SCIENCES

Biology

	COURSES	POINTS		COURSES	POINTS
Aberdeen	Biol.+	16	London		
Abertay Dundee	Biol.+	10	Imperial	Biol.+	20-24
Aberystwyth	Biol.+	16-20	King's	Biol.+	20
Anglia	Biol. Sc.+	12	Queen Mary	Biol.+	16-18
Aston	Biol.+	18-20	Royal Holloway	Biol.+	20-22
Bangor	Biol. +	14-16	UCL	Biol.+	18-24
Bath	Biol. +	20	Wye	Biol.+	14
Birmingham	Biol. Sc.+	20	Luton	Biol.	12
Brighton	Biol. Sc.+	12	Manchester	Biol.+	18-20
Bristol	Biol. +	24	Manchester Met	Biol.+	12-18
Bristol (W. of E.)	Biol.+	8	Napier	Biol. Sc.+	8
Brunel	Appl. Biol.+	18	Newcastle	Biol. Sc..+	18-22
Cambridge	Biol.+	28-30	North London	Biol. Sc.+	10-12
Cardiff	Biol.+	20-24	Northumbria	Appl. Biol.	10
Central Lancs	Appl. Biol.+	14	Nottingham	Biol.+	26-28
Coventry	Biol. Sc.+	12-16	Nott'ham Trent	Appl. Biol.+	12
De Montfort	Biol.+	8-14	Oxford	Biol. Sc.+	26-28
Derby	Biol. +	8-10	Oxford Brookes	Biol.+	8-20
Dundee	Biol. +	16	Paisley	Biol.	4-18
Durham	Biol.+	18-20	Plymouth	Biol. Sc.+	10-14
East Anglia	Biol. Sc.+	20-22	Portsmouth	Biol.+	14
East London	Biol.+	12-14	Queen's, Belfast	Biol. Sc.+	18
Edinburgh	Biol. Sc.+	22	Reading	Biol. Sc.+	18
Essex	Biol.+	18	Robert Gordon	Biol. Sci.	6
Exeter	Biol. Sc.	18	Salford	Appl. Biol.+	16-20
Glamorgan	Biol. Sc.+	8-12	Sheffield	Biol. Sc.	22
Glasgow Cal	Appl.		Southampton	Biol.+	20-22
	Bioscience	12	South Bank	Appl. Biol.+	8
Greenwich	Appl. Biol.+	10-16	St Andrews	Biol.+	22
Heriot-Watt	Biol. Sc.+	12	Staffordshire	Appl. Biol.+	12
Hertfordshire	Appl. Biol.+	13-15	Stirling	Aquaculture	16
Hull	Biol.+	18-20	Strathclyde	Biol. Sc.+	18
Keele	Biol.+	16-24	Sunderland	Appl. Biol.+	8
Kent	Biol. Sc.+	20	Sussex	Biol.+	20-22
Kingston	Appl. Biol.+	12-16	Swansea	Biol. Sc.+	20
Lancaster	Biol. Sc.+	18-22	Ulster	Biol. Sc.+	14-16
Leeds	Biol.+	20	UMIST	Biol. Sc.	20
Leicester	Biol. Sc.+	20	Warwick	Biol. Sc.+	20
Liverpool	Biol.+	20	Westminster	Biol. Sc.+	12
Liverpool JMU	Appl. Biol.+	8-10	Wolverhampton	Biol. Sc.+	8
			York	Biol.+	20-22

Biochemistry

	COURSES	POINTS		COURSES	POINTS
Aberdeen	Biochem.+	16	London		
Abertay Dundee	Biol Chem.	10	Imperial	Biochem.+	22-24
Aberystwyth	Biochem.+	16-18	King's	Biochem.+	20-22
Anglia	Cell & Molec. Biol.	10	Queen Mary	Biochem.+	16-18
Bangor	Biochem.+	14-16	Royal Holloway	Biochem.+	20
Bath	Biochem.	24	UCL	Biochem.+	20-24
Birmingham	Biochem.+	20	Wye	Biochem.+	14
Bradford	Med. Biochem.	16	Manchester	Biochem.+	22
Bristol	Biochem.+	24	Manchester Met	Med &	
Bristol (W. of E.)	Appl.			Biol. Chem.	8-10
	Biochem.+	14	Newcastle	Biochem.+	20
Brunel	Appl.		North London	Biochem.+	8
	Biochem.+	18	Northumbria	Biochem.+	10
Cambridge	Biochem.+	28-30	Nottingham	Biochem.+	20-28
Cardiff	Biochem.+	20-22	Nott'ham Trent	Biochem.+	12
Central Lancs	Appl.		Oxford	Mol. & Cell.	
	Biochem.+	14		Biochem.+	28
Coventry	Biochem.+	10-12	Oxford Brookes	Biol. Chem.	8-20
Dundee	Biochem.+	16	Paisley	Appl. Biochem.+	4-18
Durham	Molec. Biol. &		Portsmouth	Biochem.	14
	Biochem.	18-20	Queen's, Belfast	Biochem.+	18
East Anglia	Biochem.+	18-26	Reading	Biochem.+	18
East London	Biochem.+	8-12	Salford	Biochem'l Sc.	14-22
Edinburgh	Biochem.+	22	Sheffield	Biochem.+	22-24
Essex	Biochem.+	18	Southampton	Biochem.+	20
Exeter	Biol. & Medical		South Bank	Biochem.	14
	Chem.	18	St Andrews	Biochem.+	18
Glasgow	Biochem.+	18-22	Staffordshire	Biochem.+	8-12
Greenwich	Biochem.+	10	Stirling	Biochem.+	16
Heriot-Watt	Biochem.+	12	Strathclyde	Biochem.+	18
Hertfordshire	Biochem.+	13-15	Sunderland	Biochem. +	8-10
Huddersfield	Biochem.+	10-18	Surrey	Biochem.+	18-20
Keele	Biochem.+	16-22	Sussex	Biochem.+	18
Kent	Biochem.+	20	Swansea	Biochem.+	20
Kingston	Biochem.+	12-14	Ulster	Appl. Biochem. Sc.	16
Lancaster	Biochem.+	20	UMIST	Biochem.+	18-20
Leeds	Biochem.+	20-22	Warwick	Biochem.+	20-22
Leicester	Biol. Chem.+	18-24	Westminster	Biochem.+	12
Liverpool	Biochem.+	20-22	Wolverhampton	Biochem.+	8
Liverpool JMU	Appl.		York	Biochem.+	20-22
	Biochem.+	8-10			

Psychology

COURSES	POINTS		COURSES	POINTS
Aberdeen	Psychol.+	16-22	Liverpool JMU	App. Psychol.+	16-20
Abertay Dundee	Psychol.+	10	London		
Anglia	Psychol.+	14	Goldsmiths'	Psychol.+	22
Aston	Psychol.+	20-24	LSE	Psychol.+	24
Bangor	Psychol.+	18-22	Royal Holloway	Psychol.+	22-24
Bath	Psychol.+	24	UCL	Psychol.+	22-28
Birmingham	Psychol.+	24	London Guildhall	Psychol.+	10-12
Bournemouth	App. Psychol.+	14-16	Loughborough	Psychol.+	22
Bradford	Psychol.+	16-18	Luton	Psychol.+	14
Bristol	Psychol.+	24	Manchester	Psychol.+	22-26
Bristol (W. of E.)	Psychol.+	16-22	Manchester Met	Psychol.+	18
Brunel	Psychol.+	20-24	Middlesex	Psychol.+	14-18
Buckingham	Psychol.+	14	Newcastle	Psychol.+	24-26
Cambridge	Psychol.+	28-30	North London	Psychol.+	8-12
Cardiff	Psychol.+	24	Northumbria	Psychol.+	16
Central England	Psychol. +	12	Nottingham	Psychol.+	22-24
Central Lancs	Psychol.+	18	Nott'ham Trent	Psychol.+	22
City	Psychol.+	18-20	Oxford	Psychol.+	28
Coventry	Psychol.+	10-12	Oxford Brookes	Psychol.+	8-22
De Montfort	Psychol.+	10-12	Paisley	Psychol.+	12
Derby	Psychol.+	18-20	Plymouth	Psychol.+	20-22
Dundee	Psychol.+	14-20	Portsmouth	Psychol.+	20
Durham	Psychol.+	24-26	Queen's, Belfast	Psychol.+	22
East London	Psychol.+	12	Reading	Psychol.+	20-24
Edinburgh	Psychol.+	24-28	Sheffield	Psychol.+	26-28
Essex	Psychol.+	22	Sheffield Hallam	Psychol.+	20
Exeter	Psychol.+	24-28	Southampton	Psychol.+	8-24
Glamorgan	Psychol.	12-16	South Bank	Psychol.+	14-18
Glasgow	Psychol.+	18-22	St Andrews	Psychol.+	26
Glasgow Cal	Psychol.+	16	Staffordshire	Psychol.+	18
Greenwich	Psychol.+	14-16	Stirling	Psychol.+	16-22
Heriot-Watt	Psychol.	18	Strathclyde	Psychol.+	18
Hertfordshire	Psychol +.	20	Sunderland	Psychol.+	10-14
Huddersfield	Psychol.+	14-20	Surrey	Psychol.+	22
Hull	Psychol.+	20-24	Sussex	Psychol.+	24
Keele	Psychol.+	20-24	Swansea	Psychol.+	20-24
Kent	Psychol.+	22-26	Teesside	Psychol.+	10-16
Kingston	Psychol.+	16-18	Thames Valley	Psychol.+	8-12
Lancaster	Psychol.+	20-22	Ulster	Psychol.+	18-22
Leeds	Psychol.+	26	Warwick	Psychol.+	20-24
Leicester	Psychol.+	24	Westminster	Psychol.+	12-14
Lincs & Humber	Psychol.+	18	Wolverhampton	Psychol.+	18
Liverpool	Psychol.+	24-26	York	Psychol.+	24-26

SOCIAL SCIENCES

Economics

	COURSES	POINTS		COURSES	POINTS
Aberdeen	Econ.+	22	Liverpool JMU	Econ.+	12-16
Abertay Dundee	Econ.+	10	London		
Aberystwyth	Econ.+	16-20	Goldsmiths'	Econ.+	18
Anglia	Econ.+	12-14	LSE	Econ.+	24-28
Bangor	Econ.+	18	Queen Mary	Econ.+	18-22
Bath	Econ.+	22	Royal Holloway	Econ.+	20-26
Birmingham	Econ.+	22-24	SOAS	Econ.+	20-24
Bradford	Econ.+	16-18	SSEES	Econ.+	20
Bristol	Econ.+	22-24	UCL	Econ.+	20-30
Bristol (W. of E.)	Econ.+	16-22	London Guildhall	Econ.+	8-14
Brunel	Econ.+	20-24	Loughborough	Econ.+	20
Buckingham	Econ.+	12-14	Manchester	Econ.+	22-24
Cambridge	Econ.+	28-30	Manchester Met	Econ.+	14-18
Cardiff	Econ.+	22-24	Middlesex	Econ.+	12-16
Central England	Econ.+	12-14	Newcastle	Econ.+	20-24
Central Lancs	Econ.+	12	North London	Econ.+	12-14
City	Econ.+	20-22	Northumbria	Econ.+	12-14
Coventry	Econ.+	12-16	Nottingham	Econ.+	26-28
De Montfort	Econ.+	12-18	Nott'ham Trent	Econ.+	14-18
Derby	Bus. Econ.+	14	Oxford	Econ.+	26-28
Dundee	Econ.+	14-20	Oxford Brookes	Econ.+	10-22
Durham	Econ.+	24-26	Paisley	Bus. Econ.+	16
East Anglia	Econ.+	20-22	Plymouth	Econ.+	14-22
East London	Econ.+	12-14	Portsmouth	Econ.+	16
Edinburgh	Econ.+	24-26	Queen's, Belfast	Econ.+	18-22
Essex	Econ.+	18-22	Reading	Econ.+	18-22
Exeter	Bus. Econ.+	18-26	Salford	Econ.+	16-20
Glamorgan	Econ.+	12-16	Sheffield	Econ.+	22-26
Glasgow	Econ.+	22	Southampton	Econ.+	22-24
Glasgow Cal	Bus. Econ.+	14	South Bank	Econ.+	12-18
Greenwich	Econ.+	14-16	St Andrews	Econ.+	20-26
Heriot-Watt	Econ.+	18-22	Staffordshire	Econ.+	12-14
Hertfordshire	Appl. Econ.+	12-20	Stirling	Econ.+	18-20
Huddersfield	Econ.+	14	Sunderland	Econ.+	8-24
Hull	Econ.+	18-22	Surrey	Econ.+	20-24
Keele	Econ.+	20-24	Sussex	Econ.+	20-24
Kent	Econ.+	18-20	Swansea	Econ.+	20-24
Kingston	Econ.+	12-16	Teesside	Bus. Econ.+	14-16
Lancaster	Econ.+	22-28	Thames Valley	Econ.+	8-12
Leeds	Econ.+	22-24	Ulster	Econ.+	18-22
Leeds Met	Econ.+	14	Warwick	Econ.+	28-30
Leicester	Econ.+	20-24	Westminster	Econ.+	14
Lincs & Humber	Econ.+	16	Wolverhampton	Econ.+	14
Liverpool	Econ.+	18-20	York	Econ.+	20-24

Sociology

	COURSES	POINTS		COURSES	POINTS
Aberdeen	Sociology+	22	Liverpool JMU	Sociology+	12-18
Anglia	Sociology+	12-14	London		
Aston	Sociology+	18-20	Goldsmiths'	Sociology+	20-22
Bangor	Sociology+	16-18	LSE	Sociology+	24
Bath	Sociology+	20-24	Royal Holloway	Sociology+	20-26
Birmingham	Sociology+	22	London Guildhall	Social Policy+	8-14
Bradford	Sociology+	18-22	Loughborough	Sociology+	20
Brighton	Cultural &		Luton	Social St.+	12-16
	Hist. St.	12	Manchester	Sociology+	20-24
Bristol	Sociology+	22-24	Manchester Met	Sociology	12-14
Bristol (W. of E.)	Sociology+	14-22	Middlesex	Sociology+	12-16
Brunel	Sociology+	20-24	North London	Sociology+	12
Cambridge	Sociology+	28-30	Northumbria	Sociology+	14-18
Cardiff	Sociology+	20-26	Nottingham	Sociology+	22
Central England	Sociology+	12	Oxford	Sociology+	26-28
Central Lancs	Social St.+	16	Oxford Brookes	Sociology+	12-20
City	Sociology+	20	Plymouth	Sociology+	14-22
Coventry	Social St.+	12	Portsmouth	Sociology+	12-14
De Montfort	Sociology+	8-16	Queen's, Belfast	Sociology+	20
Derby	Sociology+	12	Reading	Sociology+	20-22
Durham	Sociology+	20-26	Salford	Sociology+	18
East Anglia	Sociology+	22	Sheffield	Sociology+	22-26
East London	Sociology+	12	Sheffield Hallam	Sociology+	18
Edinburgh	Sociology+	24-28	Southampton	Sociology+	18-20
Essex	Sociology+	20-22	South Bank	Sociology+	12-18
Exeter	Sociology+	18-24	Staffordshire	Sociology+	12-16
Glamorgan	Sociology+	10-14	Stirling	Sociology+	18-22
Glasgow	Sociology+	22	Strathclyde	Sociology+	18
Greenwich	Sociology+	12-18	Sunderland	Sociology+	8-10
Hertfordshire	Social Sc.	14	Surrey	Sociology+	18-22
Huddersfield	Sociology+	12-16	Sussex	Social Sc.	24
Hull	Sociology+	16-24	Swansea	Sociology+	20-22
Keele	Sociology+	20-24	Teesside	Sociology+	12-14
Kent	Sociology+	18-24	Thames Valley	Sociology+	8-12
Kingston	Sociology+	14-18	Ulster	Sociology	20
Lancaster	Sociology+	18-20	Warwick	Sociology+	20-26
Leeds	Sociology+	20-24	Westminster	Sociology+	14
Leeds Met	Social Policy+	16-20	Wolverhampton	Sociology+	12
Leicester	Sociology+	20	York	Sociology+	20-22
Liverpool	Sociology+	20			

Law

	COURSES	POINTS		COURSES	POINTS
Aberdeen	Law+	24	Lincs & Humber	Law+	16-18
Abertay Dundee	Law+	8-14	Liverpool	Law+	26-28
Aberystwyth	Law+	24	Liverpool JMU	Law+	16-20
Anglia	Law+	12-18	London		
Aston	Law+	22-24	King's	Law+	26-28
Bangor	Criminology+	18	LSE	Law+	24-26
Birmingham	Law+	28	Queen Mary	Law+	24
Bournemouth	Bus. Law+	16	SOAS	Law+	24
Bradford	Law+	16-18	UCL	Law+	26-28
Brighton	Law+	18	London Guildhall	Law+	12-20
Bristol	Law+	26	Luton	Law+	12-16
Bristol (W. of E.)	Law+	16-24	Manchester	Law+	26-28
Brunel	Law+	20-24	Manchester Met	Law+	22
Buckingham	Law+	12-18	Middlesex	Law	18
Cambridge	Law+	30	Napier	Law	12-18
Cardiff	Law+	24	Newcastle	Law+	24-26
Central England	Law+	12-18	North London	Law+	12-20
Central Lancs	Law+	14-18	Northumbria	Law+	24
City	Law+	24	Nottingham	Law+	26-28
Coventry	Law+	12-20	Nottingham Trent	Law+	22
De Montfort	Law+	14-22	Oxford	Law+	28
Derby	Law+	18-20	Oxford Brookes	Law+	8-24
Dundee	Law+	22	Plymouth	Law+	16-22
Durham	Law+	24-28	Portsmouth	Law+	18
East Anglia	Law+	24	Queen's, Belfast	Law+	26-28
East London	Law+	12-14	Reading	Law+	24-26
Edinburgh	Law+	26-28	Robert Gordon	Law+	10
Essex	Law+	22-26	Sheffield	Law+	28
Exeter	Law+	20-26	Sheffield Hallam	Law+	20
Glamorgan	Law+	18	Southampton	Law+	24-26
Glasgow	Law+	26	South Bank	Law+	12-18
Glasgow Cal	Law+	14	Staffordshire	Law+	14-20
Greenwich	Law+	12-18	Stirling	Law+	20
Hertfordshire	Law+	20	Strathclyde	Law+	22
Huddersfield	Law+	16-18	Sunderland	Bus. Law+	8-10
Hull	Law+	22-24	Surrey	Law+	18-22
Keele	Law+	20-26	Sussex	Law+	24
Kent	Law+	16-26	Swansea	Law+	20-24
Kingston	Law+	2022	Teesside	Law+	18
Lancaster	Law	26	Thames Valley	Law+	8-12
Leeds	Law+	28	Ulster	Law+	22
Leeds Met	Law	22	Warwick	Law+	24-28
Leicester	Law+	24-26	Westminster	Law+	20-22
			Wolverhampton	Law+	8-28

Politics

COURSES	POINTS		COURSES	POINTS
Aberdeen	Politics+	22	London		
Aberystwyth	Politics+	18-22	Goldsmiths'	Politics+	18
Anglia	Politics+	12-14	LSE	Gov.+	24-26
Bath	Politics+	22	Queen Mary	Politics+	20-24
Birmingham	Political Sc.+	20-24	Royal Holloway	Politics+	20-24
Bradford	Politics+	16-22	SOAS	Politics+	20-24
Bristol	Politics+	22-26	SSEES	Politics+	20
Bristol (W. of E.)	Politics+	16-22	London Guildhall	Politics+	8-14
Brunel	Politics+	20	Loughborough	Politics+	20
Buckingham	Politics+	12-16	Luton	Public Admin.+	14
Cambridge	Political Sc.+	28-30	Manchester	Politics+	22-26
Cardiff	Politics+	20-24	Manchester Met	Public Admin.+	12
Central England	Gov.	12	Middlesex	Politics+	12-16
Central Lancs	Gov.	12	Newcastle	Politics+	20-26
Coventry	Politics	10-12	North London	Politics+	12
De Montfort	Politics.+	14-18	Northumbria	Politics+	12-14
Dundee	Political Sc.+	20	Nottingham	Politics+	24-26
Durham	Politics+	22-24	Nottingham Trent	Politics+	12-18
East Anglia	Politics+	20-24	Oxford	Politics+	28
East London	Political St.	12	Oxford Brookes	Politics+	8-20
Edinburgh	Politics+	24-26	Plymouth	Politics+	14-22
Essex	Politics+	20-22	Portsmouth	Politics+	10-12
Exeter	Politics+	18-26	Queen's, Belfast	Politics+	20
Glamorgan	Politics+	8-14	Reading	Politics+	20-22
Glasgow	Politics+	22	Robert Gordon	Public Policy+	8
Glasgow Cal	Public Admin.+	12	Salford	Politics+	18
Greenwich	Politics+	10-16	Sheffield	Politics+	22-24
Hertfordshire	Politics	14	Sheffield Hallam	Public Admin.+	14
Huddersfield	Political St.	14	Southampton	Politics+	20-22
Hull	Politics+	20-24	South Bank	Politics+	12-18
Keele	Politics+	20-24	St Andrews	Int. Relations	28
Kent	Politics & Gov.+	18-22	Staffordshire	Politics+	12-16
Kingston	Politics+	14-18	Stirling	Politics+	18-22
Lancaster	Politics+	20-22	Sunderland	Politics+	8-12
Leeds	Politics+	22-24	Sussex	Politics+	22-24
Leeds Met.	Politics+	18-20	Swansea	Politics+	20-24
Leicester	Politics+	18-20	Teesside	Politics+	12-14
Lincs &			Ulster	Gov.+	18-22
Humber	Politics+	14-18	Warwick	Politics+	20-26
Liverpool	Politics+	20-24	Westminster	Politics+	14
Liverpool JMU	Politics+	12-18	Wolverhampton	Politics.+	10
			York	Politics+	22-26

VISUAL AND PERFORMING ARTS

Art & Design

	COURSES	POINTS		COURSES	POINTS
Aberdeen	Hist. of Art+	22	SOAS	Hist. of Art+	20
Aberystwth	Art+	18-22	UCL	Hist. of Art+	22-24
Anglia	Art+	14	London Guildhall	Des.+	8-18
Birmingham	Hist. of Art+	24	Loughborough	Hist. of Art &	
Bournemouth	Des.+	12-16		Des.	10-20
Brighton	Product Des.	18	Luton	Des.+	14
Bristol	Hist. of Art	22	Manchester	Hist. of Art	20-24
Bristol (W. of E.)	Art+, Des.+	14	Manchester Met	Art+, Des.+	8-12
Brunel	Des.+	18	Middlesex	Des. Tech.	8-10
Buckingham	Hist. of Art	10-12	Napier	Interior Des.	12
Cambridge	Hist. of Art	28	Newcastle	Art	18
Central England	Des.+	18	North London	Interior Des.	10
Central Lancs	Des.+	18	Northumbria	Art+	18
Coventry	Graphics	12	Nottingham	Art Hist.+	22
De Montfort	Des.+	12-18	Nott'ham Trent	Art+, Des.+,	
Derby	Art+	18		Textiles+	12-18
East Anglia	Hist. of Art+	22	Oxford	Fine Art	24-26
East London	A&D+, Fine		Oxford Brookes	Fine Art+,	
	Art+	12		Hist. of Art+	8-20
Edinburgh	Hist. of Art,		Plymouth	Art Hist.+,	
	Art+	24		Des.+	14-18
Essex	Art Hist.+	20-22	Portsmouth	Des.+	18
Exeter	Art+	20-24	Reading	Art+,	
Glamorgan	Art+, Des.+	8-12		Hist. of Art	20-22
Glasgow	Hist. of Art+	22-24	Robert Gordon	Des. for	
Hertfordshire	Art, Des.	10		Industry	16
Huddersfield	Des.+	10-14	Salford	Des.+	4
Keele	Art+	20-24	Sheffield Hallam	Art+, Des.+	12-16
Kent	Hist. of Art+	20-22	St Andrews	Art Hist.+	22-24
Kingston	Hist. of Art	14-16	Staffordshire	Art+, Des.+	12-18
Lancaster	Hist. of Art+	20-22	Southampton	Art,	
Leeds	Art+, Hist. of			Hist of Art	10-20
	Art+	20-22	Sunderland	Art+	
Leeds Met	Art+, Des.+	10-14		Hist. of Art	8-18
Leicester	Hist. of Art	20-22	Sussex	Hist. of Art+	24
Lincs &			Teesside	Des.+	14-18
Humber	Art+, Des.+	12-16	Thames Valley	Des.+	8-12
Liverpool	Hist. of Art	20-24	Ulster	Tech. & Des.	16
Liverpool JMU	Des.+,		UMIST	Textile Des.+	18
	Hist. of Art	12-20	Warwick	Hist. of Art	22-24
London			Westminster	Des.+	12-16
Courtauld Inst.	Hist. of Art	22	Wolverhampton	Des.+	8-18
Goldsmiths'	Art+	14-22	York	Hist. of Art+	22-26

Music & Performing Arts

	COURSES	POINTS		COURSES	POINTS
Aberystwth	Drama+	20	London		
Anglia	Music+	12-14	Goldsmiths'	Music, Drama & Theatre	22
Bangor	Music+	16-18	Imperial	Music+	22
Birmingham	Dance, Music+	20-28	King's	Music+	22-26
Brighton	Visual/Perf. Arts	12	Queen Mary	Drama+	26
Bristol	Drama+, Music+	14-22	Royal Holloway	Drama+, Music+	20-24
Brunel	Drama+, Music+	16-20	SOAS	Music+	20-24
Cambridge	Music	28	Loughborough	Drama+	22
Cardiff	Music	20-22	Luton	Media Perf.+	12-16
City	Music	20-22	Manchester	Drama+, Music+	22-24
Coventry	Theatre+	12-20	Manchester Met	Drama, Music, Theatre Arts	8-14
De Montfort	Perf. Arts+	10-20	Middlesex	Acting+, Dance+, Music+	12-16
Derby	Perf. Arts+	12			
Durham	Music+	20-24	Napier	Music+	10-14
East Anglia	Drama, Music+	20-26	Newcastle	Music	16-22
East London	Acting	12	North London	Theatre St.	12
Edinburgh	Music+	14-24	Northumbria	Drama	14
Essex	Music+	20	Nottingham	Music	22-24
Exeter	Music+, Drama+	20-24	Nott'ham Trent	Contemp. Arts	12
Glamorgan	Media Drama	12-14	Oxford	Music	26-28
Glasgow	Music+, Theatre St.+	22-24	Oxford Brookes	Music	8-22
Hertfordshire	Perf. Arts+, E'tronic Music	12-18	Plymouth	Drama & Theatre Arts+, Music+	14-18
Huddersfield	Music+, Theatre St.	8-12	Queen's, Belfast	Music+	20
Hull	Drama+, Music+	18-12	Reading	Film & Drama+, Music+	20-22
Keele	Music+	20-24	Salford	Music	8-12
Kent	Drama+	22-24	Sheffield	Music+	20-24
Kingston	Music+	10	Southampton	Music+	20-22
Lancaster	Music+, Theatre St.+	20-24	Staffordshire	Music Tech., Drama	12
Leeds	Music+, Theatre St.+	22-28	Strathclyde	Appl. Music	12
Liverpool	Music+	16-24	Sunderland	Music+	8-12
Liverpool JMU	Drama+, Theatre St.+	16-18	Surrey	Music+, Dance+	16-26
			Sussex	Music +	22
			Thames Valley	Music+	8-12
			Ulster	Music+, Theatre St.+	18
			Warwick	Theatre St.+	20-26
			Wolverhampton	Music, Drama	10-14
			York	Music	22

Architecture

	COURSES	POINTS		COURSES	POINTS
Bath	Arch. St.	24	London		
Brighton	Arch.+	18	UCL	Arch.+	22
Bristol (W. of E.)	Arch. & Plan'g	16-20	Luton	Arch.	16
Cambridge	Arch.+	28-30	Manchester	Arch.+	20-22
Cardiff	Arch. St.	24	Manchester Met	Arch.+	20
Central England	Arch.	14	Middlesex	Arch.+	4
De Montfort	Arch.+	16	Newcastle	Arch. St.+	24
Derby	Arch. Tech.	10	North London	Arch.	12
Dundee	Arch.	20	Northumbria	Arch. Des.+	12-16
East London	Arch.	12	Nottingham	Arch.	24
Edinburgh	Arch.+	26	Nott'ham Trent	Arch. Tech.	14
Glasgow	Arch.+	16-20	Oxford Brookes	Arch.	16
Greenwich	Arch.+	16	Paisley	Arch. St.+	14-18
Heriot-Watt	Arch.+	20	Plymouth	Arch.	18
Huddersfield	Arch.+	12-14	Portsmouth	Arch.	18
Kingston	Arch.	22	Queen's, Belfast	Arch.	20
Leeds	Arch. Eng.	18	Robert Gordon	Arch.	12
Leeds Met	Arch.	16-18	Sheffield	Arch.+	20-24
Lincs & Humber	Arch.+	14	Sheffield Hall.	Arch. Tech.	16
Liverpool	Arch.	24	South Bank	Arch.	12
Liverpool JMU	Arch. St.	18	Strathclyde	Arch. St.+	22
			Westminster	Arch.	12-14

EDUCATION

	COURSES	POINTS		COURSES	POINTS
Aberystwyth	Educ.+	14-22	Liverpool	Educ.+	20-22
Anglia	Educ.+(t)	16	Liverpool JMU	Educ.+(t)	16-18
Bangor	Educ.+(t)	8-20	London		
Bath	Educ.+(t)	18-20	Goldsmiths'	Educ.(t)	18-20
Brighton	Educ.+(t)	12-14	King's	Educ.+	8-22
Bristol	Childhood St.	20	Loughborough	Educ.+(t)	12-26
Bristol (W. of E.)	Educ.+(t)	12-22	Luton	Educ.	14
Brunel	Educ.+(t)	14-16	Manchester	Educ.+	18
Cambridge	Educ.+(t)	18-28	Manchester Met	Educ.(t)	12
Cardiff	Educ.+	20-24	Middlesex	Educ.+(t)	12-18
Central England	Educ.+(t)	4-20	Newcastle	Educ.(t)	22-24
Central Lancs	Educ. St.+	14	North London	Educ.+(t)	10-12
De Montfort	Educ.+(t)	8-16	Northumbria	Educ.+(t)	12-20
Derby	Educ.+(t)	14	Nott'ham Trent	Educ.+(t)	8-14
Durham	Educ.(t)	14-22	Oxford Brookes	Educ. St.+(t)	12-22
East London	Educ.+	12	Paisley	Educ. (t)	16
Exeter	Educ. St(t).	8-18	Plymouth	Educ.+(t)	12-18
Greenwich	Educ.(t)	10-12	Portsmouth	Educ.+	16
Heriot-Watt	Educ.+	12-14	Reading	Educ. St.(t)	14
Hertfordshire	Educ.+(t)	10-12	Sheffield Hallam	Educ.(t)	4-20
Huddersfield	Educ.+(t)	4-6	Southampton	Educ.+	22
Hull	Educ.(t)	14-20	Stirling	Educ.+(t)	16-22
Keele	Educ.+(t)	20-24	Strathclyde	Educ.+(t)	10-18
Kingston	Educ.(t)	10-12	Sunderland	Educ.+(t)	8-14
Lancaster	Educ. St.+	18-22	Warwick	Educ.+(t)	18-24
Leeds	Childhood St.	22	Wolverhampton	Educ.+(t)	8-18
Leeds Met	Educ.+(t)	12-18	York	Educ.+	20-26

9
OXBRIDGE

Oxbridge is another world when it comes to university admissions. Although part of the UCAS network, the two universities have different deadlines from the rest of the system, and applications are made direct to colleges. There is little to choose between them in terms of entrance requirements, but a formidable number of successful applicants have the maximum possible A-level score.

However, that does not mean the talented student should be shy about applying: both Oxford and Cambridge have fewer applicants per place than many less prestigious universities, and admission tutors are always looking to extend the range of schools and colleges from which they can recruit. For those with a realistic chance of success, there is little to lose except the possibility of a wasted space on the UCAS form. While a few universities are said to look askance at candidates who consider them second best to any other institution, most are likely to see an Oxbridge application as a welcome sign of ambition and self-confidence.

Overall, there are about three applicants to every place at Oxford and Cambridge, but there are big differences between subjects and colleges. As the tables in this chapter show, competition is particularly fierce in subjects such as medicine and English, but those qualified to read metallurgy or classics have a high chance of success. The pattern is similar to that in other universities, although the high degree of selection (and self-selection) that precedes an Oxbridge application means that even in the less popular subjects the field of candidates is likely to be strong.

These two universities' power to intimidate prospective applicants is based partly on myth. Both have done their best to live down the *Brideshead Revisited* image, but many sixth-formers still fear that they would be out of their depth there, academically and socially. In fact, the state sector produces about half the entrants to Oxford and Cambridge, and the drop-out rate is lower than at many other universities. The 'champagne set' is still present and its activities are well publicised, but most students are hard-working high achievers with the same concerns as their counterparts on other campuses. A joint poll by the two universities' student newspapers showed that undergraduates were spending much of their time in the library or worrying about their employment prospects, and relatively little time on the river or in the college bar.

State school applicants

Student organisations at both universities have put in a great deal of effort trying to encourage applications from state schools, and some colleges have launched their own campaigns. Such has been the determination to convince state school pupils that they will get a fair crack of the whip that a new concern has grown up of possible bias against independent school pupils. In reality, however, the dispersed nature of Oxbridge admissions discounts any conspiracy. Some colleges set relatively low-standard offers to encourage applicants from the state sector, who may reveal their potential at interview. Some admissions tutors may give the edge to candidates from comprehensive schools over those from highly academic independent schools because they consider theirs the greater achievement in the circumstances. Others stick with tried and trusted sources of good students. The independent sector still enjoys a degree of success out of proportion to its share of the school population.

Choosing the right college

Thorough research to find the right college is therefore very important. Even within colleges, different admissions tutors may have different approaches, so personal contact is essential. The college is likely to be the centre of your social life, as well as your home and study centre for at least a year, so you need to be sure not only that you have a chance of a place, but that you want one at that college. Famously sporty colleges, for example, can be trying for those in search of peace and quiet.

The tables in this chapter give an idea of the relative academic strengths of the colleges, as well as the varying levels of competition for a place in different subjects. But only individual research will suggest which is the right place for you. For example, women may favour one of the few remaining single-sex colleges (St Hilda's at Oxford; New Hall, Newnham and Lucy Cavendish at Cambridge). Men have no such option.

Neither the Norrington Table, for Oxford, nor the Tompkins Table, for Cambridge, is published by the university concerned. Indeed, Oxford has tried without success to make compilation impossible. However, both tables give an indication of where the academic power-houses lie – information which can be as useful to those trying to avoid them as those seeking the ultimate challenge. Although there can be a great deal of movement year by year, both tables tend to be dominated by the rich, old foundations.

In both universities, teaching for most students is based in the colleges. In practice, however, this arrangement holds good in the sciences only for the first year. One-to-one tutorials, which are Oxbridge's traditional strength for undergraduates, are by no means universal. However, teaching groups remain much smaller than in most universities, and the tutor remains an inspiration for many students.

Both Oxford and Cambridge give applicants the option of leaving the choice of college to the university. For those with no ready source of advice on the colleges, this would seem an attractive solution to an intractable problem, but it is also a risky one: a lower proportion gets in this way than by applying to a particular college and, inevitably, you may end up somewhere that you hate.

The applications procedure

Both universities have set a deadline of October 15 1999 for entry in 2000. The UCAS form and a Preliminary Application Form (PAF) should be submitted simultaneously to your chosen university and to UCAS. You may apply to only one of Oxford or Cambridge in the same admissions year, unless you are seeking an Organ award at both universities. Interviews take place in September for those who have left school or applied early, but in December for the majority. By the end of October, the first group can expect an offer, a rejection or deferral of a decision until January. That is when the main group of applicants will receive either a conditional offer or a rejection.

There are differences between the two universities, however. Some Cambridge colleges take into account S-levels, as well as A-levels or their equivalent, or ask candidates to sit the university's Sixth Term Examination Papers.

Oxford recently abolished its entrance examination because of claims that it favoured candidates from independent schools. Applicants are now given conditional offers in the normal way, although they may be asked to sit tests when they are called for interview. Oxford is more likely than Cambridge to make an offer as low as two E grades if it is sure that it wants the applicant.

For general information about Oxford and Cambridge universities, including student numbers and main undergraduate subject areas, *see* pages 227 and 156 respectively.

College league tables

OXFORD The Norrington Table 1998

98	97		98	97	
1	4	Jesus	16	10	Oriel
2	1	Merton	17	16	Lincoln
3	5	Wadham	18	15	Exeter
4	2	St John's	19	18	Brasenose
5	19	Balliol	20	29	St Peter'sl
6	3	University	21	23	Pembroke
7	13	Queen's	22	21	St Anne's
8	12	St Edmund Hall	23	17	Hertford
9	6	Keble	24	7	Corpus Christi
10	27	Worcester	25	8	Trinity
11	11	Magdalen	26	24	St Hilda's
12	20	Christ Church	27	22	St Hugh's
13	14	Lady Margaret Hall	28	26	St Catherine's
14	9	New College	29	25	Somerville
15	28	Mansfield	30	30	Harris Manchester

CAMBRIDGE The Tompkins Table 1998

98	97		98	97	
1	1	Trinity	13	15	Churchill
2	3	Queens'	14	9	St Catherine's
3	2	Christs'	15	16	Selwyn
4	8	Gonville and Caius	16	20	Jesus
5	7	Emmanuel	17	4	Sidney Sussex
6	11	Clare	18	23	Corpus Christi
7	6	Trinity Hall	19	21	Robinson
8	10	St John's	20	18	Newnham
9	5	Pembroke	21	22	Girton
10	14	King's	22	17	Magdalene
11	12	Downing	23	19	Peterhouse
12	13	Fitzwilliam	24	24	New Hall

Both tables are compiled from the degree results of final-year undergraduates. A first is worth five points, a 2:1 four, a 2:2 three, a third one point. The total is divided by the number of candidates to produce each college's average.

Applications and acceptances by faculty: Oxford

ARTS	Applications		Acceptances		% places to applications	
	1997	1996	1997	1996	1997	1996
Ancient and Modern History	60	51	25	13	41.7	25.5
Archaeology and Anthropology	56	64	23	24	41.1	37.5
Classics	172	204	130	136	75.6	66.7
Classics and English	26	24	15	9	57.7	37.5
Classics and Modern Languages	17	25	9	10	52.9	40.0
Economics and Management	444	416	80	69	18.0	16.6
English	879	888	262	252	29.8	28.4
English and Modern Languages	131	119	34	22	25.9	18.5
European and Middle Eastern Languages	4	12	2	5	50.0	41.7
Fine Art	126	156	21	20	16.7	12.8
Geography	223	232	102	101	45.7	43.5
Law	838	884	239	241	28.7	29.4
Law with Law Studies in Europe	247	242	24	25	9.7	10.3
Mathematics and Philosophy	46	54	22	24	47.8	50.0
Modern History	695	680	279	289	40.1	42.5
Modern History and Economics	56	45	10	11	17.9	24.4
Modern History and English	68	76	15	15	22.1	19.7
Modern History and Modern Languages	72	99	22	37	30.6	37.4
Modern Languages	381	412	204	198	53.5	481
Music	77	94	52	54	67.4	50.0
Oriental Studies	110	107	37	43	67.5	57.4
Philosophy and Modern Languages	60	46	24	17	40.0	37.0
Philosophy and Theology	56	37	22	12	39.3	32.4
Physics and Philosophy	41	53	15	12	36.6	22.6
PPE	990	986	295	278	29.8	28.2
Theology	70	76	43	56	61.4	73.7
TOTAL ARTS	**5924**	**6085**	**2013**	**1967**	**34.0**	**32.3**
SCIENCES						
Biochemistry	160	180	83	89	51.6	49.4
Biological Sciences	237	237	109	99	46.0	41.8
Chemistry	315	264	183	194	58.1	73.5
Computation	64	95	16	18	25.0	18.9
Earth Sciences (Geology)	56	46	33	30	58.9	65.2
Engineering Science	327	325	135	112	41.3	34.5
Engineering and Computer Science	58	58	19	12	32.8	20.7
Engineering Economics and Management	77	83	22	28	28.6	33.2
Engineering and Materials	9	21	5	9	55.6	42.1
Experimental Psychology	155	162	38	44	24.5	27.2
Human Sciences	91	98	46	44	50.5	44.9
Mathematics	423	446	185	183	43.7	41.0
Mathematics and Computation	77	79	36	41	46.8	51.9
Medicine	654	633	109	102	16.7	16.1
Metallurgy and MEM	38	39	23	23	60.5	59.0
Physics	438	445	184	173	42.0	39.0
Physiological Sciences	44	34	21	12	47.7	35.3
PPP	192	205	48	39	25.0	19.0
TOTAL SCIENCES	**3416**	**3450**	**1295**	**1252**	**37.9**	**36.3**
TOTAL	**9535**	**9548**	**3219**	**3397**	**33.8**	**35.6**

Applications and acceptances by faculty: Cambridge

	Applications		Acceptances		% places to applications	
ARTS	**1997**	**1996**	**1997**	**1996**	**1997**	**1996**
Anglo-Saxon	41	45	17	19	41.5	42.2
Archaeology and Anthropology	172	142	61	56	35.5	39.4
Architecture	227	216	33	33	14.5	15.2
Classics	152	122	79	63	52.0	51.6
English	994	884	212	198	21.3	22.4
Geography	279	275	88	77	31.5	28.0
History	617	573	197	173	31.9	30.2
Modern and Medieval Languages	594	680	201	208	33.8	30.6
Music	188	154	67	54	35.6	35.0
Oriental Studies	76	82	28	23	36.8	28.0
Philosophy	160	140	54	45	33.8	32.1
Theology and Religious Studies	81	81	35	32	43.2	39.5
TOTAL ARTS	**3581**	**3394**	**107**	**981**	**29.9**	**28.9**
SOCIAL SCIENCES						
Economics	745	647	161	161	21.6	24.8
Land Economy	76	79	23	27	30.3	34.2
Law	813	856	198	189	24.4	22.0
Social and Political Sciences	425	371	101	92	23.8	24.8
TOTAL SOCIAL SCIENCES	**2059**	**1953**	**483**	**469**	**23.5**	**24.0**
SCIENCE AND TECHNOLOGY						
Computer Science	295	315	79	78	26.8	24.7
Mathematics	748	785	276	248	36.9	31.6
Natural Sciences	1904	1729	607	551	31.9	31.8
Engineering	1069	1049	306	252	28.6	24.0
Medical Sciences	1273	1113	243	232	19.1	20.8
Veterinary Medicine	508	419	58	57	11.4	13.6
TOTAL SCIENCE AND TECHNOLOGY	**5797**	**5410**	**1569**	**1418**	**27.1**	**26.2**
TOTAL	**11,437**	**10,757**	**3214**	**2868**	**27.3**	**26.6**

Mathematics includes those applying for Mathematics, Mathematics with Computer Science, and Mathematics with Physics.

The tripos courses at Cambridge in Chemical Engineering and Information Sciences, History of Art, Management Studies, and Manufacturing Engineering can only be taken after a part of another tripos. The entries for these courses are recorded under the first-year subjects taken by the students involved.

OXFORD COLLEGE PROFILES

BALLIOL
Balliol College, Oxford OX1 3BJ (tel. 01865-277777)

Students: 380
Male/female ratio: 64/36

Famous as the alma mater of many prominent post-war politicians, including Harold Macmillan, Denis Healey and Roy Jenkins, the university's current Chancellor, Balliol has maintained a strong presence in university life and is usually well represented in the Union. Academic standards are formidably high, as might be expected in the college of Wycliffe and Adam Smith, notably in the classics and social sciences. A dive down the Norrington Table in 1996 was as surprising as it was temporary. PPE in particular is notoriously over-subscribed. Library facilities are good and include a 24-hour law library.

Balliol began admitting overseas students in the 19th century and has cultivated an attractively cosmopolitan atmosphere, of which the lively JCR is a natural focus. Most undergraduates are offered accommodation in college for three years, while the 147 graduate students are usually lodged in the Graduate Centre at Holywell Manor. Centrally located with a JCR pantry that is open all day, Balliol is convenient as well as prestigious.

BRASENOSE
Brasenose College, Oxford OX1 4AJ (tel. 01865-277830)

Students: 347
Male/female ratio: 66/34

Brasenose may not be the most famous Oxford college but it makes up for its discreet image with a consistently healthy academic performance, an advantageous position in the centre of town, and lesser known attractions such as Gertie's Tea Bar. Brasenose was one of the first colleges to become co-educational in the 1970s, although men still take two-thirds of the places. In its defence, the college prospectus points out that the major undergraduate office, President of the JCR, has been filled as often by a woman as a man. But BNC as the college is often known, still has the image of a rugby haven.

Named after the door knocker on the 13th-century Brasenose Hall, the college has a pleasant, intimate ambience which most find conductive to study. Law, PPE and modern history are traditional strengths and competition for places in these subjects is intense. Sporting standards are as high as at many much larger colleges and the college's rowing club is one of the oldest in the university. The college has recently restructured accommodation charges for its students. A new annex, the St Cross Building, means all undergraduates can live in. Most third-years live in the Brasenose annex at Frewin Court, just a few minutes' walk away.

CHRIST CHURCH
Christ Church, Oxford OX1 1DP (tel. 01865-276150)

Students: 420
Male/female ratio: 50/50

The college founded by Cardinal Wolsey in 1525 and affectionately known as The House has come a long way since Evelyn Waugh mythologised its aristocratic excesses in *Brideshead Revisited*. The social mix at Christ Church is much more varied than most applicants suspect and the college has gone out of its way recently to become something of a champion of political correctness. The male/female ratio has been improving steadily and a code of practice on sexual harassment has been implemented.

Academic pressure at Christ Church is reasonably relaxed, although natural high-achievers prosper and the college's history and law teaching is highly regarded. The magnificent 18th-century library, housing 100,000 books, is one of the best in Oxford. It is supplemented by a separate law library. Christ Church has its own art gallery, which holds over 2,000 works of mainly Italian Renaissance art.

Sport, especially rugby, is an important part of college life. The playing fields are a few minutes' walk away through the Meadows. The river is also close at hand for the aspiring oarsman, and the college has good squash courts.

Accommodation is rated by Christ Church students as excellent and includes flats off Iffley Road as well as a number of beautifully panelled shared sets (double rooms) in college. The modern bar adds to the lustre of a college justly famous for its imposing architecture and cathedral, the smallest in England.

CORPUS CHRISTI
Corpus Christi College, Oxford OX1 4JF (tel. 01865-276700)

Students: 225
Male/female ratio: 60/40

Corpus, until recently Oxford's smallest college, is naturally overshadowed by its Goliath-like neighbour, Christ Church, but makes the most of its intimacy, friendly atmosphere and exquisite beauty. Like The House it has an exceptional view across the Meadows.

Although the college has only 310 students including postgraduates (with men and women in equal number), it has an admirable library open 24 hours a day. Academic expectations are high and English, PPE and medicine are especially well established. Despite this, the undergraduate prospectus asserts that it is 'considered much more important to be sociable than to get good results'. The college is beginning to make the most of ties with its namesake at Cambridge, establishing a joint lectureship in history in 1999. Corpus is able to offer accommodation to all its undergraduates, one of its many attractions to those seeking a smaller community in Oxford.

EXETER
Exeter College, Oxford OX1 3DP (tel. 01865-279600)

Students: 307
Male/female ratio: 70/30

Exeter is the fourth oldest college in the university and was founded in 1314 by Walter de Stapeldon, Bishop of Exeter. Nestling halfway between the High Street and Broad Street, site of most of the city's bookshops, it could hardly be more central. The college boasts handsome buildings, the exceptional Fellows' garden and attractive accommodation for most undergraduates for all three years of their university careers.

Exeter's academic record is strong and the college is a consistent high performer in the Norrington Tables. It is, however, often accused of being rather dull. Given its glittering roll-call of alumni, which includes Martin Amis, JRR Tolkien, Alan Bennett, Richard Burton, Imogen Stubbs and Tariq Ali, this seems an accusation that on the face of it at least is hard to sustain.

College food is not rated highly by students although the bar is popular with students from other colleges. The social scene is livelier than the male/female ratio might suggest.

HARRIS-MANCHESTER
Harris-Manchester College, Oxford OX1 3TF (tel. 01865-270999)

Students: 300
Male/female ratio: 45/55

Founded in Manchester in 1786 to provide education for non-Anglican students, Harris-Manchester finally settled in Oxford in 1889 after spells in both York and London. A full University college since 1996, its central location with fine buildings and grounds in Hollywell Street is very convenient for the Bodleian, although the college itself does have an excellent library.

Harris-Manchester admits only mature students of mostly 25 years and above to read for both undergraduate and graduate degrees, predominantly in the arts. There are also groups of visiting students from American Universities and some men and women training for the ministry. Most of its members live in and all meals are provided, indeed the college encourages its members to regularly dine in hall.

The college has few sporting facilities but its students do still manage to represent Harris-Manchester in football, cricket, swimming and chess as well as playing on other college or University teams. Other outlets include the college Drama Society and also the chapel, a focal point to many there.

HERTFORD
Hertford College, Oxford OX1 3BW (tel. 01865-279400)

Students: 360
Male/female ratio: 67/33

Though tracing its roots to the 12th century, Hertford is determinedly modern. It was one of the first colleges to admit women (in 1976) though they still account for only a third of the places. Hertford also helped set the trend towards offers of places conditional on A-levels, which paved the way for the abolition of the entrance examination. It is still popular with state school applicants.

The college lacks the grandeur of Magdalen, of which it was once an annex, but has its own architectural trade-mark in the Bridge of Sighs. It is also close to the History Faculty library (Hertford's neighbour), the Bodleian and the King's Arms, perhaps Oxford's most popular pub.

Academic pressure at Hertford is not high but the quality of teaching, especially in English, is generally thought admirable. Accommodation is improving, thanks in part to the new Abingdon House Complex, and the college can now lodge almost all its undergraduates at any one time. Like most congenial colleges, Hertford is often accused of being claustrophobic and inward-looking – a charge most Hertfordians would ascribe simply to jealousy.

JESUS
Jesus College, Oxford OX1 3DW (tel. 01865-279700)

Students: 305
Male/female ratio: 67/33

Jesus, the only Oxford college to be founded in the reign of Elizabeth I, suffers from something of an unfair reputation for insularity. Its students, whose predecessors include T E Lawrence and Harold Wilson, describe it as 'friendly but gossipy' and shrug off the legend that all its undergraduates are Welsh.

Close to most of Oxford's main facilities, Jesus has three compact quads, the second of which is especially enticing in the summer. Academic standards are high and most subjects are taught in college. Physics, chemistry and engineering are especially strong. Rugby and rowing also tend to be taken seriously.

Accommodation is almost universally regarded as excellent and relatively inexpensive. Self-catering flats in north and east Oxford have enabled every graduate to live in throughout his or her Oxford career. The range of accommodation available to undergraduates is similarly good. The college's Cowley Road development is described by the student union as 'some of the plushest student housing in Oxford'.

KEBLE
Keble College, Oxford OX1 3PG (tel. 01865-272727)

Students: 440
Male/female ratio: 65/35

Keble, named after the leader of the Oxford Movement, was founded in 1870 with the intention of making Oxford education more accessible and the college remains proud of 'the legacy of a social conscience'. That said, little more than a third of undergraduates are women, so the college is still rather male dominated. With 400 undergraduates, Keble is one of the biggest colleges in Oxford, while its uncompromising Victorian Gothic architecture also makes it one of the most distinctive. Once famous for the special privileges it extended to rowers, the college is now academically strong, particularly in the sciences where it benefits from easy access to the Science Area, the Radcliffe Science Library and the Mathematical Institute. At the same time, the college's sporting record remains exemplary, providing a large number of rugby Blues in recent years.

Undergraduates are guaranteed accommodation in their first two years (or two out of three years), although rent increases in recent years have been the cause of some friction between undergraduates and the college authorities. Students who live in must eat in Hall 30 times a year. The Starship Enterprise bar is a particular attraction.

LADY MARGARET HALL
Lady Margaret Hall, Oxford OX2 6QA (tel. 01865-274300)

Students: 407
Male/female ratio: 50/50

Lady Margaret Hall, Oxford's first college for women, has been co-educational since 1978 and is now equally balanced. For many students, LMH's comparative isolation – the college is three-quarters of a mile north of the city centre – is a real advantage, ensuring a clear distinction between college life and university activities, and a refuge from tourists. Although the neo-Georgian architecture is not to everyone's taste, the college's beautiful gardens back onto the river, which allows LMH to have its own punt house. The students union describes academic life at the college as 'fairly lax' while commending its record in English, history and law.

Accommodation should soon be available to all undergraduates. The college's two tower-blocks have the remarkable attraction of private bathrooms in all their rooms. LMH shares most of its sports facilities with Trinity College though has squash and tennis courts on site. Recently, it has become one of Oxford's dramatic centres.

LINCOLN
Lincoln College, Oxford OX1 3DR (tel. 01865-279800)

Students: 270
Male/female ratio: 50/50

Small, central Lincoln cultivates a lower profile than many other colleges with comparable assets. The college's 15th-century buildings and beautiful library – a converted Queen Anne church – combine to produce a delightful environment in which to spend three years. Academic standards are high, particularly in arts subjects, although the college's relaxed atmosphere is justly celebrated. Accommodation, rated 'excellent' by the student union, is provided by the college for all undergraduates throughout their careers and includes rooms above The Mitre Hotel, a medieval inn. Students parade around Oxford in *sub fusc* (formal wear) on Ascencion Day while choristers beat the bounds. Graduate students have their own centre a few minutes' walk away in Bear Lane.

Lincoln's small size and self-sufficiency have led to the college's being accused of insularity. Lincoln's food is outstanding, among the best in the university. Sporting achievement is impressive for a college of this size, in part a reflection of the college's good facilities.

MAGDALEN
Magdalen College, Oxford OX1 4AU (tel. 01865-276000)

Students: 375
Male/female ratio: 50/50

Perhaps the most beautiful college in Oxford or Cambridge, Magdalen is known around the world for its tower, its deer park and its May morning celebrations when students throw themselves off Magdelen Bridge. The college has shaken off its public school image to become a truly cosmopolitan place, with a large intake from overseas and an increasing proportion of state-school pupils. Magdalen's record in English, history and law is second to none, while its new science park at Sandford is bound to bolster its reputation in the sciences. Library facilities are excellent, especially in history and law.

First-year students are accommodated in the Waynflete Building and allocated rooms in subsequent years by ballot. Undergraduates can be housed for all three years, since the opening of the first phase of the Grove Quad in 1996. Sets in cloisters and in the palatial New Buildings are particularly sought after. Magdalen is also conveniently placed for the wealth of rented accommodation in east Oxford.

The college bar is one of the best in Oxford and the college is a pluralistic place, proud of its drama society and choir. Enthusiasm on the river and sports field makes up for a traditional lack of athletic prowess.

MANSFIELD
Mansfield College, Oxford OX1 3TF (tel 01865 27099)

Students: 300
Male/female ratio: 56/44

Mansfield's graduation to full Oxford college status marked the culmination of a long history of development since 1886. Its spacious, attractive site is fairly central, close to the libraries, the shops, the University Parks and the River Cherwell.

With only 195 undergraduates, the community is close-knit, although this can verge on the claustrophobic. The male to female ratio is slightly better than for the University as a whole. Women may prefer the less intimidating atmosphere of Mansfield, perhaps helped by its strong representation of state school students at fifty per cent. First and third-years live in college accommodation. Mansfield students share Merton's excellent sports ground and have numerous college teams although it is in drama that its students truly excel.

Despite its former theological background, students are not admitted on the basis of religion and can read a wide variety of subjects. Mansfield is home to the Oxford Centre for the Environment, Ethics and Society (OCEES) and also the American Studies Institute, evidence of the strong links between Mansfield and the United States which is reflected by some 70 visiting students annually.

MERTON
Merton College, Oxford OX1 4JD (tel. 01865-276310)

Students: 347
Male/female ratio: 66/34

Founded in 1264 by Walter de Merton, Bishop of Rochester and Chancellor of England, Merton is one of Oxford's oldest colleges and one of its most prestigious. Quiet and beautiful, with the oldest quad in the university, Merton has high academic expectations of its undergraduates, often reflected in a position at the top of the Norrington Table. History, law, English, physics and chemistry all enjoy a formidable track record. The medieval library is the envy of many other colleges.

Accommodation is cheap, of a good standard and offered to students for all three years. Merton's food is among the best in the university; formal Hall is served six times a week. No kitchens are provided for students who live in college, however.

Merton's many diversions include the Merton Floats, its dramatic society, an excellent Christmas Ball and the peculiar Time Ceremony, which celebrates the return of GMT. Sports facilities are excellent, although participation tends to be more important than the final score.

NEW COLLEGE
New College, Oxford OX1 3BN (tel. 01865-279555)

Students: 420
Male/female ratio: 60/40

New College is large, old (founded in 1379 by William of Wykeham) and much more relaxed than most expect when first confronting its daunting facade. It is a bustling place, as proud of its excellent music and its bar as of its strength in law, history and PPE. The college has been making particular efforts to increase the proportion of state-education students, inviting applications from schools that have never sent candidates to Oxford. The Target Schools Scheme, designed to increase applications from state schools, is well established.

Accommodation is good and guaranteed for the first two years, after which most live out. The college's library facilities are impressive, especially in law, classics and PPE. The sports ground is nearby and includes good tennis courts. Women's sport is particularly strong. A new sports complex, named after Brian Johnston, opened in 1997, at St Cross Road.

The sheer beauty of New College remains one of its principal assets and the college gardens are a memorable sight in the summer. In spite of these traditional charms, the college has strong claims to be considered admirably innovative. Music is a feature of college life and the Commemoration Ball, held every three years, is a highlight of Oxford's social calendar.

ORIEL
Oriel College, Oxford OX1 4EW (tel. 01865-276555)

Students: 280
Male/female ratio:60/40

In spite of its reputation as a bastion of muscular privilege, Oriel is a friendly college with a strong sense of identity and has adjusted rapidly to co-educational admissions (women were not admitted until 1985). The student union describes the college as having 'a strong crew spirit' reflecting its traditions on the river.

Academic standards are better than legend suggests and the college's well-stocked library is open 24 hours a day. But Oriel's sporting reputation is certainly deserved and its rowing eight is rarely far from the head of the river. Other sports are well catered for, even if their facilities are considerably farther away than the boathouse, which is only a short jog away.

Accommodation is of variable quality but Oriel can usually provide rooms for all three years for those students who require them. Scholars and Exhibitioners chasing firsts in their final year are given priority in the ballot for college rooms. Extensive new accommodation is being rolled out one mile away at Nazareth House and at the Island Site on Oriel Street. Oriel also offers a lively drama society, a Shakespearian production taking place each summer in the front quad.

PEMBROKE
Pembroke College, Oxford OX1 1DW (tel. 01865-276444)

Students: 390
Male/female ratio: 60/40

Although its alumni include such extrovert characters as Dr Johnson and Michael Heseltine, Pembroke is one of Oxford's least dynamic colleges. Academic results are solid, and the college has Fellows and lecturers in almost all the major university subjects. But severe financial problems have led to confrontation with the students over rents.

Pembroke promises accommodation to 'a fair proportion' of undergraduates throughout their courses. The eight-year-old Sir Geoffrey Arthur building on the river, ten minutes' walk from the college, offers excellent facilities. College food is reasonable, though some find formal Hall every evening rather too rich a diet. Rugby and rowing are strong, with Pembroke second only to Oriel on the river, and squash and tennis courts are available at the nearby sports ground.

QUEEN'S
Queen's College, Oxford OX1 4AW (tel. 01865-279120)

Students: 465
Male/female ratio: 50/50

One of the most striking sights of the High Street, Queen's has now shed its exclusive 'northern' image to become one of Oxford's liveliest and most attractive colleges. The college's academic record is good. According to the student union, 'the general attitude to work is fairly relaxed and seems to bring good results'. Modern languages, chemistry and mathematics are reckoned among the strongest subjects. Queen's does not normally admit undergraduates for the honour school of English language and literature or geography. The library, open till 10 pm, is as beautiful as it is well stocked.

All students are offered accommodation, first-years being housed in modernist annexes in east Oxford. The college's beer cellar is one of the most popular in the university and the JCR's facilities are also better than average. An annual dinner commemorates a student who is said to have fended off a bear by thrusting a volume of Aristotle into its mouth.

ST ANNE'S
St Anne's College, Oxford OX2 6HS (tel. 01865-274800)

Students: 465
Male/female ratio: 50/50

Architecturally uninspiring (a row of Victorian houses with concrete 'stack-a-studies' dropped into their back gardens), St Anne's makes up in community spirit what it lacks in awesome grandeur. It has a high proportion of state school students. A women's college until 1979, its academic standing is questionable by Oxford's standards, although it has begun to climb the Norrington Table again since slipping to last place in the middle of the decade. The library is particularly rich in law, Chinese and medieval history texts. Opening hours are long.

Accommodation is guaranteed to all undergraduates but the college is a long way from the city centre. A new accommodation block costing £2.3 million opened in Summertown in 1997. This block provides larger rooms, including two for disabled students.

ST CATHERINE'S
St Catherine's College, Oxford OX1 3UJ (tel. 01865-271700)

Students: 450
Male/female ratio: 67/33

Arne Jacobsen's modernist design for 'Catz', one of Oxford's youngest undergraduate college and second largest, has attracted much attention as the most striking contrast in the university to the lofty spires of Magdalen and New College. Close to the university science area and the pleasantly rural Holywell Great Meadow, St Catherine's is nevertheless only a few minutes' walk from the city centre.

Academic standards are especially high in mathematics and physics though the college's scholarly ambitions are far from having been exhausted. The undergraduate prospectus used to complain that Fellows were 'increasingly eager to apply more academic pressure in college'. The well-liked Wolfson library (famous for its unusual Jacobsen chairs) is open till 1 am on most days.

Accommodation is available for first- and third-years. Rooms are small but tend to be warmer than in other, more venerable colleges. Squash, tennis and netball courts are all on the main college site. There is an excellent theatre, and the college is host to the Cameron Mackintosh Chair of Contemporary Theatre, of which recent incumbents have included Sir Ian McKellen, Alan Ayckbourn and Lord Attenborough. St Catherine's has one of the best JCR facilities in Oxford, including a bar open until 11 pm.

ST EDMUND HALL
St Edmund Hall, Oxford OX1 4AR (tel. 01865-279000)

Students: 400
Male/female ratio: 65/35

St Edmund Hall – 'Teddy Hall' – is one of Oxford's smallest colleges but also one of its most populous with 400 undergraduates swarming through its medieval quads. Some two-thirds of undergraduates are male, but the college is anxious to shed its image as a home for 'hearties', and the authorities have gone out of their way to tone down younger members' rowdier excesses. Nonetheless, the sporting culture at St Edmund Hall is still vigorous and the college usually does well in rugby, football and hockey.

Academically, the college has some impressive names among its fellowship as well as a marvellous library, originally a Norman church. The student union reports that 'a laid-back approach (to work) is the norm'. Accommodation is reasonable and is guaranteed to first- and third-years, though most second-year students live out. The college has two annexes, one near the University Parks, the other in Iffley Road, where many of the rooms have private bathrooms. Hall food is better than average.

ST HILDA'S
St Hilda's College, Oxford OX4 1DY (tel. 01865-276884)

Students: 400
Women only.

With Somerville co-educational, St Hilda's is now the last bastion of all-women education in Oxford. How long the university will allow it to remain that way is open to question. In spite of its variable academic record, the college is a distinctive part of the Oxford landscape and is usually well represented in university life. The 50,000-volume library is growing fast and plans for its extension are being considered. St Hilda's also boasts one of the largest ratios of state-school to independent undergraduates in Oxford. Accommodation is guaranteed to first-years and for one of the remaining two years. The college owns its own punts, which are available free for college members and their guests. Many of the rooms offer some of the best river views in Oxford. Social facilities are limited but the standard of food is high.

ST HUGH'S
St Hugh's College, Oxford OX2 6LE (tel. 01865-274900)

Students: 400
Male/female ratio: 60/40

One of Oxford's lesser-known colleges, St Hugh's was criticised by students in 1987 when it began admitting men. There are now fewer women than men at the college, although the male/female ratio is better balanced than at most Oxford colleges.

Like Lady Margaret Hall, St Hugh's is a bicycle ride from the city centre and has a picturesque setting. It is an ideal college for those seeking a place to live and study away from the madding crowd, and is well liked for its pleasantly bohemian atmosphere. Academic pressure remains comparatively low, although the student union says there are signs that this is changing.

St Hugh's is one of the few colleges which guarantees accommodation to undergraduates for all three years, although the standard of rooms is variable. Sport, particularly football, is taken quite seriously. The extensive grounds include a croquet lawn and tennis courts

---

ST JOHN'S
St John's College, Oxford OX1 3JP (tel. 01865-277300)

Students: 380
Male/female ratio: 60/40

St John's is one of Oxford's powerhouses, excelling in almost every field and boasting arguably the most beautiful gardens in the university. Founded in 1555 by a London merchant, it is richly endowed and makes the most of its resources to provide undergraduates with an agreeable and challenging three years. The work ethic is very much part of the St John's ethos, and academic standards are high, with English, chemistry and history among the traditional strengths, though all students benefit from the impressive library. There are still fewer undergraduates from state schools than public schools (52/48), but the college compensates to some extent by offering generous hardship funds to those in financial difficulty.

As might be expected of a wealthy college, the accommodation is excellent and guaranteed for three or four years. St John's has a strong sporting tradition and offers good facilities, but the social scene is limited.

ST PETER'S
St Peter's College, Oxford OX1 2DL (tel. 01865-278900)

Students: 325
Male/female ratio: 60/40

Opened as St Peter's Hall in 1929, St Peter's has been an Oxford college since 1961. Its medieval, Georgian and 19th-century buildings are close to the city centre and most of Oxford's main facilities. Though still young and comparatively small, St Peter's is well represented in university life and has pockets of academic excellence despite finishing near the bottom of the Norrington Table. History tutoring is particularly good. There are no Fellows in classics at the college.

Accommodation is offered to students for the first year and for one year thereafter and is generally of a high standard. A residential block opened in 1988 and accommodation at St George's Gate opened in 1995, added to the stock of rooms. The college's facilities are impressive, including one of the university's best JCRs. St Peter's is known as one of Oxford's most vibrant colleges socially. It is strong on acting and journalism and has a recently refurbished bar.

SOMERVILLE
Somerville College, Oxford OX2 6HD (tel. 01865-270600)

Students: 330
Male/female ratio: 50/50

The announcement, early in 1992, that Somerville was to go co-educational sparked an unusually acrimonious and persistent dispute within this most tranquil of colleges. Protests were doomed to failure, however: the first male undergraduates arrived in 1994 and now account for half the students. Lady Thatcher was one of those who flocked to their old college's defence, illustrating the fierce loyalty Somerville inspires. The college's atmosphere appears to have survived the momentous change, although the culture of protest reappeared when a number of students refused to pay the Government's tuition fees in 1998.

Accommodation, including 30 small flats for students, is of a reasonable standard, and is guaranteed for first-years and students sitting public examinations. Sport is strong at Somerville and the womens' rowing eight usually finishes near the head of the river. The college's hockey pitches and tennis courts are nearby. The 100,000-volume library is open 24 hours a day and is one of the most beautiful in Oxford.

TRINITY
Trinity College, Oxford OX1 3BH (tel. 01865-279900)

Students: 280
Male/female ratio: 50/50

Architecturally impressive and boasting beautiful lawns, Trinity is one of Oxford's least populous colleges. It is ideally located, beside the Bodleian, Blackwell's book shop and the White Horse pub. Cardinal Newman, an alumnus of Trinity, is said to have regarded Trinity's motto as 'Drink, drink, drink'. Academic pressure varies, as the college darts up and down the unofficial Norrington Table of academic performance. Nonetheless, the college produces its fair share of firsts, especially in arts subjects.

Trinity has shaken off its reputation for apathy, though the early gate-closing times can leave the college isolated late at night. Members are active in all walks of university life and the college has its own debating and drama societies. The proportion of state school entrants has been rising. Accommodation is of a reasonable standard and most undergraduates can live in for three years if they wish.

UNIVERSITY
University College, Oxford OX1 4BH (tel. 01865-276602)

Students: 415
Male/female ratio: 67/33

University is the first Oxford college to be able to boast a former student in the Oval Office. Indeed, the college seems certain to benefit from its unique links with President Clinton, a Rhodes Scholar at University in the late 1960s. The college is probably Oxford's oldest, though highly unlikely to have been founded by King Alfred, as legend claims.

Academic expectations are high and the college prospers in most subjects. Physics, PPE and maths are particularly strong. That said, University has fewer claims to be thought a powerhouse in the manner of St John's, arguably its greatest rival. Accommodation is guaranteed to undergraduates for all three years, with third years lodged in an annexe in north Oxford about a mile and a half from the college site on the High Street. The student union complains that facilities are poor. Sport is strong and University is usually successful on the river, but the college has a reputation for being quiet socially.

WADHAM
Wadham College, Oxford OX1 3PN (tel. 01865-277946)

Students: 440
Male/female ratio: 67/33

Founded by Dorothy Wadham in 1609, Wadham is known in about equal measure for its academic track record – the college generally ranks in the top third in examination performance – and its leftist politics. The JCR is famously dynamic and politically active, although the breadth of political opinion is greater than its left-wing stereotype suggests. And for somewhere supposedly unconcerned with such fripperies, its gardens are surprisingly beautiful. The somewhat rough-hewn chapel is similarly memorable. The college has a good 24-hour library.

Accommodation is guaranteed for at least two years and there are many large, shared rooms on offer. Journalism and drama play an important part in the life of the college, although sport is there for those who want it. Although still predominantly male, Wadham is a popular stop on the weekend social scene.

WORCESTER
Worcester College, Oxford OX1 2HB (tel. 01865-278300)

Students: 360
Male/female ratio: 60/40

Worcester is to the west of Oxford what Magdalen is to the east, an open, rural contrast to the urban rush of the city centre. The college's rather mediocre exterior conceals a delightful environment, including some characteristically muscular Baroque Hawksmoor architecture, a garden and a lake. Though academic pressure has been described as 'tastefully restrained', law, theology and engineering are among the college's strengths. The 24-hour library is strongest in the arts.

Accommodation varies in quality from ordinary to conference standard in the Linbury Building. Shortage of cooking facilities is a common complaint. The ratio of bathrooms to students (one to four) is better than in many colleges. Sport plays an important part in college life, Worcester having engaged more success recently in rowing and rugby.

CAMBRIDGE COLLEGE PROFILES

CHRIST'S
Christ's College, Cambridge CB2 3BU (tel. 01223-334900)

Undergraduates: 384
Male/female ratio: 60/40

Christ's prides itself on its academic strength. It is also one of the few colleges still to offer places on two E grades at A-level, meaning not that entry standards are low but that the college is sufficiently confident of its ability to identify potential high-flyers at interview that it is in effect prepared to circumvent A-levels as the principal criteria for entry. The college has a 50/50 state-to-independent ratio and women make up 40 per cent of the students. Though the college has a reputation for being dominated by hard-working natural scientists and mathematicians, it maintains a broad subject range.

The atmosphere is supposedly so cosy that one student described Christ's as 'a cup of Horlicks', but some complain of short bar opening hours and a poor relationship between undergraduates and fellows.

Accommodation in college is guaranteed to all undergraduates, some of whom will be allocated rooms in the infamous New Court 'Typewriter', probably the least attractive building in the city. The Typewriter houses the excellent New Court theatre, home to Christ's Amateur Dramatics Society and Christ's Films, one of the most adventurous student film societies. College sport has flourished in recent years, with teams competing to a good standard in most sports. The playing fields (shared with Sidney Sussex) are just over a mile away.

CHURCHILL
Churchill College, Cambridge CB3 0DS (tel. 01223-336000)

Undergraduates: 420
Male/female ratio: 67/33

Founded in 1960 to help meet 'the national need for scientists and engineers and to forge links with industry', Churchill consistently finishes high in the academic league tables. Maths, natural sciences, history, engineering and computer science are traditional strengths. The college also has some of the university's best computer facilities. Deferred entry is encouraged in all subjects. Churchill has the joint highest ratio of state to independent pupils (75/25) but one of the lowest proportions of women undergraduates, only one in three.

Some are put off by Churchill's unassuming modern architecture and the college's distance from the city centre; others argue that the distance offers much-needed breathing space. One undeniable advantage is Churchill's ability to provide every undergraduate with a room in college for all three years.

There are extensive on-site playing fields, and the college does well in rugby, hockey and rowing. The university's only student radio station (broadcasting to Churchill and New Hall) is based here.

CLARE
Clare College, Cambridge CB2 1TL (tel. 01223-333246)

Undergraduates: 411
Male/female ratio: 53/47

Though for many Clare's outstanding features are its gardens and harmonious buildings, hard-pressed undergraduates are just as likely to praise the rent and food charges, among the lowest in the university. Accommodation is guaranteed for all three years, either in college or nearby hostels.

As one of the few colleges which openly encourages applications from 'candidates of a good academic standard who have special talents in non-academic fields', Clare still tends to feature near the top of the academic tables. Applicants are encouraged to take a gap year. Languages, natural science and music are especially strong. The ratio of male to female students is largely balanced at 53/47, while that between private and state school pupils is almost exactly 50/50.

Music thrives. The choir records and tours regularly, and Clare Cellars (comprising the bar and JCR) is rapidly becoming the Cambridge jazz venue as well as more contemporary sounds such as drum and bass. Sporting emphasis is as much on enjoyment as competition. The women's teams have had outstanding success in recent years. The playing fields are little more than a mile away.

CORPUS CHRISTI
Corpus Christi College, Cambridge CB2 1RH (tel. 01223-338000)

Undergraduates: 266
Male/female ratio: 60/40

The only college to have been founded by town residents, Corpus's size inevitably makes it one of the more intimate colleges. It prides itself on being a cohesive community, but some find the focus on college rather than university life excessive. No one academic area is particularly favoured.

The kitchen fixed charge is above average but the college is known for a good formal hall. Almost all undergraduates are allocated a room in college or neighbouring hostels. The library is open 24 hours. There is a fairly even sexual and social balance: the independent-to-state school ratio is 42/58. The college bar has an enviable atmosphere.

The sporting facilities, at Leckhampton (just over a mile away), are among the best in the university and include a swimming pool. Corpus's size means that the college's sporting reputation owes more to enthusiasm than success, however. Drama is also well catered for, and the college owns The Playroom, the university's best small theatre.

DOWNING
Downing College, Cambridge CB2 1DQ (tel. 01223-334800)

Undergraduates: 400
Male/female ratio: 60/40

Downing's imposing neo-Classical quadrangle may look more like a military academy than a Cambridge college but the atmosphere here is anything but martial. Founded in 1800 for the study of law, medicine and natural sciences, these are still the college's strong subjects. Indeed Downing is often called 'the law college'.

A reputation for hard-playing, hard-drinking rugby players and oarsmen is proving hard to shake off. The college claims the best boat club in Cambridge. But while sport undoubtedly enjoys a high profile, pressure to conform to the sporty stereotype is never excessive.

Downing currently guarantees a place in college accommodation for two out of three years; the completion of a new accommodation block two years ago allows almost all students to be housed throughout a first degree. The new library, opened by Prince Charles in 1993, has won an award for its architecture.

There is a good balance between male and female students and state and independent school backgrounds. The new student-run bar/party room has improved college social life following three candlelit formal dinners a week.

EMMANUEL
Emmanuel College, Cambridge CB2 3AP (tel. 01223-334200)

Undergraduates: 450
Male/female ratio: 65/35

Thanks in no small part to its huge and stylish, strikingly modern bar, Emmanuel has something of an insular reputation; although the students are active in university clubs and societies. Academically, Emmanuel is a mid-table college, with no subject bias. Deferred entry is greatly encouraged. An almost even state-to-independent ratio contributes to the college's unpretentious atmosphere and one-in-three undergraduates are women. All first- and third-year students are guaranteed accommodation. Second-years are housed in college hostels. With self-catering facilities limited, most students eat in Hall. The college offers ten expedition grants to undergraduates every year, and has a large hardship fund.

In the summer, the college tennis courts and open-air swimming pool offer a welcome haven from exam pressures. The duck pond is one of the most picturesque spots in Cambridge. The sports grounds are excellent, if some distance away.

FITZWILLIAM
Fitzwilliam College, Cambridge CB3 0DG (tel. 01223-332000)

Undergraduates: 415
Male/female ratio: 60/40

Based in the city centre until 1963, the college now occupies a large, modern site on the Huntingdon Road. What it may lack in architectural splendour, Fitzwilliam makes up in friendly informality. More than 70 per cent of its undergraduates come from the state sector, and about 40 per cent are women, though the college hopes 'significantly to raise this proportion in the coming years'.

Approximately 80 per cent of undergraduates are allocated rooms in college (first- and third-years guaranteed) but many second-years are obliged to fend for themselves in the city's relatively expensive private housing market. A new accommodation block is planned.

Fitzwilliam's academic record is improving, with languages and natural sciences the strongest subjects plus economics, geography and medical sciences. Applications are also encouraged in archaeology and anthropology, classics, social and political sciences and music. As at Christs', offers of places are sometimes made on the basis of two Es only at A-level.

On the extra-curricular front, the badminton, hockey and football teams are among the best in the university. The playing fields are a few hundred yards away. The twice termly Ents (college entertainments) are exceptionally popular. Music and drama thrive.

GIRTON
Girton College, Cambridge CB3 0JG (tel. 01223-338999)

Undergraduates: 500
Male/female ratio: 50/50

The joke about needing a passport to travel to Girton refuses to die. In fact, with the city centre a 15-minute cycle-ride away, the college is closer than many hostels at other universities. But if comparative isolation inevitably encourages a strong community spirit, Girtonians still manage to participate in university life at least as much as students at more central colleges and are particularly active in university sports.

Only Trinity and St John's have more undergraduates. On the other hand, since Girton stands on a 50-acre site and the majority of second-year students live in Wolfson Court (near the University Library), there is no question of over-crowding: rooms are available for the entire course. Some find that the long corridors remind them of boarding school.

Since going co-educational in 1979, the college has maintained a balanced admissions policy. Almost 60 per cent of undergraduates are from state schools. Girton also has the highest proportion of women fellows in any mixed college (50 per cent).

The on-site sporting facilities, which include a swimming pool, are excellent. The college is active in most sports and particularly strong in football. The formal hall is excellent and popular, but held only once a week.

GONVILLE AND CAIUS
**Gonville and Caius College, Cambridge CB2 1TA
(tel. 01223-332447)**

Undergraduates: 480
Male/female ratio: 63/37

Gonville and Caius college – to confuse the outsider, the college is usually known as Caius (pronounced 'key's) – is among the most beautiful of Cambridge's colleges, as well as one of the most central. It has an excellent academic reputation, especially in medicine and history, though the humanities, law in particular, are also highly rated. Book grants are available to all undergraduates. The library has been refurbished and computer facilities improved.

Accommodation is split between the central site on Trinity Street and Harvey Court, a five-minute walk away across the river. Rooms are guaranteed for all first- and third-years. The majority of second-years live in college hostels, none of which is more than a mile away. Undergraduates are obliged to eat in Hall at least 45 times a term, a ruling some find restrictive but which at least ensures that students meet regularly.

The college has something of a Home Counties/public school reputation especially for its 'It' girls, society high-fliers. At 58/42 the independent-to-state school ratio is not excessive. However, Caius is 'eager to extend the range of its intake'.Caius tends to do well in rowing and hockey, but most sports are fairly relaxed. A lively social scene is helped by the student-run Late Night Bar.

HOMERTON
Homerton College, Cambridge CB2 2PH (tel. 01223-411141)

Undergraduates: 650
Male/female ratio: 10/90

Designated an Approved Society of the University, Homerton is a teacher-training college offering four-year BEd courses. All first-years have rooms in or around the college, but thereafter may have to take their chance in the open market. There is a 50/50 state-independent split, but with men making up no more than 10 per cent of those on the BEd course it's no surprise that the first-year atmosphere has been likened to that of a girls' boarding school.

Recent speculation over the possible sale of the college's 25-acre site to a supermarket chain has died down. Homerton looks set to stay in its present location about a mile from the city centre.

The college's position and specialised nature mean that the onus is very much on Homerton students to take the initiative if they wish to get involved in university activities. Many do, however.In most respects Homerton is no different from the other undergraduate colleges and students can take advantage of Formal Hall, sport (there are on-site playing fields), music and drama. One disadvantage of Homerton's status is that accommodation costs are higher than at many other colleges.

JESUS
Jesus College, Cambridge CB5 8BL (tel. 01223-357626)

Undergraduates: 460
Male/female ratio: 58/42

For those of a sporting inclination Jesus is perhaps the ideal college. Within its spacious grounds there are football, rugby and cricket pitches as well as three squash courts and no less than ten tennis courts, while the Cam is just a few hundred yards away. With these facilities, it is hardly surprising that sports, in particular rowing, rugby and hockey, rate high on many students' agendas. That said, sporting prowess is far from the whole story.

The music society thrives, and has extensive practice facilities. Although Jesus lacks a theatre of its own, the college is active in university drama. On the academic front, the Fellows-to-undergraduates ratio is generous and, while English and history are among the college's strong suits, the balance between arts and sciences is fairly even. There is an excellent and stylish new library.

Rooms in college are guaranteed for all first- and third-year students. The majority of second-years live in college houses directly opposite the college. Roughly half the undergraduates are state-educated and the college is keen to encourage more applications from the state sector. The college grounds – particularly The Chimney walkway to the porter's lodge – are attractive.

KING'S
King's College, Cambridge CB2 1ST (tel. 01223-331100)

Undergraduates: 380
Male/female ratio: 60/40

The reputation of King's as the most right-on place in the university has become something of an in-joke. It is true that the college has a three-to-one state-to-independent ratio and that it has banned Formal Hall and abandoned May Balls in favour of politically correct June Events. The college is involved in an initiative to increase the number of candidates from socially and educationally disadvantaged backgrounds, and is also keen to encourage applications from ethnic minorities and from women. The students' union is active politically.

The college has fewer undergraduates than the grandeur of its buildings might suggest, one result being that accommodation is guaranteed, either in college or in hostels a few hundred yards away. With the highest ratio of Fellows to undergraduates in Cambridge, it is not surprising that King's is one of the most academically successful colleges. No subjects are especially favoured. Applications are not accepted in veterinary medicine and there are few law students.

Sport at King's is anything but competitive. An extremely large bar/JCR is the social focal point, while the world-famous chapel and choir form the heart of an outstanding music scene.

LUCY CAVENDISH
Lucy Cavendish College, Cambridge CB3 0BU (tel. 01223-332190)

Undergraduates: 85
Women only

Since its creation in 1965, Lucy Cavendish has given hundreds of women over the age of 21 the opportunity to read for Tripos subjects. A number of its students had already started careers and/or families when they decided to enter higher education. The college seeks to offer financial support to those with family responsibilities, though as yet it has no child care facilities.

Accommodation is provided for all who request it, either in the college's three Victorian houses or in its three modern residential blocks. The college's small size enables all students to get to know one another. Plans to increase the intake are unlikely to alter the intimate and informal atmosphere.

Law is still the dominant subject in terms of numbers of students, but veterinary science is also strong and the college welcomes applications in the sciences and other disciplines. All the Fellows are women. For subjects not covered by the Fellowship, there is a well-established network of university teachers.

MAGDALENE
Magdalene College, Cambridge CB3 0AG (tel. 01223-332100)

Undergraduates: 318
Male/female ratio: 65/35

As the last college to admit women (1988), Magdalene has still to throw off a lingering image as home to hordes of public school hearties. In fact, just under half its undergraduates are from the state sector while about a third are women. That said, the sporty emphasis, on rugby and rowing in particular, is undeniable. The nearby playing fields are shared with St John's and the college hs its own Eton fives court.

Despite finishing closer to the foot of the academic league tables than its

Fellows would wish, Magdalene is strong in architecture, law and social and political science .Students are heavily involved in university-wide activities from drama to journalism as well as sport

Accommodation is provided for all undergraduates, either in college or in one of 21 houses and hostels, 'mostly on our doorstep'. Living in is more expensive than in most colleges. Magdalene is proud of its river frontage, the longest in the university, which is especially memorable in the summer.

NEW HALL
New Hall, Huntingdon Road, Cambridge CB3 0DF (tel. 01223-351721)

Undergraduates: 330
Women only

One of three remaining all-women colleges, New Hall enjoys a largely erroneous reputation for feminism and academic underachievement not helped by a much-publicised whitewash on University Challenge. Founded in 1954 to increase the number of women in the university, it occupies a modern grey-brick site next door to Fitzwilliam. Students are split 50/50 between state and independent schools. The college lays claim to certain paradoxes. While a rent strike early in the decade attested to a degree of political activism, tradition is far from rejected. The following year saw New Hall's first-ever May Ball, an event hosted jointly with Sidney Sussex.

Its results regularly place the college at the bottom of the academic league, but it must be remembered that women's results lag behind men's throughout the university. Natural sciences, medicine, economics, English and history are New Hall's strongest areas.

The college is known for its unusual split-level bar, but many students choose to socialise elsewhere. Sport is a good mixture of high-fliers and enthusiasts, with grounds, shared with Fitzwilliam, half a mile away. The college is particularly proud of its collection of contemporary womens' art.

NEWNHAM
Newnham College, Cambridge CB3 9DF (tel. 01223-335700)

Undergraduates: 420
All women

Newnham has long had to battle with a blue-stocking image. Its entry in the university prospectus insists that it 'is not a nunnery' and that the atmosphere in this all-women college is no stricter than elsewhere. It even has a 'Newnham Nuns' drinking club to make the point. With an even state-independent ratio, the college has also successfully cast off a reputation for public-school dominance.

Newnham is in the perfect location for humanities students, with the lecture halls and libraries of the Sidgwick Site just across the road. The college is, however, keen to encourage applications in engineering, maths and the sciences. All of the Fellows are women.

Around 95 per cent of students live in for all three years. This is not to say that ventures into the social, sporting and artistic life of the university are the exception rather than the rule. Newnham students are anything but insular.

As well as being blessed with the largest and most beautiful lawns in Cambridge, Newnham has its playing fields on site. The boat club has been notably successful, while college teams compete to a high standard in tennis, cricket and a number of minority sports.

PEMBROKE
Pembroke College, Cambridge CB2 1RF (tel. 01223-338100)

Undergraduates: 385
Male/female ratio: 60/40

Another college with a reputation for public-school dominance (the current state-to-independent ratio is around 40/60), Pembroke's image is changing. Rowing and rugby still feature prominently, but with a female population of about 40 per cent the heartiness is giving way to a more relaxed if still somewhat insular atmosphere. Around two thirds of all undergraduates live in college, including all first-years. The rest are housed in fairly central college hostels, though the standards of these are variable. A new college building will improve the situation. Academically, Pembroke is considered solid rather than spectacular. Engineering and natural sciences have the largest number of undergraduates, but the subject range is wide with geography a recent strength.

The bar is inevitably the social focal point, but a restriction on advertising means that Pembroke bops attract few students from other colleges. The Pembroke Players generally stage one play a term in the Old Reader, which also doubles as the college cinema, and many Pembroke students are involved in university dramatics. The Old Library is a popular venue for classical concerts. Indeed music is a Pembroke strength. In a city of memorable college gardens, Pembroke's are among the best.

PETERHOUSE
Peterhouse College, Cambridge CB2 1RD (tel. 01223-338200)

Undergraduates: 256
Male/female ratio: 75/25

The oldest and smallest of the colleges, Peterhouse is another that has had to contend with an image problem. But while by no means as reactionary as its critics would have it, Peterhouse is certainly not overly progressive. There is a three-to-one male-to-female split, while the state school-independent ratio is the university average at 50/50. The college's diminutive size – its entire student population is the same as one year's intake at Trinity – inevitably makes for an intimate atmosphere. But this does not mean that its undergraduates never venture beyond the college bar.

Peterhouse is known above all as 'the history college'. But while history is indeed a traditional strength, there are in fact no more history students than there are taking natural science or engineering. Academically, the college is a consistent mid-table performer.

The 13th-century candle-lit dining hall provides a fitting setting for what by common consent is the best food in the university. Rents are below average, and undergraduates live in for at least two years, the remainder choosing rooms in college hostels, most within one or two minutes' walk. The sports grounds are shared with Clare and are about a mile away. The college teams have a less than glittering reputation, not surprisingly, given its size.

QUEENS'
Queens' College, Cambridge CB3 9ET (tel. 01223-335511)

Undergraduates: 472
Male/female ratio: 63/37

There is a strong case for claiming that Queens' is the most tightly knit college in the university. With all undergraduates housed in college for the full three years, a large and popular bar (open all day) and outstanding facilities, including Cambridge's first college nursery, it is easy to see why. Queens' also has the distinction of attracting an above-average number of applicants. The state-to-independent ratio (60/40) is good, but barely more than a third of students are female.

Though not to all tastes, the mix of architectural styles, ranging from the medieval Old Court to the 1980s Cripps Complex, is as great as any in the university. In addition to three excellent squash courts, the Cripps Complex is also home to Fitzpatrick Hall, a multi-purpose venue containing Cambridge's best-equipped college theatre and the hub of Queens' renowned social scene. Friday and Saturday night bops are extremely popular. Queens' has perhaps the foremost college drama society and thriving cinema.

Law, maths, engineering and natural sciences are the leading subjects in a college with an enviable academic record. Apart from Squash, Queens' is not especially sporty. The playing fields (one mile away) are shared with Robinson.

ROBINSON
Robinson College, Cambridge CB3 9AN (tel. 01223-339100)

Undergraduates: 385
Male/female ratio: 62/38

Robinson is the youngest college in Cambridge and admitted its first students in 1979. Its unspectacular architecture has earned it the nickname 'the car park'. On the other hand, having been built with one eye on the conference trade, rooms are more comfortable than most and many have their own bathrooms. Almost all students, including all first- and third-years, live in college or in houses in the attractive gardens.

Robinson has been close to the bottom of the academic tables recently. There is no particular subject bias and one in four Fellows are women, the second highest proportion in any mixed college.

Its youth and balanced admissions policy (38 per cent are from independent schools, and there is a 38 per cent female intake) ensure that Robinson has one of the more unpretentious atmospheres. The auditorium is the largest of any college and is a popular venue for films, plays and concerts. The college fields (shared with Queens') are home to excellent rugby and hockey sides, and the boat club is also successful.

ST CATHARINE'S
St Catharine's College, Cambridge CB2 1RL (tel. 01223-338300)

Undergraduates: 420
Male/female ratio: 65/35

Known to everyone as Catz, this is a medium-sized, 17th-century college standing opposite Corpus Christi on King's Parade. The principal college site, with its distinctive three-sided main court, though small, provides accommodation for all its first year students. The majority of second-years live in flats at St Chad's Court, a ten-minute walk away.

Catz is not one of the leading colleges academically but it has a reputation as a friendly place. Geography and law are usually the strongest subjects. More than a third of the students are women, and the split between independent and state school pupils is about even. A new library and JCR have improved the facilities considerably.

College social life centres on the large bar, which has been likened, among other things, to a ski chalet or sauna. With a reputation for being sporting rather than sporty, Catz is one of the few colleges that regularly puts out three rugby XVs, and also has a good record in football and hockey. The playing fields are about a ten-minute walk away.

ST JOHN'S
St John's College, Cambridge CB2 1TP (tel. 01223-338600)

Undergraduates: 540
Male/female ratio: 65/35

Second only to Trinity in size and wealth, St John's has an enviable reputation in most fields and is resented for it. The wealth translates into excellent accommodation in college for almost all undergraduates throughout their three years as well as book grants and a new 24-hour library. First-years are housed together, which can hinder integration.

There is no particular subject bias and John's has a formidable academic record. A reputation for heartiness persists and the female intake is 35 per cent, slightly below average. The state school-independent split is about 50/50.

The boat club has a powerful reputation, but rugby, hockey and cricket are all traditionally strong. In such a large community, however, all should be able to find their own level. Extensive playing fields shared with Magdalene are a few hundred yards away and the boathouse is extremely good.

The college film society organises popular screenings in the Fisher Building, which also contains an art studio and drawing office for architecture and engineering students. Music is dominated by the world-famous choir. Excellent as the facilities are, some students find that the sheer size of St John's can be daunting and this makes it hard to settle into.

SELWYN
Selwyn College, Cambridge CB3 9DQ (tel. 01223-335846)

Undergraduates: 350
Male/female ratio: 55/45

Described by one undergraduate as 'the least overtly intellectual college', Selwyn has a down-to-earth and relatively unpressured atmosphere. Located behind the Sidgwick Site, it is in an ideal position for humanities students, and its academic prowess has traditionally been on the arts side although engineering is an merging strength. One of the first colleges to go mixed (1976),now almost half of Selwyn's undergraduates are female. The state-to-independent ratio is 54/46. Accommodation is provided for all students, either in the college itself or in hostels, all of which are close by.

As well as the usual college groups, the Music Society is especially well supported. The bar is popular if a little 'hotel-like'. In sport, the novice boat crews have done well in recent years, as have the hockey and badminton sides, but the emphasis is as much on enjoyment as achievement. The grounds are shared with King's and are three-quarters of a mile away.

SIDNEY SUSSEX
Sidney Sussex College, Cambridge CB2 3HU (tel. 01223-338800)

Undergraduates: 311
Male/female ratio: 58/42

Students at this small, central college are forever the butt of jokes about Sidney being mistaken for the branch of Sainsbury's over the road. Two other, more serious aspects of life at Sidney stand out: almost every year its undergraduates raise more for the Rag Appeal than any others; while rents are comfortably the lowest in the university (all students are housed either in college or one of 11 nearby hostels).

Exam results generally place the college in the middle of the academic leagues. It reached the upper echelons in 1997 but dived to 17th in 1998. Engineering, geography and Medieval and law are the strongest subjects.

Sidney has a good social balance, with a nearly even state-to-independent ratio, while more than 40 per cent of the undergraduates are women. There is a large student-run bar which is the venue for fortnightly bops, an active drama society (SADCO) and plenty of involvement in university activities. The sports grounds are shared with Christ's and are a 10-minute cycle ride away. Sidneyites are enthusiastic competitors, but the college does not have a reputation for excellence in any individual sports. Sidney's size means that the college is a tight-knit community. Some students find such insularity suffocating rather than supportive.

TRINITY
Trinity College, Cambridge CB2 1TQ (tel. 01223-338400)

Undergraduates: 660
Male/female ratio: 65/35

The legend that you can walk from Oxford to Cambridge without ever leaving Trinity land typifies Cambridge undergraduates' views about the college, even if its is not true. Indeed, the college is almost synonymous with size and wealth. Founded by Henry VIII, its endowment is almost as big as the other colleges' put together. However, the view that every Trinity student is an arrogant public schoolboy is less easily sustained. That said, it is true that only about a third of Trinity undergraduates are women, the lowest proportion in any of the mixed colleges. On the other hand, there is little obvious bias towards independent schools in the admissions policy.

Being rich, Trinity offers book grants to every student as well as generous travel grants and spacious, reasonably priced rooms in college for all first- and third-year students as well as many second-years. The college generally features in the top ten academically and has topped the Tompkins Table for the last two years.The strongest subjects are English, maths and natural sciences.

Trinity rarely fails to do well in most sports, with cricket in the forefront. The playing fields are half a mile away. A new and larger bar should improve the social scene. The Trinity Sweatys attract students from all over the university.

TRINITY HALL
Trinity Hall, Cambridge CB2 1TJ (tel. 01223-332500)

Undergraduates: 345
Male/female ratio: 55/45

The outstanding performance of its oarsmen has ensured the prevailing view of Trinity Hall as a 'boaty' college, but it is also known for its drama, music and bar. The Preston Society is one of the better college drama groups and stages regular productions both in the college theatre and at other venues. Weekly recitals keep the Music Society busy. The small bar is invariably packed. Not surprisingly, many undergraduates rarely feel the need to go elsewhere for their entertainment.

The college is strong academically. Law is a traditional speciality, though the natural sciences are also well represented. Approaching half of the undergraduates are women and around half are from state schools.

All first-years and approximately half the third year live in the college, which is situated on the Backs behind Caius. The remainder take rooms either in two large hostels close to the sports ground (a mile from college), or in college accommodation about five minutes' walk away.

Part 2

UNIVERSITY LISTINGS

9
UNIVERSITY PROFILES

Some famous names are missing from our university listings: the Open University, the separate business and medical schools, Birkbeck College and Cranfield University among them. Their omission is no reflection on their quality, simply a function of their particular roles. The guide is based on provision for full-time undergraduates and the factors judged to influence this.

The Open University, though Britain's biggest university, with 75,000 students, could not be included because most of the measures used in our listings do not apply to it. As a non-residential, largely part-time institution, Birkbeck College, London, could also not be compared in many key areas.

Several universities have been omitted because they are mostly postgraduate institutions. Although Cranfield, for example, offers undergraduate degrees in two of its campuses, the institute is primarily for graduate students. Manchester and London business schools were excluded for the same reason.

Similarly, specialist institutions such as the Royal College of Art and the medical schools could not fairly be compared with generalist universities. A number of colleges with degree-awarding powers also do not appear because they have yet to be granted university status. The profiles include teaching quality ratings published by the Higher Education Funding Councils. Assessments are carried out by teams of subject specialists, and departments graded differently in England, Scotland and Wales. Since April 1995, in England and Northern Ireland, subjects have been rated on six criteria, each attracting a maximum score of four points. Scotland also went over to this system in 1998. The listings in this chapter give the aggregate scores. Before this system was introduced, subjects were rated as 'excellent', 'satisfactory' or 'unsatisfactory'. Ratings published since October 1998, when the latest round of reports was completed in England, have not been included.

Student numbers are expressed as full-time equivalents, using the Funding Councils' conversion formula for part-time places. Full-time student equivalent numbers exclude those on franchised courses, those studying at further education level and overseas distance-learning students. They are for 1996-97, as are the percentages for mature and overseas students and the male/female ratios. Overseas students are those from outside the European Union.

Comments on campus facilities apply to the universities' own sites only. New universities, in particular, operate 'franchised' courses at further education colleges, which are likely to have lower levels of provision. Prospective applicants should check out the library and social facilities before accepting a place away from the parent institution.

UNIVERSITY OF ABERDEEN
Regent Walk, Aberdeen AB9 1FX (tel. 01224-272090)

Founded 1495
Times ranking: 35 *(1998 ranking: 33)*

Enquiries: Schools liaison office
Total students: 9,500
Male/female ratio: 49/51
Mature students: 21%
Overseas students: 12%

Main subject areas: arts and social sciences; divinity; engineering; law; medicine; science.

Teaching quality ratings 1993-98
Rated excellent: cellular biology; economics; French; geography; medicine; organismal biology; sociology.
Rated highly satisfactory: accounting; chemistry, civil engineering; English; geology; history of art; law; mathematics; mechanical engineering; philosophy; politics; psychology, theology.
From 1998: European languages 22; planning and landscape 19.

Aberdeen styles itself the "balanced university" because half of its students are men and half women, half study medicine, science or engineering, half the arts or social sciences. The proportions are valued both socially and academically in an institution which strives to be the classic Scottish university, offering its students the broadest possible choice of subjects. The modern university has overcome its funding difficulties of the 1980s and strengthened its senior academic staff. A complete reorganisation of the medical departments, which are among the university's main strengths, has taken place. The new Institute of Medical Sciences, which brings together all Aberdeen's work in this area, is mainly a research initiative. But the concentration of medical departments on the Foresterhill site and the appointment of a dozen professors, with supporting lectureships, is bringing benefits for undergraduates. New chairs have also been established in subjects as diverse as Celtic and Spanish, international relations and environmental and occupational medicine.

Recent teaching assessments have been very complimentary. All but one of the five subjects assessed in 1996-97 were rated excellent and only three – business and management, computer studies and electrical and electronic engineering – have ever been considered less than highly satisfactory. Research assessments were less impressive, with only law in the top two categories.

The university's modular courses are so flexible that the majority of students change their intended degree before graduation. The compact prospectus includes current entry requirements as well as an unusually detailed description of courses. Biblical studies, medicine and law are among the university's traditional strengths. Biological sciences are second only to social sciences in size. Plant and soil science and zoology are also well-regarded, as are geology and land economy.

The original King's College buildings are the focal point of an appealing and quiet campus, complete with cobbled main street and some sturdily handsome Georgian buildings, about a mile from the city centre. A bus service links the two main sites with the Hillhead residential complex. The students' union runs free late-night buses.

The university finds accommodation for about half its students and guarantees a hall place for all first-years from outside the Aberdeen area. More than a quarter of the students come from Northern Scotland. The oil industry created accommodation problems for students and, as a result, the university is committed to adding 500 residential places every year. Three of the halls are linked into the university's computer network. Other students have 24-hour access to classroom-based machines. There are 1,000 computers available for student use.

Today's university is a fusion of two ancient institutions which came together in 1860. Indeed Aberdeen likes to boast that for 250 years it had as many universities as the whole of England.

The students' union has good facilities and is also one of the cheapest places in the city to eat and drink. A separate students' representative council carries out the political functions. Students seem to like Aberdeen on the whole, despite its remoteness (to the sizeable English contingent at least) and the long and often bitter winters.

Thirty bursaries of £1,000 a year are available to counter the impact of tuition fees. There are also specialist bursaries, including a few for golfers.

UNIVERSITY OF ABERTAY DUNDEE
Bell Street, Dundee DD1 1HG (tel. 01382-308080)

Royal charter 1994, formerly Dundee Institute of Technology
Times ranking: 82 *(1998 ranking: 79)*

Enquiries: Information and recruitment office
Total students: 4,300
Male/female ratio: 50/50
Mature students: 30%
Overseas students: 7%

Main subject areas: accountancy; construction and environment; engineering; informatics; life sciences; health and nursing and social sciences; management and law. Most subjects available at diploma level as well as at degree level.

Teaching quality ratings
Rated excellent: economics.
Rated highly satisfactory: cellular and molecular biology; chemistry;

civil engineering; mechanical engineering; mathematics and statistics; psychology.

Britain's newest university was made to wait for its upgrading from a central institution, but was already well established in the higher education system. Even as Dundee Institute of Technology, teaching in economics was rated more highly than in some of Scotland's elite universities. Subsequent assessments have been solid, without quite living up to that early promise. More than half of the subjects have been graded better than satisfactory.

Based mainly in the centre of Dundee, Abertay plays to its strengths with a limited range of courses. Even the business school, in the imposing Dudhope Castle, is only a 15-minute walk from the three main sites. Entrance requirements are modest in most subjects, with one student in six entering through clearing last year.

Courses are predominantly vocational, the modular scheme introduced in September 1994 allowing students to move on to a degree in most subjects on successful completion of a diploma. The majority of courses are now divided into modules for extra flexibility, most students taking five modules per semester. Many degrees have a sandwich structure, students either spending a year or two six-month periods at work. Several courses also include a language, and involve a period of study abroad, and about 300 students a year take part in European exchanges of at least a month's duration. The benefit are seen in Abertay's employment rate, with two-thirds of graduates at work six months after leaving.

With barely 4,000 full-time students, including a growing number of postgraduates, Abertay is among the smaller universities. But more programmes are being added every year. European business law and forest products technology are among recent examples. The library has been replaced by a purpose-built learning resources centre with 400 study places opened by the Queen in 1998, which is among the most advanced in Britain. A powerful computer network links all departments, and students have access to the media centre for project work.

First-years take priority in the allocation of more than 800 residential places, enough to house 80 per cent of new students requiring accommodation. Most university places are self-catering, and Dundee is one of the less expensive student centres for those who find themselves in the private market. More than half of Abertay's students are local, so many live at home.

The university has few sports facilities of its own, but Abertay students have access to a nearby college complex, as well as three sports centres in the city. An annual fee of £12.50 buys access to six sports centres, a golf course and water sports facilities. The students' association is not large, but its premises have been refurbished recently.

ANGLIA POLYTECHNIC UNIVERSITY
Victoria Road South, Chelmsford, Essex CM1 1LL (tel. 01245-493131)

University status 1992, formerly Anglia Polytechnic
Times Ranking: 67 *(1998 ranking: 66)*

Enquiries: Senior admissions officer (tel. 01223-63271)
Total students: 11,400
Male/female ratio: 41/59
Mature students: 37%
Overseas student: 14%

Main subject areas: advanced nursing, midwifery and health studies; applied science, business, design and communication systems; arts, languages and social studies; education; humanities; law. Also a range of diploma courses.

Teaching quality ratings
Rated excellent 1993-95: English; music; social work.
April 1995-97: modern languages 21; building and civil engineering 20; sociology 20; land management 19; town planning 19; history of art 18; media studies 18.

It's all change at the last university to retain the polytechnic title. The name will change as soon as the Privy Council permits, one of the three campuses closes in 1999 and a state of the art replacement has already opened. Anglia hopes to be come the University of Eastern England although objections are likely to delay a decision long enough to ensure that entrants in 1999 will still be using the old name. Potential applicants and employers were confused by the mixture of titles, and the university feels that the change will increase the flow of applications after recent problems in some areas.

Two well-established colleges, the Essex Institute of Higher Education and Cambridgeshire College of Arts and Technology, came together in 1989 to form the first regional polytechnic. Even as one of the centres of population growth over the last 20 years, East Anglia always lagged behind other parts of England for the number of students going on to higher education. The university boasts of teaching across four counties through a network of 20 partner colleges in Suffolk, Norfolk, Essex and Cambridgeshire. The two main centres are at Chelmsford and Cambridge. A former teacher training college at Brentwood is closing as part of the reorganisation but a country house management centre near Chelmsford will remain. Teacher training is moving to a new riverside campus in Chelmsford, which already houses a range of student facilities, a high-tech learning resource centre and more than 500 residential places. The development has eased previously cramped conditions at the town centre campus where most of the Chelmsford-based courses are taught.

The university has a strongly European outlook, encouraging students to take a language option and providing opportunities to take a part of many courses abroad. There are partner institutions in Malaysia and China, as well as several in the United States and 30 in Europe. The four-year European business degree is a prime example, giving students two years studying in Germany and a placement with a German company.

Employers play a part in course planning, contributing to Anglia graduates' good record in the jobs market. Criminology and forensic science were among the subjects added in 1998, with degrees in internet technology and artificial intelligence following in 1999. Law and computing are popular, as is European social policy, which gives students six months in the Netherlands. Teaching quality ratings have been respectable, but the university's foray into research assessment has been rather less so. Fewer than a quarter of the academics were entered, but still no subject featured in the top four of the seven categories. A notable exception is Anglia's ULTRALAB learning technology research centre. As well as producing educational material for CD-ROM and internet use, the staff have advised ministers on future policy.

Increasing numbers placed a strain on facilities at both main centres. A £1 million library extension has opened in Cambridge and 250 residential places will be added in 1999. But, even with 1,800 rooms in university-managed property, only about a third of first-year students can be housed by Anglia itself. Priority goes to students with special needs and those who live more than 80 miles from their place of study. Social life and recreational facilities vary according to location. Students say that, although there are shared services and a common students' union, for most purposes Anglia is a single institution in name only.

ASTON UNIVERSITY
Aston Triangle, Birmingham B4 7ET (tel. 0121-359 6313)

Founded 1895, royal charter 1966
Times ranking: 49 *(1998 ranking: 47)*

Total students: 4,600
Male/female ratio: 52/48
Mature students: 9%
Overseas students: 3%

Main subject areas: engineering and applied science; life and health sciences; languages and European studies; management.

Teaching quality ratings
Rated excellent 1993-95: none.
April 1995-97: French 22; German 22; electrical and electronic engineering 21; civil engineering 20; chemical engineering 19.

As befits a one-time college of advanced technology, Aston's strength is on the science side although peer assessments of engineering have been solid rather than spectacular. However, business, arts and social science students are now in a majority, and recent modernisation and landscaping has left the university unrecognisable from its parent institution. All departments have purpose-built accommodation, and there are modern and extensive computing facilities, especially in the library.

Aston has faced financial difficulties for most of the decade, partly because it refused to follow the trend for wholesale expansion. The funding council has had to provide special help several times to avoid damaging budget cuts. The university's financial position has now improved sufficiently, with the help of improved research ratings and big grants from industry, to allow for a staffing boost. Six new professors were among 25 senior appointments in 1997, mainly in business, engineering and languages, with more following in 1998. The strategy is something of a gamble designed to secure still better research ratings in 2000, with the financial rewards that would bring. The new posts are also expected to help generate more income from research contracts, overseas student recruitment and short courses.

The academic structure has also changed, reducing the number of schools of studies to four to break down barriers between departments. Seven out of ten undergraduates take sandwich courses, with beneficial effects on graduate employment prospects. Even in the difficult jobs market of recent years, at least three-quarters of those leaving Aston have been in work six months after graduation. There is a wide range of combined honours programmes for those who want to avoid excessive specialisation.

Teaching ratings have also picked up. None of the first six subjects to be assessed was rated excellent, but language departments inspected in the last two years have come out well. Pharmacy and optometry are among the top-rated degrees. Engineering with European studies, with one of five years abroad for an MEng, is particularly popular, and management courses have fared well in *The Times* rankings. Aston is flexible about the entry requirements for mature students, but those with A levels are generally asked for at least 20 points (the equivalent of a B and two Cs). The university prides itself on its information technology facilities. There are 12 computer suites, most of which are available 24 hours a day, and a £4-million local area network links the entire campus with data and video channels.

The 40-acre campus is a ten-minute walk from the centre of Birmingham. A £16-million building plan will concentrate all Aston's residences on campus by early in the next decade. The first students are expected to move into the new accommodation in autumn 1999. Already, two-thirds of the full-time students are in university accommodation and all first-years from outside the West Midlands are offered a place.

Students are issued with 'smart cards' giving them access to university facilities and enabling them to make purchases on campus, once they have money in their accounts. Most describe the university as lively and welcome its proximity to the city centre. The campus boasts two sports centres, but the playing fields are seven miles away in Walsall.

UNIVERSITY OF BATH
Claverton Down, Bath BA2 7AY (tel. 01225-826826)

Founded 1894 (in Bristol), royal charter 1966
Times ranking: 15 *(1998 ranking: 15)*

Enquiries: Registrar
Total students: 6,100
Male/female ratio: 57/43
Mature students: 12%
Overseas students: 6%

Main subject areas: architecture and civil engineering; biological sciences; chemical and mechanical engineering; chemistry; education; electronic and electrical engineering; management; mathematical sciences; materials science; modern languages; pharmacy; physics; social sciences.

Teaching quality ratings
Rated excellent 1993-95: architecture; business and management; mechanical engineering; social policy.
April 1995-97: civil engineering 22; chemical engineering 20; modern languages 19; sociology 19

Still a small technological university, Bath's high placing in *The Times* table reflects all-round strength in its field. The university passed up the opportunity to grow substantially and change character by merging with the city's college of higher education. But students still have the advantage of being part of a higher education community of more than 30,000 in Bath and Bristol.

Although expansion is under way, the accent is still on quality. The universities' Academic Audit Unit gave Bath a good report, complimenting the university particularly on its sandwich programmes. The majority of undergraduates choose this route to a degree, helping to produce the best graduate employment record among the traditional universities.

Research is Bath's greatest strength, with mathematics and computer science, chemical engineering and materials science all highly rated. The schools of architecture, mechanical engineering, social policy and business administration were top-rated in the first rounds of the funding council's teaching quality assessment. Civil engineering achieved the best score in recent teaching assessments. The American vice-chancellor, David VandeLinde, is making only gradual changes. His priorities are to raise Bath's international profile and to make its courses more flexible, but some restructuring is taking place, including the establishment of a new department of continuing and distance education.

All first-years can expect one of almost 2,000 residential places on campus, some of which are reserved for disabled students. The university occupies modern buildings overlooking one of Britain's prime tourist cities. A £5-million expansion of teaching accommodation has made room for increases in student numbers over three years. More than 20 new professorships have been established in the 1990s, and the university is helping to develop a new institution in Swindon.

Students find the campus quiet at weekends and struggle to afford some of Bath's attractions, but most value its location. There is a strong tradition in competitive sports, encouraged by the university in the form of sports scholarships - something which Bath introduced to Britain 20 years ago. intended for performers of international calibre, they are worth up to £12,000 a year and involve an extra year's study taken at the student's convenience. An international-standard swimming pool and running track have been added recently and with two artificial pitches, 38 acres of conventional playing fields and a well-equipped sports hall, the university is among the best provided in Britain.

UNIVERSITY OF BIRMINGHAM
Edgbaston, Birmingham B15 2TT (0121-414 3374)

Founded 1828, royal charter 1900
Times ranking: 16 *(1998 ranking: 14)*

Enquiries: Director of admissions
Total students: 17,500
Male/female ratio: 52/48
Mature students: 9%
Overseas students: 8%

Main subject areas: Full range of subjects in seven faculties: arts; commerce and social science; education; engineering; law; medicine and dentistry; science.

Teaching quality ratings
Rated excellent 1993-95: English; geography; geology; history; music.
April 1995-97: electrical and electronic engineering 24; sociology 24; Middle Eastern and African studies 23; Russian and East European studies 23; American studies 22; Iberian languages 22; Italian 22; chemical engineering 21; civil engineering 21; drama, dance and cinematics 21; materials science 20; German 19; French 18.

Firmly re-established among the leading group of universities, Birmingham offers an unusually wide range of degrees. Funding council ratings for teaching and research are confirming a growing reputation for quality across the board. Birmingham draws students from 100 countries, but enjoys particularly high prestige in its own region. A MORI poll showed that teachers, parents and university applicants from the West Midlands all regarded the university as the next best thing to Oxbridge.

More than a third of departments reached the top two categories for the last assessments, with anatomy, materials science, Middle Eastern and African studies and European studies rated internationally outstanding.

Sociology and electrical and electronic engineering have both managed maximum points for teaching quality. An independent audit of academic procedures commended the university for its monitoring of teaching standards and for its student counselling service.

The 230-acre campus in leafy Edgbaston includes one of the top university libraries in Britain and extensive facilities run by the guild of students. An intricate model of the campus with a sound commentary enables blind or partially sighted students to find their way around. Only the dentists are located elsewhere. Most of the halls of residence and university flats are conveniently placed in an attractive parkland setting near the main campus. The remainder are about ten minutes away by bus, or train to the campus station. The 5,300 places include family units. First-years are guaranteed accommodation, although they may have to share rooms. Home students are either interviewed or invited to one of the open days the university holds each spring, the largest of their kind in Britain. There is also an admissions forum in September.

Sports facilities have improved considerably in recent years, and include the Raymond Priestley Centre 170 miles away in the Lake District for water sports and other outdoor pursuits. The main playing fields are five miles from the university, served by coaches and minibuses. The unique Active Lifestyles Programme offers about 150 courses a term, mainly at beginner or improver level. Birmingham students have never gone in for the political extremism seen on other campuses. They tend to identify with the city, and speak highly of the quality and cost of university accommodation.

UNIVERSITY OF BOURNEMOUTH
Talbot Campus, Fern Barrow, Poole, Dorset BH12 5BB (tel. 01202-524111)

University status 1992, formerly Bournemouth Polytechnic, originally Dorset Institute of Higher Education
Times ranking: 96 *(1998 ranking: 96)*

Enquiries: Academic secretary
Total students: 9,200
Male/female ratio: 57/43
Mature students: 25%
Overseas students: 2%

Main subject areas: business; conservation sciences; design engineering and computing; finance and law; health and community studies; media arts and communication; service industries.

Teaching quality ratings
Rated excellent 1993-95: none.
April 1995-97: communication and media studies 22; television and video production 22; electrical engineering 19; mechanical engineering 18; modern languages 14.

Always a university with an eye for the distinctive, Bournemouth starts at the top as the only institution with women as chancellor and vice-chancellor. Professor Gillian Slater, the vice-chancellor, leaves prospective students under no illusion about Bournemouth's approach to higher education, stressing in her introduction to the prospectus that they will not find 'traditional academic disciplines'. Yet the university claims a number of national firsts in its growing portfolio of courses, notably in the areas of tourism, media studies and conservation, which won a Queen's Anniversary Prize in 1994.

In the early 1980s, the future for the-then Dorset Institute for Higher Education looked bleak when the only degree course (a BEd) closed. There is now a wide range of undergraduate and postgraduate programmes in seven academic schools. Teaching ratings have improved after a mediocre start in which modern languages recorded an unusually low score, especially for its learning resources. University status came only two years after success was achieved in a long-running battle to become a polytechnic. In four years, however, numbers doubled to near 10,000, including more than 1,000 postgraduates. New teaching accommodation has been added in recent years, both on the main campus and in the centre of Bournemouth.

Bournemouth's forte is in identifying gaps in the higher education market and filling them with innovative courses, usually with a highly vocational slant. A National Centre of Computer Animation opened in 1996. Degrees in retail management, public relations, taxation and revenue law, and heritage management are other examples. Media-based courses are a particular strength, as recent assessments have confirmed. Entry requirements for them are far above the university's modest overall average. Many courses include a language element, and all students are given an opportunity to improve their linguistic skills. A majority of undergraduates take sandwich courses, and 70 per cent of all students do placements.

The town and the subject-mix attract mainly middle-class students from the Midlands and the south of England. Bournemouth's familiarity to European language students has also helped to establish a small but regular intake from across the Channel. The main campus is situated two miles from the centre of Bournemouth, and there are associate colleges in Yeovil and Poole and on the Isle of Wight.

Student accommodation is relatively cheap and plentiful on the private market, and the university been increasing its own stock. There are almost 1,000 places, including 250 in a student village on the main campus, for which first-years are given priority. Other first-years are placed by the university in hotels and guest houses, which welcome the out-of-season business students bring them. Student facilities have improved, with a purpose-built centre including a nursery and medical unit. The student union's conversion of an old fire station adds to already plentiful nightlife in town.

UNIVERSITY OF BRADFORD
Richmond Road, Bradford BD7 1DP (tel. 01274-733466)

Royal charter 1966, college of advanced technology 1957-66
Times ranking: 52 *(1998 ranking:53)*

Enquiries: Schools liaison office
Total students: 8,300
Male/female ratio: 54/46
Mature students: 22%
Overseas students: 12%

Main subject areas: applied social studies; archaeological, biomedical and environmental sciences; business and management; chemical, civil, electrical and mechanical engineering; chemistry; computing; electronic imaging; health studies; human, European and peace studies; industrial technology; mathematics; modern languages; optometry; pharmacy.

Teaching quality ratings
Rated excellent 1993-95: none
April 1995-97: chemical engineering 20; civil engineering 20; general engineering 20; modern languages 18; sociology 17.

Ravaged by cuts in the early 1980s, Bradford began to grow again before many of the traditional universities. Although still not large by modern standards, student numbers had increased by more than a third at the end of the decade, and have gone on rising. In particular, Bradford has carved out a niche for itself with mature students, who account for almost a quarter of the undergraduates. Admissions tutors let it be known that they are less obsessed with A-level grades than many of their rivals in the old universities.

The relatively small, lively campus is close to the city centre. Apart from the newly incorporated Bradford and Airedale College of Health, only business and management students are taught elsewhere. The highly-rated management centre is three miles away in a period building surrounded by parkland. More than half of the undergraduates take sandwich courses, a legacy of the university's previous existence as a college of advanced technology and one which regularly places Bradford near the top of the graduate employment league.

There have been positive signs for the quality of courses recently. Previously modest research ratings improved, with civil and mechanical engineering, business and management studies and European studies leading the way. The university also received a good report from the vice-chancellors' Academic Audit Unit. Engineers and scientists, who form the majority of the students, can take management or language courses alongside their main subjects. There is an inter-disciplinary human studies programme, which includes philosophy, psychology, literature and sociology, aimed at the social scientists. Students have access to an advanced computer network with 1,000 workstations and 3,000 possible connection points throughout the campus, an unusually large total for the number of students. Having upgraded the facilities, the university is now increasing the use of computer-assisted learning.

First-years are guaranteed one of the 2,370 residential places either on campus or in halls only a short walk away. Others tend to live out in the cheap and plentiful flats and houses available in the private sector. Town and gown relations are good, and students generally become attached to Bradford. More southerners are being attracted by the low cost of living. The sports centre has been extended recently and a purpose-built hall of residence added for overseas students. A £3.5 million extension linking the library and computer centre is the latest project.

UNIVERSITY OF BRIGHTON
Mithras House, Lewes Road, Brighton BN2 4AT(tel. 01273-600900)

University status 1992, formerly Brighton Polytechnic
Times ranking: 60 *(1998 ranking: 61)*

Enquiries: Admissions office
Total students: 12,100
Male/female ratio: 45/55
Mature students: 38%
Overseas students: 12%

Main subject areas: art, design and humanities; business and management; education, sport and leisure; engineering and environmental studies; health; information technology. Also many certificate and diploma courses.

Teaching quality ratings
Rated excellent 1993-95: none.
April 1995-97: civil engineering 21; history of art and design 21; modern languages 20.

Three sites in Brighton and one in Eastbourne house the six faculties. The credit ratings system recognises prior learning and allows for easy transfer between the university and other institutions in Britain and Europe. Numerous European links give most courses an international flavour, often involving a period of study on the Continent. The university has a cosmopolitan air, with more overseas students than most of the former polytechnics. There is also close collaboration with neighbouring Sussex University. A joint degree in engineering was the first such venture between a university and a polytechnic and masters degrees are run at the joint Sussex Technology Institute.

Brighton has a strong faculty structure, each occupying its own building. The modular academic system allows students many options within their degree area, and sometimes across fields. Most undergraduates are allocated a personal tutor, who will advise on combinations. The university's main strength is in art and design, which was rated nationally excellent for research as well as recording a good score for teaching the history of design. The Design Council's national archive is lodged on campus. The four-year sandwich degree in fashion textiles design has also acquired an international reputation. Work placements are organised in the United States, France and Italy, as well as Britain.

Most of the 1,650 hall places in Brighton and Eastbourne are allocated to new students. The university also manages 500 units of accommodation, as well as offering access to a network of 2,500 landlords and landladies, so all first-years are given the option of organised places. Three-quarters of them can be housed in hall, and more places are planned.

Students like Brighton, although the cost of living can be high. They warn that the different sites each have their own character. Student union facilities are limited, but the acquisition of a club in Brighton has improved matters. Provision for sport is good, especially at Eastbourne, where the university has an Olympic-sized swimming pool, and a new gym and the sauna and sunbeds are very popular.

UNIVERSITY OF BRISTOL
Senate House, Bristol BS8 1TH (tel. 0117-9289000)

Founded 1876, royal charter 1909
Times ranking: 9 *(1998 ranking: 8)*

Enquiries: Admissions officer
Total students: 12,400
Male/female ratio: 51/49
Mature students: 13%
Overseas students: 9%

Main subject areas: Full range of disciplines in six faculties: arts; engineering; law; medicine (including dentistry and veterinary science); science; social science.

Teaching quality ratings
Rated excellent 1993-95: chemistry; English; geography; law; mechanical engineering; social work.
April 1995-97: electronic and electrical engineering 24; aeronautical engineering 22; civil engineering 22; Iberian languages 22; German 21; Italian 21; sociology 21; French 20; Russian 20.

Bristol is a traditional alternative to Oxbridge, favoured particularly by independent schools but drawing highly-qualified applicants from all sectors. the university has emerged apparently unscathed from brief but serious financial difficulties at the start of the 1990s. It is still recovering its financial strength, but peer review suggests few academic problems. Half the staff assessed for research are in internationally rated departments, and teaching ability scores have been impressive.

A moderately successful funding appeal forms the basis for a new phase of expansion in a variety of fields, allowing the university to establish new chairs and embark on several building projects. The highly-rated chemistry department is the latest to benefit, with a well-appointed new centre due to open in 2000. Several charitable trusts have put money into an Access for Deaf Students Initiative, prompting Bristol to declare itself the leading university for the hard of hearing. Private funding has assumed added importance because, like most universities, Bristol's grant has failed to keep pace with inflation. The university is aiming to increase student numbers gradually, after a five-year period in which they grew by 50 per cent.

Only geography achieved the coveted 5-star rating in the last research rankings, but 20 subjects were in the next category. Electrical and electronic engineering has produced the outstanding score for teaching, with maximum points from the assessors. A modular system is now well established, although the traditional single or joint honours degrees are still available. It is proving popular with applicants, who numbered 13 for every place in 1997. Entry requirements also reached record levels, ranging from an average of 26 A-level points for science and engineering to 28.7 for medicine.

The main library has more than one million volumes, and 12 other libraries serve individual departments and faculties. The computer centre is open 24 hours a day. Departments are located close to the city centre, with the halls in the traditional student areas of Clifton and Stoke Bishop. The university has more than 4,000 residential places, so can still accommodate all first-years. Bristol was one of the original members of the European Credit Transfer System, enabling students to take part of a degree abroad, and is committed to a more European outlook. Links are growing with universities in Eastern Europe as well as within the EC.

Students like the way the university merges into the city, although private sector rents and other living costs are high. But sports facilities are good. The students' union is the largest in the country.

BRUNEL UNIVERSITY
Uxbridge, Middlesex UB8 3PH (tel. 01895-274000)

Royal charter 1966
Times ranking: 54th equal *(1998 ranking: 50)*

Enquiries: Admissions officer
Total students: 11,400
Male/female ratio: 58/42
Mature students: 32%
Overseas students: 3%

Main subject areas: business management; economics; education; design; engineering and technology; government; law; pure and applied sciences; psychology; sociology.

Teaching quality ratings
Rated excellent 1993-95: anthropology; social policy.
April 1995-97: drama and dance 23; general engineering 22; sociology 22; American studies 21; electrical and electronic engineering 21; materials science 20; mechanical engineering 20.

Brunel has made a quantum leap in size by teaming up with the former West London Institute of Higher Education (now known as Brunel University College), a teacher-training centre with an illustrious reputation in sport. At the same time, it is going it alone in management after years of collaboration with Henley Management College.

The majority of the university's undergraduates are on four-year sandwich courses, although three-year degrees are creeping in. A thin sandwich system gives students six months in each of the first three years at work. The course structure and technological emphasis serves graduates well in the employment market. The system can also leave Brunel's students in a healthier financial state than some others – most of the placements are paid. All students have the option of including language or business programmes in their courses.

Only 5,500 students share the spacious, if uninspiring, main campus on the edge of west London. A former college of higher education provides a smaller, more picturesque site on the Thames, at Runnymede. Brunel University College is south of the river, in Twickenham and Osterley. Courses generally do not require students to travel between campuses, but a university bus service links the four sites to allow full use of the facilities.

Poor research ratings in the 1980s pushed Brunel in the direction of a predominantly teaching university although, as the last research assessments demonstrated, a determination to revive research performance has begun to pay off. Design was rated internationally outstanding and anthropology reached the next mark. Law, sociology and electronic and electrical engineering are all well regarded but the film, television and drama courses have achieved the highest rating for teaching. There is also a special four-year engineering programme designed to train future project leaders.

Unusually, most applicants in all subjects are interviewed. Brunel was also among the first of the traditional universities to establish access courses, run in further education colleges, to bring underqualified applicants up to the necessary standards for entry. Bursaries are available for promising musicians and sportsmen and women taking mainstream academic courses. All first-years who accept a place before clearing will be offered one of the university's 2,800 residential places, which are mostly on campus. Student union facilities are good and students like Brunel's intimacy, although some feel cut off at Runnymede.

UNIVERSITY OF BUCKINGHAM
Buckingham MK18 1EG (tel. 01280-814080)

Founded 1974, royal charter 1983

Enquiries: Assistant registrar (admissions)
Total students: 737
Male/female ratio: 56/44
Mature students: 74%
Overseas students: 78%

Main subject areas: accounting; business studies; computer science;
English; history; history of art and heritage management; hotel management and economics; law; politics; psychology.

Teaching quality ratings: not carried out because the Higher
Education Funding Council has no jurisdiction.

By far the smallest of the universities, Buckingham has now lost the distinction of being the youngest. Britain's only private university was a
Conservative experiment of the 1970s, which had to wait almost a decade
for its royal charter, but is now an accepted part of the university system.
Although in 1992 Buckingham installed Lady Thatcher as its chancellor
and her former minister, Sir Richard Luce, as vice-chancellor, the university now sees itself as a non-partisan institution. American-born Professor
Bob Taylor has since succeeded Sir Richard.

Buckingham's private status excludes it from the funding council's
assessments of teaching and research, making it impossible to place in our
league table. However, the university's degrees are fully accepted in academic circles and teaching standards are high. Law and accounting are both
popular. The law school is one of the largest in Britain, and is developing
computer-aided packages to supplement face-to-face teaching. Biological
sciences, too, are strong, with a growing research record.

Buckingham runs on calendar years, rather than the traditional academic variety. Between October and December, before enrolling, all students
have the opportunity to attend specially designed language courses at a
French, German or Spanish university. Degree courses run for two 40-week
years, minimising the length of career breaks for the university's many
mature students. Half of all undergraduates are from overseas, but the proportion from Britain is growing, even with fees of more than £10,000 for 1998.

The two-year degree, which Buckingham pioneered and which is now
being examined elsewhere, has been fully assessed by Dr John Clarke, who
has worked at the university since its establishment. Although hardly neu-
tral, he takes the view that the special circumstances of Buckingham enable
the system to succeed. Students enjoy considerable (and expensive) individual tuition, which is only possible through the maintenance of unusually generous staffing levels.

Campus facilities are improving, although they do not yet compare with
those available at traditional universities. The students' union is still

developing both socially and politically, and sports facilities have been expanded. First-years are guaranteed one of more than 500 residential places.

As its rivals become ever larger and more impersonal, Buckingham hopes to make a virtue of its size and become more selective. A new business school opened in 1996 and a new academic centre, containing more lecture theatres and a language centre, are giving the university the focal point that it lacked previously.

UNIVERSITY OF CAMBRIDGE
University Registry, The Old Schools, Cambridge CB2 1TN (tel. 01223-337733)

Founded: 1209
Times ranking: 1 *(1998 ranking: 1)*

Enquiries: Administrative Secretary, Intercollegiate Applications Office, Kellet Lodge, Tennis Court Road, Cambridge CB2 1QJ
Total students: 20,800
Male/female ratio: 57/43
Mature students: 6%
Overseas students: 10%

Main subject areas: full range of disciplines divided into five faculties: arts; engineering; medicine and veterinary science, science and mathematics; and social sciences.

Teaching quality ratings
Rated excellent 1993-95: anthropology; architecture; chemistry; computer science; English; geography; geology; history; law; music.
April 1995-97: chemical engineering 23; general engineering 23; Middle Eastern and African studies 23; history of art 22; modern languages 22.

Top of *The Times* league every year since it was first published, Cambridge remains at the pinnacle of the university system in many subjects. Traditionally supreme in the sciences, where an array of subjects boast top ratings for teaching and research. The university has added strength in the arts and social sciences, as well as opening a management school. All but one of the subjects assessed in the first rounds of teaching quality ratings were considered excellent and none has dropped more than two points out of 24 under the new system. Almost two-thirds of the academics entered for research assessment were top-rated.

More students now come from state schools than the independent sector, and the university and its colleges are trying hard to attract more applicants from comprehensives. The tripos system was a forerunner of the currently fashionable modular degree, allowing students to change subjects (within limits) mid-way through their degrees as well as providing two degree classifications.

The students, in a lively alternative prospectus, say there is no such thing as Cambridge University, just a collection of colleges. However, teaching is university-based while a shift of emphasis towards the centre is taking place with the aid of a successful £250-million funding appeal. The university's pre-eminent place in British higher education was underlined by its success in attracting Microsoft's first research base outside the United States. It was one of a series of recent technological partnerships with the private sector several of which benefit undergraduates as well as researchers.

See chapter 9 for information about individual colleges.

UNIVERSITY OF CENTRAL ENGLAND IN BIRMINGHAM
Perry Barr, Birmingham B42 2SU (tel. 0121-331 5595)

University status 1992, formerly Birmingham Polytechnic
Times ranking: 87th equal *(1998 ranking: 76)*

Enquiries: Recruitment unit
Total students: 17,300
Male/female ratio: 44/56
Mature students: 46%
Overseas students: 6%

Main subject areas: art and design; built environment; business and management; computing and information studies; education; engineering and computer technology; health and community care; law and social science; music. Also a wide range of diploma courses.

Teaching quality ratings
Rated excellent 1993-95: music.
April 1995-97: communication and media studies 21; mechanical engineering 19; land and property management 18; sociology 18.

The new university made its intentions clear by opting out of the funding council's 1992 research assessment exercise, the first to include the new universities. Although it did not repeat the gesture, Central England's view of itself as primarily a teaching establishment has not changed.

In fact, the university enjoys a healthy income from research and consultancy, but most activity is in applied fields, where Central England expects to compete successfully with longer-established rivals. Undergraduate courses are designed with a similar eye to the market, often in collaboration with business or industry. The built environment faculty, for example, runs inter-professional courses that promote teamwork between students of architecture, surveying and planning.

Students have their say on the quality of courses and facilities through a well-developed consultation process that is becoming a model for other universities. A quarter of students take part each year, and the results are taken seriously. Almost £1 million was spent on library stock when the survey revealed concern on that score in 1993. The initiative is just one of the activities of the influential Centre for Research into Quality, which is headed by one of the university's most senior academics.

About half the full-time students come from the West Midlands, many from ethnic minorities. Almost as large a share of the total student population are part-timers, making Central England the biggest provider of higher education in the region. Many students enter through the network of 15 associated further education colleges, which run foundation and access programmes.

The university's best-known feature is its conservatoire, which is housed in part of Birmingham's new convention centre and has Sir Simon Rattle as its president. Courses from opera to world music have given it a reputation for innovation, which was recognised in an 'excellent' rating in the funding council's assessment of teaching.

Nine sites are spread around Birmingham, from the main campus in Perry Barr, via a clutch of city-centre buildings two miles away, to teacher training in the southern suburb of Edgbaston. The Institute of Art and Design, refurbished at a cost of £20 million, spreads even further south to Bourneville, where it occupies part of the Cadbury's 'village'. It is the largest in Britain, and includes a school of jewellery with a popular exhibition area in the city centre.

There are six self-catering halls of residence, with fewer than 1,400 beds but the high proportion of local students eases pressure on accommodation. The total will rise dramatically when Central England buys out halls in a student village presently shared with Aston University. The university controls another 1,100 residential places through a leasing scheme and reckons to house 90 per cent of first-years requiring accommodation. Only the main campus and the Edgbaston site have student union offices, but catering services are provided elsewhere. Students have been critical of the sports facilities.

UNIVERSITY OF CENTRAL LANCASHIRE
Preston PR1 2HE (tel. 01772-201201)

University status 1992, formerly Lancashire (originally Preston) Polytechnic
Times ranking: 81 *(1998 ranking: 84th equal)*

Enquiries: Student recruitment officer
Total students: 15,700
Male/female ratio: 50/50
Mature students: 50%
Overseas students: 2%

Main subject areas: business studies; cultural studies; design and technology; health; legal studies; social studies; science. Also a wide range of certificate and diploma courses.

Teaching quality ratings
Rated excellent 1993-95: none.

April 1995-98: American studies 24; linguistics 22; media studies 22; modern languages 21; agriculture 20; general engineering 20; history of art 19; sociology 18; electrical and electronic engineering 15.

Having revamped its pioneering credit accumulation and transfer system, Central Lancashire now gives undergraduates more than 500 courses to choose from. Electives are used to broaden the curriculum, so that up to 11 per cent of time is spent on subjects outside the students' normal range. Students are encouraged to include a modern language in their portfolio, and more than 2,000 did so in 1997. One in 10 also took advantage of various international exchange schemes to spend part of their course abroad. Central Lancashire has some 70 partner institutions in Europe and the United States, and is one of the most active participants in EU programmes. The new university is strong in art, design and astrophysics, with two observatories, including Britain's most powerful optical telescope. Journalism is acquiring a growing reputation, while health-related courses benefit from a successful partnership with the Royal Preston Hospital.

Central Lancashire's main base is a predominantly modern campus in the centre of Preston. Ambitious construction projects have eased the pressure on teaching and residential space. The prime example, which opened in 1994, consists of a 500-seat lecture theatre, computing facilities for 130 students, more catering and a new home for the Faculty of Health. The library has been refurbished and extended at a cost of £5 million to seat 1,000 students.

With the university's doubling in size in recent years, the extra space was much needed. Stories of disgruntled Central Lancashire students being bussed in from a holiday camp used to mark the start of each academic year, but there are now 2,000 places in university halls, flats and houses. As a result, first-years are guaranteed accommodation.

The university took in an agricultural college at Newton Rigg, in Cumbria, in 1998. Further education courses in land-based subjects are continuing there and there will be new programmes at degree and post-graduate level in a county with little higher education provision. The college has residential accommodation for 280 students and sports facilities, including an equestrian centre.

A high proportion of students are local people in their 20s or 30s, many of whom have taken advantage of the well-established Life Long Learning networks run in colleges throughout the Northwest. There is a thriving access unit, and university courses can be taken elsewhere in Lancashire and Cumbria. Unlike some universities involved in 'franchising', Central Lancashire has carried out a thorough review of the quality of such programmes.

Sports facilities are good. The university won £8 million from the National Lottery for a sports complex at Ingol, two miles from the campus. A £1-million refectory with seating for 800 opened in 1994, but the students' union is crowded. Like other parts of the university, it is feeling the strain of rapid expansion, although an official survey showed that three-quarters of students would recommend Central Lancashire to a friend.

CITY UNIVERSITY
Northampton Square, London EC1V 0HB (tel. 0171-477 8000)

Founded 1894, royal charter 1966
Times ranking: 44 *(1998 ranking: 44)*

Enquiries: Admissions office (tel. 0171-477 8028)
Total students: 7,300
Male/female ratio: 51/49
Mature students: 34%
Overseas students: 19%

Main subject areas: actuarial science; business and management; engineering; health sciences; informatics; mathematics; music; studies related to medicine; social science.

Teaching quality ratings
Rated excellent 1993-95: business and management; music.
April 1995-97: electrical and electronic engineering 21; civil engineering 19; land management 19; mechanical engineering 19; sociology 19.

In spite of its history as a college of advanced technology, City now has more students taking arts, business and social science subjects than on the science side. It has acquired a strong reputation for music in association with the Guildhall School of Music and Drama, and for business studies, for which its teaching is rated excellent. Recent teaching ratings – electrical engineering apart – have been mediocre, however, and only library and information studies were top-rated for research. Most courses have a vocational slant and many, such as air transport engineering and clinical communication studies, are highly specialised. A number of degrees can be taken either as four-year sandwich programmes or on a three-year, full-time basis. The university is another to feature regularly at the head of graduate employment lists. Almost half the university's students are on postgraduate courses, mainly in the large schools of engineering and journalism or in the Barbican-based business school. The rest are in a cluster of buildings on the borders of the City of London.

Students numbers have almost doubled in the past five years, partly because of the incorporation of a nursing and midwifery college at nearby St Bartholomew's Hospital. Four new large lecture theatres have been added in anticipation of further expansion. Two floors have been added to the library and the number of reading spaces increased from 480 to 720.

First-years from outside London who accept a place by the middle of May are guaranteed a residential place. The university has three halls of residence and two blocks of flats, housing more than 1,000 students within easy reach of the campus. All the halls have workstations linked to the university's mainframe computer.

Students find the cost of living high, both in and out of the university, and complain about the food. They speak highly of the staff, who are considered unusually supportive. In spite of this, drop-out rates are relatively high. Sports facilities are good, but those for outdoor games are inconveniently placed south of the river. A new students' union opened in October 1995.

COVENTRY UNIVERSITY
Priory Street, Coventry CV1 5FB (tel. 01203-631313)

University status 1992, formerly Coventry (originally Lanchester) Polytechnic
Times ranking: 73 *(1998 ranking: 65)*

Enquiries: Academic registry (tel. 01203-838482)
Total students: 11,900
Male/female ratio: 59/41
Mature students: 40%
Overseas students: 9%

Main subject areas: applied science; art and design; business; engineering; international studies; law; social, biological and health sciences. About a third of students on certificate or diploma courses.

Teaching quality ratings
Rated excellent 1993-95: geography; mechanical engineering.
April 1995-98: building 22; modern languages 21; sociology 21; town planning 19; electrical and electronic engineering 18; media studies 18; aeronautical and manufacturing engineering 18.

Though not among the most fashionable, Coventry has always been considered among the leading new universities. It scored consistently in the polytechnics' quality ratings for teaching, and has begun to make a mark in the new system. A thriving research and consultancy base has also been built up. A rough balance is maintained between arts and science students in order to preserve an all-round educational environment. Coventry courses are also run in 24 further education colleges from Gloucester to Hereford.

The university specialises in practical and socially oriented activities, linking higher education with business and industry. Recent innovations have included a degree in international disaster management and a BA in equine studies. Its reputation has attracted hundreds of managers from the former Soviet Union, learning everything from how to privatise the Lada car works to selling baked potatoes on the streets of Moscow. The university's priorities are closer to home, however. One project has seen an old welfare building converted into a self-help centre for local people with business ambitions. Degrees such as automotive engineering design have been developed in collaboration with the city's motor industry.

Most full-time and sandwich students construct their own degree programme within faculty limits. They are encouraged to take a foreign language and to develop computer skills. Each module is assessed separately and credited towards the final degree classification. The university also runs 'minimodules' in the evening and at weekends for students and members of the public to broaden their knowledge. A disused factory has been refurbished to add teaching room to the city-centre campus, which was beginning to feel the strain of considerable expansion. Numbers have levelled off in recent years. But further growth is planned.

Coventry's experience of research assessment was disappointing, with almost a third of the academics entered finishing in the bottom category, although art and design did well. Teaching ratings have been better, especially in geography, mechanical engineering and building.

The university has over 2,600 residential places and guarantees to find all first-year students accommodation, either of its own or in the relatively cheap private sector. A new hall of residence at Singer Hall, with 622 bedrooms, includes many rooms designed for those with disabilities. Students say that town and gown relations are not always good, but the union provides a good social base, especially since the opening of Planet, a £3 million entertainments complex, which has allowed the union to attract bigger-name artists.

DE MONTFORT UNIVERSITY
The Gateway, Leicester LE1 9BH (tel. 01162-551551)

University status 1992, formerly Leicester Polytechnic
Times ranking: 70 *(1998 ranking: 62nd equal)*

Enquiries: Academic registrar

Total students: 18,600
Male/female ratio: 50/50
Mature students: 38%
Overseas students: 3%

Main subject areas: applied physical sciences; arts; built environment; business; combined studies; computing and mathematical sciences; design and manufacture; engineering; health and life sciences; law.

Teaching quality ratings
Rated excellent 1993-95: business and management.
April 1995-98: land management 23; dance and cinematics 22; history of art and design 21; town planning 21; building 20; media studies 20; electrical and electronic engineering 19; general engineering 19; materials technology 19; modern languages (Bedford) 19; modern languages 17; sociology 17; agriculture 16.

Like the 13th-century earl of Leicester, after whom the university is named, De Montfort University has a fiefdom of sorts: it is made up of a network of campuses in a 50-mile radius. Based on what was Leicester Polytechnic, the new university has been spreading ever outwards. The addition of a nursing and midwifery college has provided a third campus in Leicester, and there is a substantial outpost at Milton Keynes. Bedford College of Higher Education and the Lincolnshire Colleges of Art and Design, and Agriculture and Horticulture have also joined the fold.

The latest additions brought teacher training, craft-related art and design, conservation, restoration, agriculture and horticulture into the curriculum as well as a profitable farm. There are now ten campuses altogether, with 3,000 staff and more than 30,000 students when the many part-timers are included. The 11 per cent taking further education courses represent the largest proportion in any university.

Professor Kenneth Barker, the vice-chancellor, makes no bones about De Montfort's academic ambitions. 'Higher education has been too busy chasing Nobel prizes, instead of giving industry and the community the service they really need,' he has asserted. Law, mathematics and art and design are strong. Teaching ratings were patchy until recently, however, with only one of the first 11 subjects to be assessed considered excellent. There has since been a marked improvement, with only one of the last five assessments awarding fewer than 20 points out of 24. Land management was particularly successful, achieving a near-perfect score. The limited range of postgraduate programmes has been growing steadily. De Montfort entered the highest proportion of academics of any of the new universities in the 1996 research assessment exercise. Energy and music were both rated nationally excellent.

De Montfort now has more than 2,000 residential places on its various campuses, with many more students accommodated through a head tenancy scheme. Priority is given to first-years who live farthest from their campus, most of whom are found accommodation. Extra accommodation is being developed. The energy efficient School of Engineering and Manufacture, which opened in 1993, has won architectural awards. Other buildings inherited from the local authority are less than beautiful, but are being renovated gradually.

UNIVERSITY OF DERBY
Kedleston Road, Derby D22 1GB (tel. 01332-622222)

University status 1992, formerly Derbyshire College of Higher Education
Times ranking: 92 *(1998 ranking: 91)*

Enquiries: Registry
Total students: 10,200
Male/female ratio: 43/57
Mature students: 43%
Overseas students: 2%

Main subject areas: art and design; business; education; environmental and applied sciences; engineering; European and international studies; health and community studies; management; mathematics and computing; social sciences.

Teaching quality ratings
Rated excellent 1993-95: geology.
April 1995-87: American studies 21; civil engineering 19; electrical and electronic engineering 19; drama, dance and cinematics 18; modern languages 18; sociology 18; media studies 17.

Derby is unrecognisable from the institution that was the only college of higher education to be granted university status with the polytechnics. Student numbers more than doubled in four years, the residential stock increased fivefold and 30,000 square metres of teaching space have been added.

The city had long claimed to be the largest in Europe without a major higher education institution. The college, which was the product of a series of mergers in the 1970s and 1980s, was the only one to meet both the academic and physical criteria for promotion. A plan to make the university considerably larger foundered when one of two local further education colleges earmarked for merger pulled out of the arrangement. Derby is still planning to expand its further education base, however.

The pace of expansion has inevitably imposed strains on the new university, which was the only one to receive two 'unsatisfactory' verdicts in the funding council's initial teaching assessments. Both the law degree and the computer studies and information systems courses have since been declared satisfactory after the normal revisit. Recent assessments have shown an improvement, with American studies scoring particularly well.

The last government's decision to cap student numbers came at an awkward moment for Derby. Applications had doubled with university status, and the aim was to have 15,000 students by 1996. The university had already embarked on a £40-million development plan to this end. Nonetheless, a science and technology block with two 180-seat lecture theatres has been added on the main Kedleston Road site, which has also acquired new premises for the schools of business and management. Library facilities have also been improved, with 1,200 study spaces and a high-speed electronic network linked to student residences and a piazza-style concourse constructed to give students a focal point. The next stage involved a £4 million redevelopment plan to bring together all of the university's art and design provision. There are four main sites in and around Derby.

Accommodation is now available on eight sites , with most of the 2,700 residential places newly built. The university has housing for 90 per cent of the first-year students who require it, and those who miss out are invited to a pre-term househunting weekend hosted by the students' union. More than half of the students are from Derbyshire or neighbouring counties and, including part- timers, 60 per cent are 21 or over and close on the same proportion are women.

As in many new universities, business and management are easily the most popular subjects. Courses are modular and a foundation programme allows students to begin work at a partner college before transferring to Derby. There is particular emphasis on the development of new teaching methods, and the university was one of nine chosen for a national technology programme. Derby's role in the project is to produce an interactive video system for use by lecturers.

UNIVERSITY OF DUNDEE
Dundee DD1 4HN (tel. 01382-223181)

Founded 1881, part of St Andrews University until 1967
Times ranking: 31st equal *(1998 ranking: 38)*

Enquiries: Schools liaison enquiry service (tel. 01382-344160)
Total students: 8,600
Male/female ratio: 49/51
Mature students: 22%
Overseas students: 4%

Main subject areas: architecture; arts and social science; environmental management; fine art; hotel and catering management; law; medicine and dentistry; nursing and midwifery; science and engineering.

Teaching quality ratings
Rated excellent 1994-97: cellular biology; English; finance and accounting; graphic and textile design; medicine; organismal biology; psychology.
Rated highly satisfactory: civil engineering; dentistry; environmental science; fine art; history; hospitality studies; law; mathematics; physics; politics; social work; statistics.
From 1998: Planning and landscape 21

Though the recent merger with the Duncan of Jordanstone College of Art has added another 1,200 students, creating a new faculty in the process, and the addition of nursing and midwifery further increased the size of the university, Dundee remains relatively small. Only the medical school, set in 20 acres of parkland, lies outside the compact campus near the centre the city.

The medical school and Centre for Medical Education, at nearby Ninewells Hospital, rate as world leaders in a number of fields, including nursing studies and treatment of wounds. A new Cancer Research Centre will doubtless add to the medical departments' reputation, which was reflected in an excellent rating for teaching and in a Queen's Anniversary prize awarded in 1998. A new social centre for students and staff is among £12m of projects being undertaken at Ninewells.

In recent years, Dundee has been among the leaders for graduate employment. Law, computing and information technology were particularly well regarded in a recent employers' survey. The school of design, based at Duncan of Jordanstone, was rated the best in Scotland in the funding council's teaching assessments. Textile and graphic design were seen as the school's chief strengths. Biochemistry is the other flagship department, and is recognised as one of Europe's top centres for the subject. Its academics hold research grants worth more than £10 million, and were among the first in Britain to be invited to participate in Japan's Human Frontier Science Programme. A £13-million Wellcome Trust Building for Biochemistry opened in September 1997, as the department celebrated Dundee's only 5-star rating for research. The law department is the only one in Scotland to offer an English LLB, as well as Scottish and Northern Irish qualifications. It was one of a string of subjects to be rated 'highly satisfactory'. Computer science, by contrast, attracted one of the few 'unsatisfactory' ratings for teaching, but went on to be rated nationally excellent for research. Civil engineering and art and design also won 5-star ratings for research. Vocational degrees predominate, but a number of combinations, such as American or European studies, are now available. Transfers between courses are relatively easy. Interviews are usual only in medicine, dentistry, architecture and town planning. However, others offered a place are invited to visit Dundee before committing themselves.

Dundee guarantees to accommodate all first-years who live outside the area in one of more than 1,000 residential places. One student in five lives at home and the rest find private rented accommodation. A new student village, being built at a cost of £3.5 million, is claimed to be 'probably the best student accommodation available anywhere in Britain'. Designed according to the wishes of 700 Dundee students, each room has a safe, a colour television and a computer point.

The student association has spacious premises for the size of university, and sports facilities are good. The Royal and Ancient Club, at St Andrews, offers bursaries to the most promising golfers. Students find the city unattractive, if welcoming, but there are compensations in the magnificent countryside and coastline, both within easy reach. The campus is the focal point of social activity, featuring an £8-million arts centre built with lottery money.

UNIVERSITY OF DURHAM
Old Shire Hall, Durham DH1 3HP (tel. 0191-374 2000)

Founded 1832
Times ranking: 18 *(1998 ranking: 13)*

Enquiries: Academic registrar
Total students: 10,400
Male/female ratio: 50/50
Mature students: 14%
Overseas students: 4%

Main subject areas: full range of disciplines except art, medicine, dentistry and veterinary science. Faculties of arts; social sciences; and science.

Teaching quality ratings
Rated excellent 1993-95: anthropology; chemistry; English; geography; geology; history; law; social work.
April 1995-97: Engineering 22; French 22; German 22; linguistics 22;

Middle Eastern and African studies 22; sociology 21; Italian 20; Russian 20; Iberian languages 16.

Long established as a leading alternative to Oxbridge, Durham even delays selection to accommodate those applying to the ancient universities. A collegiate structure and picturesque setting are further attractions for a predominantly middle-class student body many of whom come from independent schools. Those who receive offers without interview are invited to a special open day to see if Durham is the university for them. Since 84 per cent of undergraduates come from outside the Northeast, most are seeing the small cathedral town for the first time. Applications have to be made to one of the 12 colleges, all but one of which are mixed. Another is planned to open in 1999. The colleges range in size from 300 to 900 students and form the focus of social life, though all teaching is done in central departments.

Only geography reached the pinnacle of the last research assessment exercise, although a dozen subjects were considered excellent. Most of the teaching assessments have also produced top ratings. Mathematics and chemistry are particularly strong on the science side, history and theology among the stars on the arts'. Only Oxford and Cambridge have higher entry standards overall.

Durham is determinedly traditional. Whenever possible, teaching takes place in small groups and most assessment is by written examination. Resits are permitted only in the first year, although the dropout rate is among the lowest in the country. The university has broken out of its traditional mould with two recent projects, however. The first saw the establishment in the city of the Teikyo University of Japan, allowing students of Japanese access to another excellent library. The second was the opening of a college at Stockton in partnership with Teesside University.

There are 80 single-degree subjects and 24-hour computing. Sir Kenneth Calman, formerly the Government's Chief Medical Officer, and now Durham's new vice-chancellor, is hoping to realise the university's ambition to recover the medical school it lost when Newcastle University was established. The modular system includes a variety of "free elective" modules – generalist courses open to all undergraduates on subjects such as history of science, personal learning and teaching English as a foreign language.

In addition to the facilities available in colleges, there is a large central students' union overlooking the river. The university dominates the town, but Newcastle is only a short train journey away for those looking for a change of scene. Sport occupies an important place in university life. Representative teams have outdone Oxford and Cambridge in some of the most prestigious pursuits, including rugby, cricket and rowing.

The university finds accommodation for more than 65 per cent of its 7,000 students, and normally provides two years in residence, including the first. Students stress the importance of finding the right college, since they all have their own character. Some feel uncomfortable with the high proportion of colleagues from independent schools.

UNIVERSITY OF EAST ANGLIA
Norwich NR4 7TJ (tel. 01603-456161)

Royal charter 1964
Times ranking: 37 *(1998 ranking: 29)*

Enquiries: Assistant registrar (admissions) and secretary (tel. 01603 592216)
Total students: 9,600
Male/female ratio: 49/51
Mature students: 34%
Overseas students: 6%

Main subject areas: art; biological, chemical and environmental sciences; development studies; economic and social studies; education; English and American studies; health; history; information systems; law; management; mathematics; modern languages; music; physics; social work.

Teaching quality ratings
Rated excellent 1993-95: development studies; environmental studies; law; social work.
April 1995-97: communication and media studies 23; history of art 22; drama, dance and cinematics 21; electrical and electronic engineering 19; modern languages 19; sociology 16.

The University of East Anglia (UEA) has completed an ambitious building programme to provide housing for all first-year, overseas and disabled students. The campus, two miles from the centre of Norwich, has gained two environmentally sound blocks, while the rest of those given rooms are housed in the student village a few minutes away. Following expansion, the official target of 8,000 students by the end of the century has long since been exceeded with the university housing 3,500 of them itself.

With most students coming from outside the region, and a relatively large proportion from overseas, the university feels obliged to make its own provision for growth. Recent construction projects have included two academic buildings for use by the highly regarded School of Social Work and the School of Occupational Therapy and Physiotherapy, where physiotherapy can also be studied.

Health-related studies are among UEA's fastest-developing areas. Although there is no medical school, the university validates courses in nursing, and several highly rated research teams are involved in the field. Environmental sciences (which includes the option of a four-year degree, including a year in the United States) is particularly well thought of. The Climatic Research Unit is one of the leaders in the investigation of global warming. Law, development studies and social work were among the subjects rated 'excellent' for teaching, with communications and media studies only narrowly missing the maximum score in the new assessments.

The modular scheme allows students to construct their own degrees, with the help of an academic adviser, who monitors progress right through to graduation. A new development in 1999 gives most undergraduates the opportunity of course-related work experience, while the EmployAbility service puts students in touch with local firms to help with the bank balance. Schools of studies encourage broad combinations of subjects. The biggest are economic and social studies, and English and American studies. Although now retired, Malcolm Bradbury's association with the creative writing course has attracted a string of big names and made English degrees particularly popular. Art history is another strong subject, aided by the presence of the Sainsbury Centre for the Visual Arts, perhaps the greatest resource of its type on any British campus. The centre, which acquired a new wing in 1991, houses a priceless collection of modern and tribal art. Social and sporting facilities are good with a new £10m sports park intended to attract big events to the university as well as catering for the students. Most students enjoy the campus life, even if some find communications from Norwich frustratingly slow.

UNIVERSITY OF EAST LONDON
Romford Road, London E15 4LZ (tel. 0181-590 7722)

University status 1992, formerly Polytechnic of East London, originally North East London Polytechnic
Times ranking: 89 *(1998 ranking: 92)*

Enquiries: Communications and publicity office
Total students: 9,900
Male/female ratio: 45/55
Mature students: 61%
Overseas students: 15%

Main subject areas: built environment; business; engineering; health sciences; social science. Certificate and diploma courses are also offered.

Teaching quality ratings
Rated excellent 1993-95: architecture; English.
April 1995-97: civil engineering 21; sociology 19; mechanical engineering 18; modern languages 18; media studies 16; electrical and electronic engineering 15.

The opening of a £40 million docklands campus will transform a university which had struggled to recapture the sparkle it had as a pioneering polytechnic. Financial problems and occasional student unrest were clouding an otherwise impressive recovery. Although still low in *The Times* rankings, the new university had begun to do better in assessments of teaching. Cultural studies is the star attraction, achieving a rare 5-star ranking for a new university department in the 1996 research assessment exercise to add to a top rating for teaching. Architecture is also top-rated for teaching. All new lecturers are required to take a teaching qualification if they do not already have one.

Most degrees are vocational, but UEL covers a wide range of subjects for a new university. Employers – notably Ford, with whom there is a long-standing relationship – are closely involved in academic planning. About one student in seven is on a sandwich course and a quarter are part-timers.

The two original university campuses are in Barking and Stratford, and the university caters particularly for the large ethnic minority population, who take almost half of the places. A mentoring programme for black and Asian students is well used and has been so successful that it is to become a national scheme. Classes in English as a second language, designed mainly for overseas students, are available free of charge. Students with special educational needs are catered for with dyslexic workshops and a RNIB centre for the visually impaired.

The new docklands campus represents a triumph of perseverance, as well as providing valuable new facilities close to London City Airport. Financial support from Government and business was a long time coming, and East London had to take over the scheme from a consortium of universities before it came to fruition. There are student residences and recreational facilities, as well as academic buildings which will eventually cater for 7,000 students. At the heart of the development will be a technology centre involving Queen Mary and Westfield College and London Guildhall University as well as UEL.

UEL already has more residential accommodation than many of the former polytechnics. The large numbers living at home leave room for a good proportion of first-years, who take priority in the 1,200 places owned or controlled by the university.

UNIVERSITY OF EDINBURGH
Old College, South Bridge, Edinburgh EH8 9YL (tel. 0131-650 1000)

Founded 1583
Times ranking: 8th equal *(1998 ranking: 7)*

Enquiries: Schools liaison office
Total students: 15,600
Male/female ratio: 51/49
Mature students: 10%
Overseas students: 7%

Main subject areas: complete range of disciplines in eight faculties: arts; divinity; law; medicine; music; science and engineering; social sciences; veterinary medicine.

Teaching quality ratings 1993-98
Rated excellent: biology; cellular biology; chemistry; computing; electrical and electronic engineering; finance and accounting; geology; history; mathematics and statistics; physics; organismal biology; social policy; social work; sociology; veterinary medicine.

Highly satisfactory: architecture; business and management; civil engineering; English, French; geography; history of art; law; medicine; music; nursing; philosophy; politics; psychology; theology.
From 1998: European languages 21; chemical engineering 19

Having overcome a cash crisis at the start of the decade, Edinburgh is setting out to build on its reputation as Scotland's leading university. The ability to attract a former vice-chancellor of London University and head of the schools inspectorate, Sir Stewart Sutherland, as principal, gives some indication of its status.By contrast, only six years ago, staff appointments were frozen as the university grappled with a £5-million deficit. But that is in the past and new developments are under way. Chief among them is an expansion in student numbers, which have now exceeded 17,000, including part-timers.

The university provides accommodation for around 6,000 students, nearly half of them in traditional halls of residence. First years living outside the city are guaranteed accommodation. Many university flats have phones supplied under a novel agreement with British Telecom and all students have their own e-mail address. The mix of students and the setting in Scotland's capital city gives Edinburgh a cosmopolitan flavour. Some 15 per cent of places, almost 2,700 in all, are taken by overseas students, many from the Continent. Scots, although still the largest group, now make up less than half the student body. Much of the slack has been taken up by English students, with whom Edinburgh has always been popular. It remains to be seen whether an extra year's fees deters these traditional applicants.

The university buildings are scattered around the city, but most of the buildings border the historic Old Town. There is also a science campus two miles to the south, and from this August 1998 Moray House Institute of Education will join the fold. A four-year integration programme will see the institute's Cramond site closed eventually.

Six of the first ten departments to be assessed for teaching were rated as excellent. By its own high standards, a single 5-star rating for research in electrical and electronic engineering was disappointing. But more departments came in the next category and many more have since followed. Among the large number of subjects in which Edinburgh enjoys a high reputation are medicine, chemistry, physics, mathematics and languages. The law faculty is the largest in Scotland.

Departments organise visiting days in October for those interested in applying and in the spring for candidates holding offers. There is also an annual open day in June. Some £850,000 has been spent making the university more accessible to disabled people, and a disability office opened at the end of 1997.

The university is collaborating with district and regional authorities in the development of a 'science city', known as the 'Edinburgh Technopole', on its 230-acre Bush Estate near the airport. Library facilities are outstanding, the students' association extensive and well organised. Scientists sometimes feel isolated, but the cost of living is one of the few other sources of complaint for most of Edinburgh's students.

UNIVERSITY OF ESSEX
Wivenhoe Park, Colchester CO4 3SQ (tel. 01206-875333)

Royal charter 1965
Times ranking: 29 *(1998 ranking: 24)*

Enquiries: Admissions officer (tel. 01206-873666)
Total students: 5,400
Male/female ratio: 53/47
Mature students: 27%
Overseas students: 22%

Main subject areas: accounting, finance and management; art history; biology; computer science; economics; electronic systems engineering; government; history; language and linguistics; law; literature; mathematics; philosophy; physics; psychology and sociology.

Teaching quality ratings
Rated excellent 1993-95: law.
April 1995-97: electronic engineering 24; history of art 22; sociology 22; linguistics 21

After years living in the shadow of its radical past, Essex has today long since put behind it its days as a hotbed of student unrest in the 1960s and 1970s. A reputation for high-quality research, especially in the social sciences, is ousting what was once an all-pervading image of Essex as a byword for political activism. The university was prevented from finishing higher in *The Times* ranking only by its small size and arts bias.

Law was top rated in the teaching quality assessment, while sociology is also strong, having attracted a series of prestigious research projects as well as favourable ratings for teaching. Electronic engineering achieved maximum points for teaching quality to add to an improved research rating. The subject can be taken over three, four or five years with the option of a European component. Computer science is also strong. Although still the junior partners, the sciences have been growing in strength and the newly-merged biological and chemical sciences department is the largest in the university. Research ratings are good, with government and sociology considered internationally outstanding. Art history, economics and law also did well.

But improvements in the university's real function have been unable to disguise that the university's glass-and-concrete campus outside Colchester is showing distinct signs of a quarter of a century of wear. Teaching and administration blocks cluster around a network of squares which are being refurbished; most residential accommodation is in six less-than-lovely tower blocks nearby. The university has embarked on a programme of refurbishment at the same time as expanding student facilities.

Essex was originally expected to grow rapidly to become a medium to large university, but government cuts intervened and it has remained among the smallest. The latest plan is to have 6,000 students by the turn of the century. The library has been extended to provide 950 reader spaces and almost 80 hours access per week. More than 1,000 residential places are being added to make room for the new arrivals, complemented by the biggest university nursery in the country and extra teaching accommodation. The university already has beds for 2,500 students, allowing it to guarantee accommodation to all first-years.

Many of the lecturing staff are high-flying academics attracted to Essex by its pioneering broad approach to subjects. In each school, undergraduates follow a common first year before specialising, allowing choice of degree to be delayed. More than a third of the students are over 21 on entry, an unusually high proportion for a traditional university and there is a high proportion of overseas students. Essex has been more flexible than most of its rivals about entry qualifications, and has encouraged applications from comprehensive schools in deprived areas of east London and its own county. Social and sporting facilities are good, partly because they were designed for a larger student population. Town and gown relations in the garrison base of Colchester have not always been smooth, and the campus can be bleak in winter, but students do not doubt the academic quality.

UNIVERSITY OF EXETER
Northcote House, Queen's Drive, Exeter EX4 4QJ (tel. 01392-263263)

Royal charter 1955
Times ranking: 40*(1998 ranking: 36th equal)*

Enquiries: Admissions officer
Total students: 8,800
Male/female ratio: 49/51
Mature students: 13%
Overseas students: 5%

Main subject areas: biological sciences; business and economics; chemistry; classics and theology; drama and music; education; engineering and computer science; environmental science; English; geography and archaeology; historical, political and sociological studies; law; mathematics; modern languages; physics; psychology.

Teaching quality ratings
Rated excellent 1993-95: computer science; English; geography.
April 1995-97: German 24; drama, dance and cinematics 22; French 22; Italian 22; materials technology 21; sociology 21; general engineering 20; Iberian languages 20; Russian 20; linguistics 16.

Judged in terms of applications per place, Exeter is one of the country's most popular universities, especially on the arts side. Total applications dropped in 1997, but the number making Exeter their first choice held up well. For some, however, its principal handicap is its image as an alternative to Oxbridge for undergraduates from independent schools. So seriously did the university take this apparent problem that at one point in the 1980s it established a quota of places for state-school pupils.

The main campus, close to the centre of Exeter, is one of the most attractive in Britain. The highly rated school of education is a mile away in the former St Luke's College. The university has also established a foothold in Cornwall by taking on the Camborne School of Mines, a development it would like to expand with a more wide-ranging campus near Penzance.

There is a long tradition of European integration, exemplified by the European Law degree. All students are offered tuition in European languages and a number of degrees now include the option of study abroad. Language degrees have scored well in the teaching assessments, with German achieving maximum points. Exeter recorded a solid performance in the last research assessments, but had no top-rated subjects and few in the next category.

The university has undergone a complete academic and administrative reorganisation, going over to semesters in all of the 17 schools, which replaced the old faculty system. Assessment is also being streamlined on a single model of examination and course work. Modular degrees have been introduced gradually beginning with arts, law and social studies. Students construct a programme from a wide range of courses at the end of their first year.

Unlike many rivals, Exeter is satisfied to remain relatively small although it has begun to go into the franchising business, both at home and abroad. The university has been growing at under 10 per cent a year, and has already exceeded its target of 10,300 students, so dramatic growth is not expected.

Exeter's greatest strength is in the arts, with history, English literature and drama among the most heavily subscribed courses in their fields though the computer science department was one of only seven in the country to be given top marks for teaching. This small department is now moving away from its origins in artificial intelligence, but still runs a cognitive science degree.

The Northcott Theatre, on the main campus, is one of the cultural centres of the region, and sporting facilities are excellent. The Guild of Students has a prize-winning radio station. More than half of all students live in university accommodation. All first-years are offered a room, mostly in halls of residence. Some students may fight shy of the green welly image, but most value the easy access to beautiful countryside and beaches.

UNIVERSITY OF GLAMORGAN
Pontypridd, Mid Glamorgan CF37 1DL (tel. 01443-480480)

University status 1992, formerly Polytechnic of Wales
Times ranking: 80*(1998 ranking: 68th equal)*

Enquiries: Admissions office
Total students: 9,000
Male/female ratio: 58/42

Mature students: 21%
Overseas students: 6%

Main subject areas: 13 departments in three faculties: environment studies; professional studies; technology studies. Also certificate and diploma courses in all three areas.

Teaching quality ratings
Rated excellent: accounting and finance; biology; business studies; creative writing; drama; earth studies; electrical and electronic engineering; English; information and library studies; media; mining surveying; public sector schemes; Welsh.

Wales's second university was the smallest of the polytechnics. Although still not huge, Glamorgan is expanding rapidly, largely by franchising its courses to colleges at home and abroad. Twinning programmes operate in five overseas centres, while in Wales a growing number of further education colleges are also offering the university's certificate, diploma or degree courses. Moving between institutions is made easier by the university's credit-transfer scheme and modular-degree structures. Glamorgan has also made Pembrokeshire College an associate college, providing an outpost in west Wales. Students will be guaranteed places on diploma or degree courses if they fulfil set conditions. The university's own campus is 20 minutes by train from Cardiff in Treforest, overlooking the market town of Pontypridd. Originally based in a large country house, the university now has purpose-built premises for the science and technology departments. The law, nursing and midwifery schools are housed in Glyntaff in new multi-million corporate style premises, a short walk from the campus.

The best-known degrees are in engineering and professional studies. Electrical and electronic engineering are also strong, and have been at the forefront of the university's thriving company business teaching. Business studies is one of several subjects rated 'excellent' in the teaching quality assessment.

Glamorgan is committed to retaining its vocational slant. A diploma in management has been tailored to the needs of the Driver and Vehicle Licensing Agency, for example. A new degree in theatre and media drama, produced in collaboration with the Welsh College of Music and Drama, caters for would-be production staff as well as actors. The approach has paid dividends for graduate employment, which is consistently high.

Many of the 10,000 full-time undergraduates choose to live in Cardiff, which is both livelier than Pontypridd and a better source of accommodation. The university has more than 1,300 hall places, for which students from outside the county get priority although to be pretty sure of a place in university-arranged accommodation, you have to accept your offer by the end of March. Recent spending has been on a three-storey recreation centre to capitalise on a fine sporting tradition, especially in rugby.

The students' union, which has also been extended recently, is the focus of social life. Its bars are the only areas in the university excluded from an otherwise blanket no-smoking policy.

UNIVERSITY OF GLASGOW
Glasgow G12 8QQ (tel. 0141-339 8855)

Founded 1451
Times ranking: 21 *(1998 ranking: 20)*

Enquiries: Academic registrar
Total students: 17,100
Male/female ratio: 46/54
Mature students: 11%
Overseas students: 9%

Main subject areas: 100 departments in eight faculties: arts; divinity; engineering; law and financial studies; medicine; science; social sciences; veterinary medicine.

Teaching quality ratings 1993-98
Rated excellent: cellular biology; chemistry; computer studies; English; French; geography; geology; medicine; physics; philosophy; psychology, organismal biology; social policy, sociology; veterinary medicine.
Highly satisfactory: civil engineering; dentistry; drama; finance and accounting; history; history of art; law; mathematics and statistics; mechanical engineering; music; nursing; politics; social work; theology.
From 1998: European languages 22.

Glasgow is among Scotland's largest and oldest universities. It has the rare distinction of having been established by Papal Bull, and began its existence in the Chapter House of Glasgow Cathedral. Eighty per cent of students are from north of the border.

It was the first university to have a school of engineering and the huge science faculty – the biggest outside London – is strong, having received top ratings for teaching assessment in chemistry, physics, computing science, geology, biology and geography. Applications for science degrees reflect this quality, having risen by 25 per cent since the mid-1990s. Overseas recruitment has also been strong, especially in engineering. Only computer science and town planning reached the pinnacle of the research assessment exercise, but five other subjects reached the next category. With more than half the academics assessed in the third grade of seven, Glasgow might have hoped for better. The university has won two Queen's Anniversary Prizes for innovation, however. A 1994 award for opening up its artistic, cultural and scientific resources was followed in 1998 by a prize for teaching and outreach work in computing. Both are examples of an outward-looking style fostered by the Principal, Sir Graeme Davies.

The impressive, compact campus, with 99 listed buildings, is in the city's lively West End. The vets are on a greenfield site four miles away. Most of the 4,000 residential places are within easy walking distance of the main campus. First-years are usually given a place if they live outside daily commuting distance.

Interviews are usual only in medicine, dentistry, veterinary science and nursing. Good A-level passes should secure admission to the second of four years in some science, engineering and arts degrees. But 70 per cent of entrants come with Highers, reflecting the university's traditional recruiting ground in the Glasgow area. There was a high proportion of home-based students long before Glasgow became fashionable among traditional universities. The library is large, with 30 miles of shelves and 2,500 reader places as well as a number of valuable collections. Recent refurbishment has placed all undergraduate services under one roof. The Hunterian museum and art gallery are similarly noteworthy.

Students can choose between two independent student unions, until recently segregated by sex. The Queen Margaret Union and the more rumbustious Glasgow University Union both run bars and leisure facilities, while the students' representative council has responsibility for student political activities. It also has its own shops and a travel agent.

Most students like the combination of campus and city life, although the relatively high drop-out rate remains something of a worry. Sports facilities are well-used and were upgraded in January 1996 in response to student demands for better indoor facilities. There is a separate membership fee for the athletic union.

GLASGOW CALEDONIAN UNIVERSITY
Cowcaddens Road, Glasgow G4 0BA (tel. 0141-331 3000)

University status 1992, formerly Queen's College (founded 1875) and Glasgow Polytechnic (founded 1972)
Times ranking: 71st equal *(1998 ranking: 71)*

Enquiries: Registry
Total students: 12,500
Male/female ratio: 42/58
Mature students: 32%
Overseas students: 3%

Main subject areas: business; engineering and construction; health; management and social sciences; science. Diploma courses are also offered.

Teaching quality ratings 1993-98
Rated excellent: chemistry; physiotherapy.
Highly satisfactory: biology; cellular biology; consumer studies; finance and accounting; mathematics and statistics; mass communications; nursing; nutrition and dietetics; occupational therapy; physics; psychology; social work; sociology.

The loss, in 1997, of its third principal following the announcement of a Funding Council inquiry into the university's management was a setback

Glasgow Caledonian could have done without. Dramatic expansion had put facilities under strain, but the estate was improving, as were teaching ratings. The inquiry cleared the university of academic malpractice, after allegations that examination results has been falsified, but was still critical of the way Caledonian was run.

It has been a difficult start for the new, merged institution which wanted to called itself The Queen's University, Glasgow. Objections from Queen's in Belfast meant a long hiatus over a title. In the end, the institution became the only university to have its name determined by the students and staff. A ballot in December 1992 produced the name Caledonian from four possibilities acceptable to the authorities.

There are three sites: City, adjoining Glasgow's Queen Street and central bus stations; Park, in the tree-lined West End; and the more outlying Southbrae, housing the health faculty opened by Princess Diana in 1991 and where the health facilities are among the most extensive in Britain. These have been further improved by an occupational health unit at the City campus, and research laboratories and a podiatry department at the Southern General Hospital. A £17-million Faculty of Health, including a training hospital wing, opened in 1998 making the university the third-biggest in Scotland.

Chemistry was given a top rating from the Funding Council for teaching and a variety of other sciences and social sciences have also scored well. Civil engineering, however, had to follow a council-imposed action plan after failing the quality check. Degrees are strongly vocational, and are complemented by a range of professional courses. A high proportion of the students are on part-time or sandwich courses. Among the full-time programmes, the unique BA in risk management is especially popular. The polytechnic pioneered credit accumulation and transfer in Scotland, and the scheme is still the country's largest, covering the full range of courses. The fully modular system and two-semester year has expanded this flexibility.

Links with Europe are developing from a strong base in the two partner institutions, both of which offer courses taught partly abroad. There are three affiliate colleges within Glasgow providing linked entry to the university.

Queen's had a strong majority of women among its students, but the proportion of women to men is now more balanced. Residential accommodation is limited, despite the addition of 320 places in self-catering flats, so it is just as well that 80 per cent of the students live at home, as this enables the university to accommodate a high proportion of first-years from farther afield. Sports facilities have improved with the opening of a new sports centre, and a new union bar and disco have also featured in a £38 million programme of building projects launched to cope with expansion. The main library was also on the list, catering facilities have been upgraded and extended and a financial services centre added. Services for disabled students have also been upgraded.

UNIVERSITY OF GREENWICH
Wellington Street, Woolwich, London SE18 6PF (tel. 0800-005006)

University status 1992, previously Thames Polytechnic
Times ranking: 75th equal *(1998 ranking: 72)*

Enquiries: Course enquiries officer
Total students: 11,700
Male/female ratio: 51/49
Mature students: 60%
Overseas students: 5%

Main subject areas: built environment; business; education; health and community studies; science and technology; social sciences and humanities. Also a wide range of certificate and diploma courses.

Teaching quality ratings
Rated excellent 1993-95: architecture; environmental studies.
April 1995-97: town and country planning 24; sociology 23; communication and media studies 22; building 21; civil engineering 21.

Having straggled across south London in polytechnic days, the new university is now even more dispersed. There are no fewer than six separate campuses, in the Docklands and Kent, as well as in its traditional base in southeast London. The acquisition of part of the Royal Naval College in Greenwich proper should enable some rationalisation. Previous growth, achieved by absorbing a number of colleges of art and education in and around London, has left the university with a wider range of courses and more accommodation than many of the new universities. It is one of the few to guarantee a residential place for first-years and now has some 2,500 beds.

Although an imaginative deal with the local council has ensured that the university remains rooted in the London Borough of Greenwich, recent expansion is focused on the populous county of Kent, which has only one university of its own. In 1996 Greenwich took over the Natural Resources Institute at Chatham, which specialises in overseas aid. Courses in the built environment are based at Dartford, while those in earth sciences have moved to Chatham. There was once talk of a Continental base, and the university now hopes to attract business through the Channel Tunnel. The sites include Roehampton in west London and Woolwich in the east. The new student village on the Avery Hill campus, built around an impressive Victorian mansion, forms a focal point for student life. Among the largest teacher training centres in the country, Avery Hill is one of the few to offer primary, secondary and further education courses.

The university has strong links with European institutions. There are formal exchange arrangements with universities or colleges in France, Germany, Greece, Ireland and Spain. There are also several associated colleges, mostly in Kent, which teach Greenwich courses.

As a polytechnic, Thames was highly rated for architecture, engineering and technology, science and education. Architecture and environmental sciences were assessed as excellent in the first teaching assessments, and a near-maximum score for sociology has led a clutch of good ratings under the new system. Recent innovations include BScs in multimedia technology and media production, both taught at South East Essex College in Southend. Courses in exercise physiology and nutrition and a BA in heritage management have been added to the main university portfolio.

There are libraries and bars on all sites. The students' union operates on five. Sports facilities are widely spread but comprehensive. The Dartford campus used to house a physical education college. At Woolwich, there is access to a dry ski slope. Student accommodation is spread between Avery Hill (which will eventually have 2,000 places), Dartford, Roehampton, Woolwich and the Medway towns. As in most multi-site institutions, the facilities vary according to the subject chosen.

HERIOT-WATT UNIVERSITY
Edinburgh EH14 4AS (tel. 0131-449 5111)

Founded 1821, royal charter 1966
Times ranking: 42 *(1998 ranking: 45)*

Enquiries: Admissions officer
Total students: 4,400
Male/female ratio: 67/33
Mature students: 22%
Overseas students: 13%

Main subject areas: art and design; education; engineering; economic and social studies; environmental studies; science; textiles.

Teaching quality ratings 1993-98
Rated excellent: electrical and electronic engineering.
Rated highly satisfactory: cellular biology; chemistry; civil engineering; computer studies; finance and accounting; mathematics and statistics; mechanical engineering; physics.
From 1998: chemical engineering 19.

Although best known outside the academic community for its degree in brewing and distilling, Heriot-Watt has a variety of such vocational programmes, as well as more conventional degrees, offshore engineering and actuarial mathematics and statistics among them. Petroleum engineering is the top-rated department for research, while electrical and electronic engineering was the first course to achieve the maximum score for teaching.

The range of subjects has been extended by the addition of Moray House College of Education, Edinburgh College of Art and the Galashiels-based Scottish College of Textiles. Science, engineering, economic and social studies are located on a single parkland campus at Riccarton, six miles from the centre of Edinburgh. The Riccarton campus which has seen investment totalling £100 million during the 1990s, contains half of the 2,300 residential places, including a 250-bed hall with en-suite facilities in every room. Accommodation is guaranteed to all first-years from outside Edinburgh as long as they apply by early September.

Heriot-Watt is technologically based, with business and language courses complementing its strengths in science and engineering. The combination is fitting for a university which commemorates James Watt, pioneer of steam power and George Heriot, financier to King James VI. The university has just completed the move to fully modular degrees, although it has kept a traditional three-term structure.

More than a third of the students come from outside Scotland, including 13 per cent from overseas. Despite some financial difficulties, the university has been expanding. It received substantial increases in its teaching budget recently and has a healthy income from research. The large and growing commercial research park at Riccarton was the first of its type in Europe.

Heriot-Watt has also been a leader in the use of information technology for teaching, harnessing the most advanced computing facilities to allow students to work at their own pace. A huge research and development programme with the computer giant Digital has smoothed the way.

Students praise the extensive sports facilities and the modern union at Riccarton. They have also enjoyed among the best employment prospects of all the universities in recent years. The campus is far enough from the city centre to be the inevitable centre of social life.

UNIVERSITY OF HERTFORDSHIRE
College Lane, Hatfield, Herts (tel. 01707-28400)

University status 1992, formerly Hatfield Polytechnic
Times ranking: 83rd equal *(1998 ranking: 86)*

Enquiries: Admissions office
Total students: 12,300
Male/female ratio: 51/49
Mature students: 40%
Overseas students: 8%

Main subject areas: business; education; engineering; health and human sciences; humanities; information sciences; natural sciences. Certificate and diploma courses also offered in most areas.

Teaching quality ratings
Rated excellent 1993-95: environmental studies.
April 1995-97: electrical and electronic engineering 20; general engineering 20; linguistics 20; building 19; civil engineering 18; sociology 17; modern languages 16; drama, dance and cinematics 15.

One of the few genuinely rural universities, Hertfordshire has four spacious sites, as well as an observatory and biology field-station. The main campus is in Hatfield, there is a business school at Hertford, while humanities and education are based at Wall Hall, near Watford, and law in St Albans. Art and design recently moved into the former British Aerospace premises in Hatfield.

As a result, many students have to commute from the surrounding towns and villages, and Hertfordshire runs the most extensive university bus network in Britain to help them do so. First year students who confirm their acceptance of a place by the end of August take priority in the allocation of on-site accommodation. There are no distance restrictions. Nearly all the rest of the students can be accommodated in university-controlled rooms in the private sector. Some rooms are adapted for the disabled and all sites have wheelchair facilities.

Hatfield Polytechnic's reputation was built on engineering, science and computer science. However, arts and humanities have grown substantially, and there are now 2,000 health-care students. European links are a speciality. Exchange programmes operate with many other universities and colleges. A credit-transfer scheme allows experience at other institutions to count towards a degree.

Courses are modular, giving a degree of flexibility that especially suits those students over 25 (almost a third of the student body), many of whom are taking a career break. Half the undergraduates study a language option, and they are encouraged to take 'free choice' courses in subjects outside their degree programmes, which can contribute to their final results. The university also has a well-developed sandwich course system. Half of the full-time students include work placements in their degrees, and the close links with employers have brought in valuable research and consultancy contracts.

Hertfordshire's academics have always been strong on research, particularly in areas such as medical electronics. Results in the last research assessment exercise were mixed, but physics and computer science did well to achieve a grade 4 (out of 5). Higher education's largest learning resources centre (with 1,600 study spaces and 800 computer workstations) has recently opened at Hatfield to cope with a 30 per cent expansion over the last five years. There are similar centres at each of the other campuses, though on a smaller scale. Sports and student union facilities are good and you can use facilities on any campus, though you will be based at just one academically. Students value the university's proximity to London, but some find the immediate surroundings quieter than they would like.

UNIVERSITY OF HUDDERSFIELD
Queensgate, Huddersfield HD1 3DH (tel. 01484-422288)

University status 1992, formerly Huddersfield Polytechnic
Times ranking: 78 *(1998 ranking: 83)*

Enquiries: Assistant registrar (admissions)

Total students: 11,200
Male/female ratio: 51/49
Mature students: 29%
Overseas students: 1%

Main subject areas: accountancy; applied sciences; business; computing; design technology; education; human and health sciences; humanities; law; management studies; mathematics; music. Also a wide range of certificate and diploma courses.

Teaching quality ratings
Rated excellent 1993-95: music; social work.
April 1995-97: food science 20; media studies 18; drama, dance and cinematics 17; modern languages 15.

Huddersfield has made a fresh start under a new vice-chancellor following a torrid period in which the previous management attracted highly public criticism from within the university and further afield. Normal service has been resumed since the departure of Professor Kenneth Durrands, who had been at the helm since polytechnic status arrived in 1970.

A tradition of vocational education dates back to 1841, and the university has a long-established reputation in textile design and engineering. But there are less obvious gems, such as music and social work, both of which were rated as excellent for teaching and scored a creditable grade 4 (out of 5) for research. Many arts courses, which now attract the majority of students, have a vocational slant. Politics, for example, includes a six-week work placement. A third of the students take sandwich courses, and most have some element of work experience. Another third are part-timers. Most courses are now included in a modular scheme, which has broadened the range of options available. Six modules are taken and assessed in each semester.

The main campus is on a cramped site near the centre of Huddersfield, with teacher training and the International Office two miles away. Huddersfield is one of only four centres training teachers for further education. Other education courses specialise in craft, design and technology, and retraining mature students with business experience to teach business studies in secondary schools.

Canalside, a refurbished mill complex, has eased the pressure on the main Queensgate campus, providing teaching and administration space for mathematics and computing. A student village (Storthes Hall Park), with accommodation for 1,500 on an 366-acre site, opened in September 1996. It is five miles from the main campus but has its own shuttle bus service. Expansion has now slowed after reaching 13 per cent a year earlier in the decade, though more building is planned. Among the new university's first projects was the provision of a new students' union, which opened in 1993. The development has split the union in two, but provided much-needed additional catering facilities.

The student village has eased growing accommodation problems. There are now more than 2,000 hall places, many within easy walking distance of lectures, but the private housing market is limited, if relatively cheap. First-years have priority for university accommodation, but there is still only room for about half of them. Some others are housed by the council.

Town and gown relations are good, and students like the university's communal atmosphere. Concerns over the pressure on space have eased, although some teaching groups are still large. The completion rate for undergraduates starting out at Huddersfield is among the highest in the country.

UNIVERSITY OF HULL
Hull HU6 7RX (tel. 01482-346311)

Founded 1928, royal charter 1954
Times ranking: 33rd equal *(1998 ranking: 31)*

Enquiries: Assistant registrar (admissions)
Total students: 9,500
Male/female ratio: 50/50
Mature students: 11%
Overseas students: 7%

Main subject areas: arts; education (postgraduate only); engineering; law; mathematics; science; social sciences; technology.

Teaching quality ratings
Rated excellent 1993-95: chemistry; history; social policy; social work.
April 1995-97: drama 24; Iberian languages 24; American studies 23; Italian 22; French 21; German; 21; Dutch 20; sociology 20; Scandinavian 19.

After 20 years with no new academic buildings, Hull has begun to redevelop its 94-acre campus. Although the university is still not large by modern standards, with less than 14,000 students, buildings are being used beyond their intended capacity. A clutch of new buildings and extensions will ease the pressure on teaching space and make room for 2,000 more students. The campus, with its art gallery and well-stocked and highly automated library, is less than three miles from the centre of Hull. Although neither would be considered fashionable, both the university and the city inspire strong loyalty among students. As Philip Larkin, once the university librarian, said: 'People are slow to leave, quick to return.'

One reason is the modest cost of living. Hall fees are among the lowest in the traditional universities, and private accommodation is even cheaper. First-years are guaranteed one of 4,200 residential places, 900 of which are in private housing leased through the university. More than half of all full-time students can be accommodated. The most modern halls of residence have been built with an eye to the conference market and its rooms have access to the university's computer network. None is more then ten minutes' walk from the main campus.

Strength in politics is reflected in 12 graduates in the House of Commons, Euromindedness in the fact that every EU language except Greek can be taken at degree level. Iberian languages achieved maximum points in the teaching assessment, as did drama. The Queen's Anniversary Prize was won for Social Work, which has also been rated excellent for teaching. History, another top-rated teaching department, recorded the best score in an otherwise unspectacular research assessment.

The university has always tried to maintain a roughly equal balance between science and technology and the arts and social sciences in the belief that this promotes a harmonious atmosphere. In the absence of a traditional medical school, the university is collaborating with the local health authority to develop a postgraduate school with nine departments. The new School of Health opened in 1996 and a Postgraduate Medical School a year earlier.

Semesters were introduced in 1995 to accommodate the modular course structure. Full details are contained in the compact prospectus, which is also available over the internet. An Institute for Learning was established in 1997 to try to put research findings into practice. There is a particular focus on continuing education and lifelong learning, as well as a development centre producing training courses for university lecturers.

First-class degrees are hard to come by, but drop-out rates are low. A refurbished students' union, which recently acquired a £1 million extension, and a new health-and-fitness centre have added to the recreational facilities.

UNIVERSITY OF KEELE
Staffordshire ST5 5BG (tel. 01782-621111)

Founded 1949 (as University College of North Staffordshire)
Times ranking: 41 *(1998 ranking: 39th equal)*

Enquiries: Admissions office
Total students: 7,900
Male/female ratio: 50/50
Mature students: 20%
Overseas students: 9%

Main subject areas: computational, mathematical and neuro-sciences; earth sciences; health studies; humanities, history and American studies; management and economics; political and social sciences; resource management; science and engineering.

Teaching quality ratings
Rated excellent 1993-95: music; social work.
April 1995-97: American studies 24; sociology 22; French 20; Russian 20; German 19.

The breadth of Keele's courses has always been its biggest selling point. Nine out of 10 undergraduates are on dual honours programmes and about a quarter take four-year degrees with a general foundation year. All students combine two main subjects with a subsidiary from the other side of the arts/science divide for the first year, specialising only in year two. Most combinations provide the opportunity of a semester abroad, at one of Keele's many partner universities. The aim is for a quarter of all undergraduates to do so by 2000. American studies, international relations and the many dual honours degrees – especially those featuring politics and music – are among the university's strengths. Science subjects have been improving, as the university demonstrated by attracting two top scientists from ICI to run the inorganic chemistry and materials science group.

All courses at Keele are now modular, and the traditional academic year has been replaced by two 15-week semesters, with breaks at Christmas and Easter. The university is committed to ensuring that there is at least one member of staff for every 15 students throughout the period of expansion, a much more generous ratio than is expected in the new universities.

Keele has resisted pressure to concentrate on teaching, rather than research, with the notable exception of general engineering, although research ratings are mostly modest. To head-off funding council worries the postgraduate population tripled in five years as the number of undergraduates doubled. The policy seems to have worked, with external research income growing fast. The university topped a funding council 'worry list' in 1990 but is now out of the red and expanding.

Student numbers rose by 75 per cent in five years although Keele is still not large by modern university standards, with new departments of visual arts, physiotherapy, and nursing and midwifery. But the 617 acres of scenic campus can take many more. Plans are under way for major development of the campus, starting with an arts complex. A relatively small student body has had its advantages, but has limited the variety of courses Keele has been able to offer and restricted the size of research groups. Its objective is to be the leading interdisciplinary university in Britain.

Keele also expects to continue accommodating at least 75 per cent of its full-time students on campus, guaranteeing residential places for all first-years. Students have criticised the standard and size of the library, but the university has promised improvements.

UNIVERSITY OF KENT AT CANTERBURY
Canterbury CT2 7NZ (tel. 01227-764000)

Royal charter 1965
Times ranking: 47*(1998 ranking: 49)*

Enquiries: Admissions office
Total students: 8,200
Male/female ratio: 50/50
Mature students: 22%
Overseas students: 21%

Main subject areas: humanities; information technology; management science; natural sciences; social sciences. Also postgraduate medical studies.

Teaching quality ratings
Rated excellent 1993-95: anthropology; computer science; social policy.
April 1995-97: drama and theatre studies 24; history of art 22; electrical and electronic engineering 21; sociology 21; modern languages 19.

Kent has been a pioneer among the traditional universities in the adoption of flexible degree programmes and a strong European emphasis. Interdisciplinary study is encouraged, and a number of courses include the option of a year elsewhere in Europe. Almost a quarter of the undergraduates take a language for at least part of their degree, and European studies are among the most popular subject combinations. The theme carries through into research as well as teaching. Like other universities established in the 1960s, Kent has always encouraged students to broaden their studies, allowing changes of specialism up to the end of the first year. The university also has a joint stake in 26 access courses throughout the county, allowing more than 500 students to upgrade their qualifications to degree entry standard.

The regional role was extended in 1997 with the establishment of the Bridge Warden's College in the old Chatham dockyard. The initial programme concentrates on short courses and Masters degrees, but the aim is to diversify as the area's needs become clear.

The university is generally stronger in the arts than sciences with two-thirds of the students taking arts or social sciences. Social policy and administration is the top-rated research area and is also assessed as excellent for teaching. Kent's research ratings were generally disappointing, but the combination of sociology and social anthropology has proved successful. Science subjects have not been neglected, and are being actively built up with engineering scoring well for teaching. Computer science is well regarded, having a top-rating from the first teaching assessment, while drama and theatre studies achieved a perfect score more recently. Degrees in the recently established business school are also in demand. Graduates of all disciplines have fared well in the employment market. A jobless rate below 4 per cent is particularly impressive from an arts-dominated university.

Students are attached to one of four colleges, which include lecture theatres as well as study bedrooms and social facilities. Nine out of 10 first-years, and more than half of all Kent's students, live in university-owned accommodation. All new students are offered a residential place. The modern campus, overlooking Canterbury, has a cosmopolitan feel, enhanced by the presence of Chaucer College, an independent Japanese university, which opened in 1992. Though Kent is particularly popular with American students, those from other countries are also well represented.

Students complain that the campus is often quiet at weekends, and worry about the effects of expansion on Canterbury's limited housing market. Although the university is building accommodation on a rolling basis and future increases in student numbers should be less dramatic than in recent years, the plans are for growth. A new students' centre, containing a nightclub and bars as well as shops and an employment service, will help cope with the influx. The development also takes the onus off the colleges to act as the main social centre.

KINGSTON UNIVERSITY
Penrhyn Road, Kingston upon Thames, Surrey KT1 2EE (tel. 0181-547 2000)

University status 1992, formerly Kingston Polytechnic
Times ranking: 65th equal *(1998 ranking: 67)*

Enquiries: Admissions officer
Total students: 11,000
Male/female ratio: 51/49
Mature students: 22%
Overseas students: 3%

Main subject areas: business; design; education; healthcare sciences; human sciences; law; science; technology. Certificate and diploma courses are also offered.

Teaching quality ratings
Rated excellent 1993-95: business and management; English; geology.
April 1995-97: electrical and electronic engineering 21; modern languages 21; sociology 21; history of art 20.

Big changes are under way at Kingston. A £13 million building programme made a start on the physical side and a Commission on the Future of the University is following up with academic recommendations. The senior management has been reorganised, more investment planned for research and more attention given to student information and advice. A £100,000 scholarship scheme has been launched and could be supplemented from a centenary appeal.The first phase of expansion of facilities at one of Kingston's four campuses was completed in 1997. The stylish development was much needed: although student numbers have steadied recently, a doubling in the early years of the decade had imposed inevitable strains. The new buildings on the 40-acre Kingston Hill site are primarily for 1,000 healthcare students, but a 60 per cent increase in library space coupled with the new high-tech learning resources centre will benefit all six faculties. The four sites in southwest London are linked by an unusually extensive, 700-terminal computer network. Two of the four are close to Kingston town centre, while Kingston Hill's health and business students are two miles away. A new technology block at Roehampton Vale has replaced teaching accommodation once used to build Sopwith Camels and Hawker Hurricanes.

Kingston's attempt to break the traditional universities' domination of the research rankings has not been particularly successful, with art and design the highest-placed area. But teaching ratings have been good, with business, geology and English leading the way. Education was an exception, with a poor report on the small primary course endangering the future of the much larger secondary provision for a time.

Private research income is healthy, with all staff encouraged to extend their interests beyond teaching. The business school has been especially successful. The Small Business Unit, for example, has won formal recognition as a national centre of excellence. Other prime teaching areas include design, technology and music, which are run in collaboration with the Gateway School of Recording and Music Technology. Kingston is also a world leader in GIS – geographical information systems.

The number of hall places has doubled to more than 2,000 in the last four years, enabling Kingston for the first time to guarantee first-years accommodation. Another 650 students benefit from a university scheme to sub-let private flats and houses, controlling rents in an otherwise notoriously high-priced area.

Sports facilities are adequate, and lectures are not held on Wednesday afternoons to encourage students to make use of them. The main students' union is lively, and there are branches on the other sites. The university claims to have some of the safest campuses in Britain following the introduction of extra security measures. Most students like the university's location on the fringe of London, but complaints about the high cost of living are common.

UNIVERSITY OF LANCASTER
University House, Lancaster LA1 4YW (tel. 01524-592028)

Royal charter 1964
Times ranking: 14 *(1998 ranking: 16)*

Enquiries: Admissions office
Total students: 8,300
Male/female ratio: 48/52
Mature students: 27%
Overseas students: 7%

Main subject areas: engineering; humanities; management; science; social sciences.

Teaching quality ratings
Rated excellent 1993-95: business and management; English; environmental studies; geography; history; music; social policy; social work.
April 1995-97: linguistics 23; sociology 21; French 20; Italian 20; German 19.

Lancaster is another of the campus universities of the 1960s which has always traded on its flexible degree structure. Unless they are training to be teachers, undergraduates take three subjects in their first year, and only select the one in which they intend to specialise at the end of it. Combined degree programmes, with 200 courses to choose from, are especially popular.

Some offer 'active learning courses', in which outside projects count towards final results.

Lancaster showed its strength in research in the 1996 assessment exercise, when seven of the 27 departments achieved maximum scores and 10 improved their ratings. Social work, which has more than a dozen applications for every place, attracted one of a number of glowing reports for teaching. Linguistics narrowly missed the maximum score. The large Management School, in new premises and with an arm in Prague, was judged the best in Britain for research in accountancy and has also achieved an excellent rating for teaching. Of the other departments assessed so far, nine have reached the top category. The main cloud on the horizon is financial, with an official inquiry questioning the wisdom of a £35-million bond issue. The university plunged into debt in the middle of the decade and at one time faced a £16-million shortfall for 1999. Staff have accused Lancaster's management of complacency.

Almost a quarter of the entrants are mature students, a high proportion for a traditional university. An innovative scheme, subsequently developed in the polytechnics, allows adults to join courses through their local further education college. Provision for students with special needs won one of the first Queen's Anniversary Awards.

New residential accommodation, including some for single parents, allows Lancaster to house 5,000 of its students. Most are in one of the nine campus colleges, which take between 400 and 800 students each. All students and academic staff are attached to a college, whether or not they are residents. Non-scientific departments are also based in the colleges, but students are not matched to their host college's specialism.

First-years are guaranteed a residential place, but accommodation is becoming more of a problem for those who then move out, as most do. The opening of Pendle College helped and a new residence has already opened in Lancaster itself, three miles from the campus. A regular bus service connecting the campus to the city centre takes ten minutes. The university has been trying to cement its relationship with the city, basing continuing education and the Archaeology Unit there. Lancaster also has an outpost in the heart of the Lake District. Almost 700 students are enrolled at Charlotte Mason College at Ambleside, training to be primary school teachers. Outdoor studies are a speciality.

Even the main campus has the Lake District within easy reach, although some students find the university more isolated than they expected. There are few complaints about the facilities, however. The students' union lacks a building of its own but manages events at the Sugarhouse, the largest entertainments venue in Lancaster. The university is well equipped for sports and the 35 clubs are organised by the Athletic Union, part of the students' union.

UNIVERSITY OF LEEDS
Leeds LS2 9JT (tel. 0113-243 1751)

Founded 1874, royal charter 1904
Times ranking: 23 *(1998 ranking: 22nd equal)*

Enquiries: Taught courses office
Total students: 20,900
Male/female ratio: 52/48
Mature students: 8%
Overseas students: 7%

Main subject areas: full range of subjects in seven faculties: arts; economics and social studies; education (postgraduate only); engineering; law; medicine, dentistry and health; science.

Teaching quality ratings
Rated excellent 1993-95: chemistry; English; geography; geology; music.
April 1995-97: French 22; German 22; Iberian languages 22; Russian 20; sociology 20; chemical engineering 19; Italian 19; linguistics 17.

Always one of the big guns of the university system, Leeds now has more full-time students than any institution outside London. It is also among the most popular universities, thanks partly to its unusually wide range of degrees. Applicants have more than 500 undergraduate programmes to choose from. The university occupies a 140-acre site near the city centre and its Metropolitan counterpart. More than 1,100 academic staff teach over 21,000 students, with many more taking short courses.

Leeds has followed the fashion for modular courses, enabling its students to take full advantage of a growing range of interdisciplinary degrees as an alternative to traditional single honours. Communications, broadcasting studies, women's studies and international studies are among the options.

Mechanical engineering, food science, Italian and town planning were the subjects ranked most highly for research in 1996, when 40 per cent of the academics entered were in the top two categories. The large English department is also highly rated. Teaching ratings have generally been good. The impressive Brotherton Library, with over 2.5 million items, is one of the top university libraries. Students also have access to a particularly powerful computer network, with more than 1,300 terminals. Recent building has provided new premises for biological and biomolecular sciences.

Leeds is an enthusiastic participant in European exchange programmes, with some 100 Continental partners. One undergraduate in 10 takes a language course, and there is a free-standing language unit. There are also ten colleges and affiliated institutions in the Yorkshire area, for which separate applications are needed. Employment prospects, which took an unexpected dip early in the decade, have largely recovered. Leeds was the first of the traditional universities to introduce a careers education module into the general curriculum. The university has also introduced special facilities for deaf students, providing subtitles for lectures.

Residential accommodation has been added as the university has grown. First-year students are guaranteed one of the 6,500 places, and most then move into the relatively cheap private sector, assisted by an efficient accommodation service. The students' union is one of the biggest in Britain, and long famed as a venue for rock concerts. Sports facilities are also plentiful, although the playing fields are four miles away. Students like the broad mix of backgrounds within the university, which includes more than 1,000 from overseas, and value the good town/gown relationship that the city-centre location fosters.

LEEDS METROPOLITAN UNIVERSITY
Calverley Street, Leeds LS1 3HE (tel. 0113-283 2600)

University status 1992, formerly Leeds Polytechnic
Times ranking: 86*(1998 ranking: 84th equal)*

Enquiries: Course enquiries officer
Total students: 13,700
Male/female ratio: 51/49
Mature students: 49%
Overseas students: 2%

Main subject areas: business; cultural and educational studies; environment; health and social care; information and engineering systems. Also a full range of certificate and diploma courses.

Teaching quality ratings
Rated excellent 1993-95: none
April 1995-97: cinematics 22; media studies 19; modern languages 19; mechanical engineering 17.

The incorporation of a large further education college in Harrogate will hasten the transformation of Leeds Metropolitan into a "comprehensive" post-school institution, in which students will be able to take courses at all levels and progress through a network of qualifications. The move came as the university completed a complete review of its activities to prepare for the new century.

Always a popular choice among students - there are at least twoapplicants to every full and part-time place - its commitment to openaccess and emphasis on teaching, rather than research, have depressed its place in recent Times rankings The move to a modular, semester-based system, together with the adoption of the credit accumulation and transfer scheme has eased the way for part-time students, who now make up over half the university. Personal contacts with academic staff are being reserved mainly for seminar groups and small group teaching. The system is supported by libraries that, even before the new learning centre opens, are larger than normal among the new universities, with 2,300 study spaces, 500 of them wired up to electronic networks, and 500,000 books.

Hotel catering, sport and recreation, personnel management and environmental studies are all well regarded. Students are included on the committees that design and manage all courses.

The new university has two campuses in Leeds: the main site close to the city centre and Leeds University, and Beckett Park three miles away in 100 acres of park and woodlands. The latter boasts outstanding sports facilities and many of the university's residential places, as well as teaching accommodation for education, informatics, law and business. Over 7,000 students take part in some form of sporting activity. Only half of all first-years can be accommodated in university property, but a £17-million development has provided another 1,000 places. An accommodation agency run jointly with Leeds University has a large register of property, which is relatively cheap and plentiful.

Almost half the higher education students are over 21 at entry, many living at home, which eases some of the pressure on accommodation. Almost 40 per cent come from Yorkshire and Humberside. A minority are on conventional, full-time degrees because of the popularity of both sandwich and part-time courses, which in turn produce a good employment record. Students praise the level of social and leisure facilities. The students' union is large and active, while the physical education college which formed part of the polytechnic has left a legacy of success in sporting competition.

UNIVERSITY OF LEICESTER
University Road, Leicester LE1 7RH (tel. 0116-252 2295)

Founded 1918, royal charter 1957
Times ranking: 31st equal *(1998 ranking: 22nd equal)*

Enquiries: Admissions office
Total students: 10,400
Male/female ratio: 49/51
Mature students: 16%
Overseas students: 9%

Main subject areas: arts; education (postgraduate only); law; medicine; science; social science.

Teaching quality ratings
Rated excellent 1993-95: chemistry; English; history; law.
April 1995-97: German 21; general engineering 20; Italian 20; French 19; sociology 19.

Though Leicester celebrated its 80th anniversary in 1998, the university is only now approaching the size of most of its traditional counterparts, this despite growing by 60 per cent in recent years. There was even debate on a merger with nearby Loughborough University at the start of the 1990s, but all that remains of the venture is some collaboration in research. Growth in full time numbers has now halted for the moment but, with more than 5,000 on distance learning courses, undergraduates are now in a minority overall.

More departments reached the top rungs of the research ladder in the latest rankings, although only pharmacology achieved a 5-star rating. Chemistry, economic and social history, law, history and English were all rated excellent in the first teaching assessments. Leicester is also a leader in space science and hosts the National Space Science Centre after attracting a big grant from the Millennium Commission. The medical school, built in the 1970s, is the newest in the country and it is hoping to expand through a joint venture with Warwick University. The siting of a medically based interdisciplinary research centre at the university is a sign of the school's growing strength, while undergraduates are catered for in new facilities at the city's General Hospital.

Other than in clinical medicine, all teaching and most residential accommodation is concentrated in a leafy suburb little more than a mile from the city centre. The campus is a mixture of Georgian and modern architecture in sometimes uneasy combinations. Recent developments have included a new arts and social science centre. Computing facilities have been resited and modernised, providing 1,000 microcomputers and 750 workstations for student use. An audiovisual centre is also heavily used for teaching.

With almost 4,000 residential places at its disposal, the university is well able to guarantee accommodation to first-years, as long as they accept a place by the end of May. Some 40 per cent of undergraduates stay in university accommodation throughout their time at Leicester. Five of the six halls are in a complex at Oadby, two miles from the campus, to where there has a regular bus link. The main sports ground and sports hall are also at Oadby. Social facilities, both in the halls and on campus, are good and reasonably priced. The students' union, refurbished in 1995, includes a nightclub, The Asylum.

Leicester has an equal opportunities code for admissions, which has helped to raise the proportion of mature students. The university also boasts the prize-winning Richard Attenborough Centre for Disability and the Arts, which has a variety of specialist facilities. Only a minority of departments interview candidates as a matter of course, but those offered places are invited to visit.

UNIVERSITY OF LINCOLNSHIRE AND HUMBERSIDE
Cottingham Road, Hull HU6 7RT (tel. 01482-440550)

University status 1992. Humberside University until August 1996, previously Humberside Polytechnic
Times ranking: 97 *(1998 ranking: 95)*

Enquiries: Admissions office
Total students: 9,600
Male/female ratio: 50/50
Mature students: 57%
Overseas students: 8%

Main subject areas: art, architecture and design; business, engineering and information technology; business and management; food, fisheries and environmental studies; media and communications; policy studies; social and professional studies. Certificate and diploma courses also offered.

Teaching quality ratings
Rated excellent 1993-95: none.
April 1995-97: food science 20; media studies 17; sociology 16.

In perhaps the most dramatic transformation of any university in recent times, Humberside has not only opened Britain's newest campus, but has even given its new location pride of place in its title. The purpose-built campus near Lincoln station is an equal partner in the new, split-site institution, with courses disappearing from the university's at Grimsby in 1999. To make the most of contrasting locations 40 miles apart, the university is marketing its two sites separately: as the Humberside University campus and Lincoln University campus. The approach makes sense, since the big city of Hull will appeal to a different clientele to smaller Lincoln's more genteel image, and courses have been allotted accordingly. Hull will have the lion's share of the business courses, with their high proportion of part-time students, while Lincoln concentrates on social sciences.

The opening of the 40-acre waterfront campus in Lincoln, which attracted architectural as well as educational interest, represented the end of a saga. The cathedral city had been seeking a university presence for some time, and initially chose Nottingham Trent University to provide it. But the Conservative government's cap on student numbers stopped the deal going ahead. Humberside was able to capitalise by transferring existing places rather than expanding its existing sites.

Lincoln opened with criminology, health studies, management, humanities, international relations and tourism. Communications, law, economics and psychology were added in 1997. The university offers the luxury of one of the best computer-to-student ratios in the country: one for every 20 of them. There are 322 study bedrooms on the Lincoln campus, most en suite and with shared kitchens and on the doorstep of the main academic building. A warehouse conversion added another 200 places in Hull, producing one of the best accommodation records among the new universities.

The Lincoln development will accentuate the arts and social sciences bias already evident at Humberside although a £3 million science and research centre is on the way on the new campus. Engineering, technology, computing and information systems are available in Hull but the university is better known for business and design. Humberside has also pioneered European links, with more than 40 formal partnerships.

All students take the Effective Learning Programme, which uses computer packages backed up by weekly seminars to develop necessary study skills and produce a detailed portfolio of all their work. Research into teaching and learning methods is aided by a £1-million fund given by BP, with which the university has close relations. The process will be smoother for the completion of a £1.5-million broad-band telecommunications network linking the campuses.

Humberside recorded an unexpectedly low finish in 1998's *Times* league table, partly because of preparations for the Lincoln development. But it won a Charter Mark for exceptional service and has been among the leading new universities in previous years. The new-style university can be expected to climb the table in the next few years. Student facilities are sparse as yet in Lincoln, although the city is beginning to adapt to its new visitors. In Hull they are well-established and supplemented by neighbouring Hull University's.

UNIVERSITY OF LIVERPOOL
Liverpool L69 3BX (tel. 0151-794 5928)

Founded 1881
Times ranking: 38th equal*(1998 ranking: 32)*

Enquiries: Faculty admissions office
Total students: 13,700
Male/female ratio: 51/49
Mature students: 17%
Overseas students: 9%

Main subject areas: full range of degree courses in seven faculties: arts; engineering; law; medicine and dentistry; science; social and environmental studies; veterinary science.

Teaching quality ratings
Rated excellent 1993-95: English; geology; history; law.
April 1995-97: French 22; Iberian languages 21; sociology 21; German 19.

The original redbrick university, Liverpool has added to a well-established reputation for research with a series of good teaching reports. It has been among the top dozen recipients of research council funds for two decades, with outside income increasing dramatically in recent years. Expansion by 50 per cent in five years has also brought more money for teaching, much of which has been invested in new educational technology. The library has been extended recently and the former Liverpool Royal Infirmary converted into extra teaching accommodation to cope with the influx. Almost 2,000 students are postgraduates, but recent expansion has been concentrated on first degrees.

Excellent ratings for law, history, geology, economic and social history and English established a sound foundation in the teaching assessments. Music, physiology and materials science are the top-rated research departments. The university prides itself on its strength across the board, with one in five of the academics entered for the research assessment placed in one of the top two categories. Interdisciplinary courses have been expanded, introducing engineering with management and European studies, for example, and geophysics, mathematics and information studies.

Undergraduate courses are divided into eight units per two-semester year. Many courses have examinations at the end of each semester. The traditional three terms have survived for the moment, but consideration is being given to a more radical reconstruction in the future. Liverpool was among the first of the traditional universities to run access courses for adults without traditional academic qualifications. A relatively high proportion of undergraduates for a traditional university are over 21 at entry, and the trend is expected to continue.

The university precinct, which includes the large and well-equipped guild of students, is only half a mile up the hill from the city centre. Recent developments have included a new student services centre, which includes specialist advice on money matters. The conversion of the former Liverpool Royal Infirmary will provide new facilities for health care, pharmacy and technology transfer. Eight halls of residence, on two parkland sites two and a half miles from the university, contain 2,300 places. The university also has room for another 1,250 students in self-catering flats closer to hand. First-years who accept a place by the end of May are guaranteed accommodation. Excellent sports facilities have been enhanced by the opening of an impressive new sports centre, although there is a nominal charge for their use. There are three sports grounds and an outdoor activities centre in Snowdonia. Both the university and the city have a loyal following among students, a state of affairs not wasted on the recruiters: the Beatles and both Liverpool's football teams feature on the first page of the prospectus.

LIVERPOOL JOHN MOORES UNIVERSITY
Rodney House, 70 Mount Pleasant, Liverpool L3 5UX (tel. 0151-231 2121)

University status 1992, formerly Liverpool Polytechnic
Times ranking: 74 *(1998 ranking: 77)*

Enquiries: Admissions
Total students: 14,700
Male/female ratio: 50/50
Mature students: 34%
Overseas students: 8%

Main subject areas: art, media and design; built environment; business; education and community studies; engineering and technology management; information science and technology; law; natural sciences and health sciences; social science; social work and social policy. Diploma courses are also offered.

Teaching quality ratings
Rated excellent: none.
April 1995-97: media studies 22; modern languages 19; sociology 18; town planning 18.

Naming itself after a football pools millionaire was just the start for one of the most innovative of the new universities. Among other initiatives was the launching of Britain's first student charter, which has become a template for others. At the same time, and this before before university status had even been confirmed, JMU announced an ambitious plan to turn itself, over 10 years and at a cost of £80 million, into a huge, futuristic, multi-media institution. Two learning resource centres, serving different academic areas, and a media centre have seen the project largely completed. Among the new initiatives are the replacement of many lectures by computer-based teaching methods, thus freeing teaching staff for face-to-face tutorials. A 65 per cent increase in six years has already taken student numbers to 20,000, including part-timers.

It's a far cry from the recent past. Under local authority control in the dim, dark days of Militant, the polytechnic once came to the brink of closure. Perhaps in compensation, since gaining independence JMU has seemed to make a point of celebrating its escape with a series of showy occasions to mark new developments. Even before university status, the mission statement opened with a desire to be a 'prestigious' as well as progressive institution. There is, however, no intention of abandoning the range of diploma courses which have traditionally supplemented the largely vocational degree programmes. The new university, which is mainly concentrated in an area between the city's two cathedrals, is already one of Britain's biggest. The IM Marsh campus, once a teacher training college, is three miles away in the suburbs. JMU has retained a local commitment, with more than 60 per cent of the students drawn from the Merseyside area. A new 'learning federation' embraces four further education colleges, in St Helen's, Southport and Liverpool itself. There is also a partnership agreement with Dublin Business School, Ireland's largest independent business college.

A growing research reputation is a source of particular pride, and is reflected in an unusually large number of postgraduates for a new university. JMU was one of the few new universities to achieve two grade 5s in the 1996 research rankings. General engineering and sports science also had a clutch of good scores. Media studies has produced the best teaching score by far. All courses are now fully modular.

University-owned residential accommodation is scarce for the size of institution, although refurbishment of the newly acquired North Western Hall has now been completed. There are about 2,000 places in halls or self-catering flats. First-years who live more than 25 miles from Liverpool are given priority, but cannot be guaranteed a place. Private accommodation is plentiful and cheap, but students may find themselves travelling up to eight miles to lectures. The Liverpool Student Homes (LSM) run jointly by Liverpool John Moores University and the University of Liverpool, organises 'House hunting receptions' after A level results come out to help students find houses. The students' union is lively, with the refurbished Cooler bar and nightclub the centrepiece, open until at least 1am six nights a week.

UNIVERSITY OF LONDON
Senate House, Malet Street, London WC1E 7HU (tel. 0171-636 8000)

Founded 1836

Enquiries: To individual colleges, institutes or schools
Total students: 89,500
Male/female ratio: 49/51
Mature students: 32%
Overseas students: 15%

The federal university is Britain's biggest by far, even if some of the most prestigious members have considered going their own way. Indeed its colleges and institutes have already seen their autonomy increased considerably. They are bound together by the London degree, which enjoys a high reputation worldwide. The colleges are responsible both for the university's academic strength and its apparently precarious financial position.

London students have access to some joint residential accommodation, sporting facilities and the University of London Union. But most identify with their college, which is their social and academic base.

Colleges not listed separately but admitting undergraduates:
Birkbeck College, Malet Street, London WC1E 7HX (tel. 0171-580 6622). 12,400 students, mainly part-time. Apply direct, not through UCAS.
Charing Cross and Westminster Medical School, The Reynolds Building, St Dunstan's Road, London W6 8RP (tel. 0181-846 7202). Degrees in medicine and BSc. 848 students.
Courtauld Institute of Art, Somerset House, Strand, London WC2R 0RN (tel. 0171-873 2645). History of art degree. 115 undergraduates.
Heythrop College, Kensington Square, London W8 5HQ (tel. 0171-795 6600). Theological college. 130 undergraduates.
Imperial College School of Medicine at St Mary's, Norfolk Place, Paddington, London W2 1PG (tel. 0171-723 1252). Degrees in medicine and BSc. 631 students.
Jews' College, Albert Road, London NW4 2SJ (tel. 0181-203 6427). Degree in Jewish studies. 25 undergraduates.
Royal Academy of Music, Marylebone Road, London NW1 5HT (tel. 0171-935 5461). Music degree. 530 students.
Royal College of Music, Prince Consort Road, London SW7 2BS (tel. 0171-589 3643). Music degree. 580 students.
Royal Free Hospital School of Medicine, Rowland Hill Street, London NW3 2PF (tel. 0171-794 0500). Medical degree. 800 students.
Royal Veterinary College, Royal College Street, London NW1 0TU (tel. 0171-468 5000). Degrees in veterinary medicine and BSc. 600 students.
St Bartholomew's and the Royal London School of Medicine and Dentistry, Turner Street, London E1 2AD (tel. 0171-377 7611). Degrees in medicine and dentistry. 1,100 students.
St George's Hospital Medical School, Cranmer Terrace, London SW17

ORE (tel. 0181-672 9944). Degrees in medicine and BSc. 1,100 students.
School of Pharmacy, 29-39 Brunswick Square, London WC1N 1AX (tel.
0171-753 5800). Degrees in pharmacy and toxicology. 780 students.
School of Slavonic and East European Studies, London WC1E
7HU (tel. 0171-637 4934). Arts degrees only. 332 undergraduates.
United Medical and Dental Schools (Guy's and St Thomas's),
Lambeth Palace Road, London SE1 7EH (tel. 0171-928 9292). Degrees in
medicine, dentistry and BSc. 2,400 students.
Wye College, Ashford, Kent TN25 5AH (tel. 01233 812401). Degrees in
agriculture, rural development and environmental studies. 1,710 students.

GOLDSMITHS' COLLEGE
**Lewisham Way, New Cross, London SE14 6NW (tel. 0171-919
7971)**

Founded 1891, royal charter 1990
Times ranking: 50th *(1998 ranking: 51st equal)*

Enquiries: Registry
Total students: 5,100
Male/female ratio: 33/67
Mature students: 47%
Overseas students: 15%

Main subject areas: anthropology; design; drama; education; English;
European languages; history; mathematical and computing sciences;
media studies; music; professional and community education; psychology;
social studies; sociology; visual art.

Teaching quality ratings
Rated excellent 1993-95: music
April 1995-98: Drama, dance and cinematics 22; media studies 22;
sociology 21; history of art 19; modern languages 17.

London University's newest college has a long history of community-based
courses, mainly in education and the arts. Evening classes are still as popular
as the conventional degree courses. A tradition of providing educational
opportunities for women is now reflected in the largest proportion of
female students in the British university system – almost two-thirds.

Determinedly integrated into its southeast London locality, the college
precincts have a cosmopolitan character. More than half of all students are
over 21 on entry, many come from the area's ethnic minorities, and there is
a growing proportion of overseas students. Goldsmiths' has also become
highly fashionable among the trendier elements of the new left, especially
since the arrival of political biographer Ben Pimlott as Warden. The older
premises have been likened to a grammar school, with their long corridors
of classrooms. But new building has included a purpose-built library with

longer opening hours than those of many other university libraries, and a nearby site is now being developed.

Goldsmiths' has a well-established reputation in the visual arts, numbering Graham Sutherland and Mary Quant among its alumni over the years. Education, which caters mainly for primary teachers, is also well regarded. A spectacular performance in the 1996 research rankings saw design studies and visual arts rated internationally outstanding, with anthropology, music and sociology in the next highest category. Their successes promise to transform the financial position of the college, which was already building a high-tech information services centre. Courses are fully modular and are included in the Credit Accumulation and Transfer Scheme, allowing experience gained at other institutes to count towards a degree.

Nine halls of residence accommodate all first-years from outside London. The college now has more than 1,000 residential places, the majority within walking distance, and the New Cross area is cheaper than many in the capital for those who prefer, or have, to live out. The sports facilities which, in keeping with the college's philosophy, are open to the public, areadequate, with the main ground eight miles away in Sidcup, Kent. Social life revolves around a well-equipped, highly political students' union, which has a reputation for attracting up-and-coming rock bands.

IMPERIAL COLLEGE OF SCIENCE AND TECHNOLOGY
South Kensington, London SW7 2AZ (tel. 0171-589 5111)

Founded 1907
Times ranking: 2 *(1998 ranking: 3)*

Enquiries: Assistant registrar for admissions
Total students: 7,800
Male/female ratio: 71/29
Mature students: 15%
Overseas students: 22%

Main subject areas: aeronautics; biochemistry; biology; chemical engineering; chemistry; civil engineering; computing; earth resources and management; electrical and electronic engineering; environmental technology; geology; physics; mathematics; materials; mechanical engineering; medicine.

Teaching quality ratings
Rated excellent 1993-95: business and management; chemistry; computer science; geology.
April 1995-97: electrical and electronic engineering 24; materials science 24; general engineering 23; aeronautical engineering 22; chemical engineering 22; civil engineering 21.

After years of running Oxford close in *The Times* rankings, London's specialist science and engineering college has finally moved ahead and into second place in the table. Over 800 academic staff include Nobel prize-winners and 35 Fellows of the Royal Society. More than a quarter of the academics entered for the last research assessment exercise were in departments considered internationally outstanding and almost three-quarters were in one of the top two categories. Teaching scores have been up to the same high standard, with electrical and electronic engineering and materials science achieving maximum points. Imperial is not recommended for academic slouches, but tough entry requirements ensure that they are a rare breed in any case. There are eight applicants to every place and, on average, entrants in 1997 had better than an A and two Bs at A level.

Though Imperial has contemplated severing its already loose link with London University, the current rector, Sir Ron Oxburgh, has made it clear that the college will remain within the federation, where it already enjoys more autonomy than others in the university. However, 1997 did see the merging of the Imperial College School of Medicine with St Mary's and with the Charing Cross and Westminster medical schools. The National Heart and Lung Institute joined in August 1995. The school, with 200 undergraduate places, is one of the largest in the country. It has the status of a constituent college and handles its own admissions.

The college has been expanding its range of courses, such as the new MSci in physics with a year in Europe, which offer the opportunity of a year's study abroad. Imperial also operates exchange programmes with a variety of prestigious technological institutions on the Continent.

The campus, in the heart of South Kensington's museum district, is being expanded with the construction of a new biomedical sciences building and an extension to the library. More residential accommodation is also planned. The college already had almost 2,000 residential places, enough to guarantee accommodation for all first-years. Private housing is expensive, but second- and third-years can apply for one of 1,700 college-controlled rooms or for one of the newly built college flats in South Ealing about 10 miles away. Excellent indoor sports facilities are available on campus, but it is 15 miles to the outdoor pitches, served by coaches on Saturdays and Wednesday afternoons, when there are no lectures. There is also a boathouse at Putney. The students' union is well equipped and largely apolitical.

KING'S COLLEGE LONDON
The Strand, London WC2R 2LS (tel. 0171-836 5454)

Founded 1829
Times ranking: 17 *(1997 ranking: 17th equal)*

Enquiries: Registry
Total students: 10,800
Male/female ratio: 42/58
Mature students: 19%
Overseas students: 10%

Main subject areas: arts and music; education; engineering; law; life sciences; mathematics and physical sciences; medicine and dentistry; theology.

Teaching quality ratings
Rated excellent 1993-95: geography; history; law; music.
April 1995-97: Portuguese 23; Spanish 22; French 21; electrical and electronic engineering 20; German 20.

Following a merger with Chelsea College and Queen Elizabeth College, Kensington, King's is now the second largest of London's colleges. More than 60 departments offer over 200 degrees in a wide range of subjects. The merger partners' sites, in Kensington and Chelsea, are being phased out and replaced by a new complex on the south bank of the Thames. Medical subjects are the main growth point. Two nursing schools were amalgamated within the college to form the Nightingale Institute, which offers nursing qualifications, complementing the College's long-standing BSc in nursing studies, while the merger in summer 1998 of the United Medical Schools of Guy's and St Thomas's Hospitals will give King's one of the largest medical schools in Europe with 2,500 students training to become doctors or dentists. Another property deal will bring together the college's libraries at the former Public Record Office in Chancer Lane.

Residential places are more widely spread across London, but are sufficiently plentiful to allow many undergraduates two years in hall. A student village in Hampstead, opened five years ago, enables the college to guarantee accommodation for all first-years who accept places before the end of May. Residences opened in the last three years have brought the number of college places to more than 3,000, including 900 en-suite apartment rooms.

War studies, theology and classics, education, Greek and mechanical engineering are among the top-rated research subjects. More than a quarter of academics assessed for research were in such departments. History and music are in the top category for both teaching and research. Science students remain in the majority, however, and are now able to take some novel interdisciplinary combinations, such as chemistry and philosophy or French and mathematics. King's was an early convert to modular degrees, and also flirted with the possibility of two-year degrees during a turbulent period which saw the resignation of the previous principal. The two-year option was dropped, and the college has resumed more conventional expansion.

The strength of the college's academic ambition is clear from its mission statement, which includes the aim of having all teaching and research rated excellent by the start of the new century. King's is a solid bet for a good degree for those who can satisfy the demanding entry requirements. Every student is allocated a personal tutor, and much of the teaching is in small groups. Over 60 per cent are generally awarded a first or upper-second class degree. Students' union facilities are good and those for sport adequate, if distant for outdoor sports.

LONDON SCHOOL OF ECONOMICS AND POLITICAL SCIENCE
Houghton Street, London WC2A 2AE (tel. 0171-405 7686)

Founded 1895
Times ranking: 4 *(1998 ranking: 4)*

Enquiries: Undergraduate admissions office
Total students: 6,300
Male/female ratio: 58/42
Mature students: 24%
Overseas students: 48%

Main subject areas: accounting and finance; anthropology; economic history; economics; geography; government; industrial relations; international history; international relations; language studies; law; philosophy, logic and scientific method; social psychology; social policy and administration; sociology; statistics and mathematics.

Teaching quality ratings
Rated excellent 1993-95: anthropology; applied social work; management; history; law; social policy.
April 1995-98: media studies 22; sociology 20

As the LSE adjusts to a new director the school remains at something of a crossroads. The LSE has taken on a new lease of life under its latest director, signing up big-name social scientists from Oxford, Harvard, Yale and other top universities. Although most are visiting professors or on short-term appointments, the new blood is revitalising one of Britain's best-known seats of learning. The school is still anxious to increase student numbers, but a series of development plans have come to grief. Not only has the government put the brake on expansion nationally, but attempts to break out from the cramped site near London's Law Courts have so far been frustrated. The most ambitious – a bid for County Hall – was blocked by the last government, while the option of a move to Docklands was rejected by the school itself. The governors left themselves the option of shoring up the LSE's finances by charging students top-up fees but the Labour government's own scheme ensured that the plans were stillborn. Proposals to divide the institution into undergraduate and graduate schools have been dropped, but the school still wants to concentrate on masters degrees. The result may be to make the LSE even more difficult to get into: only Oxbridge has higher average entry scores. Already half the students are postgraduates, and the accent on research has seen income from this area treble in three years.

The school has the highest proportion of overseas students in the country, with the nationals of more than 100 countries taking up nearly half the places. Alumni are in influential positions all over the world, not forgetting Britain, where 30 sitting MPs are LSE graduates. Such achievements not only make the LSE one of the most prestigious institutions but give it an unusual degree of financial independence. Only 26 per cent of its income comes from the Higher Education Funding Council.

Areas of study range much more broadly than the school's name implies. Law, management and history are among the subjects top-rated for teaching, while research in economic history, economics, politics and social policy is internationally recognised. All achieved top ratings in the last research assessment exercise. Almost half the academics assessed for research were in top-rated departments, the highest proportion outside Oxford and Cambridge.

Most of the 2,100 residential places, which are enough to guarantee accommodation for all first-years, are within a mile of the school. The LSE has doubled its accommodation stock in three years, and now houses almost 40 per cent of its students. Those who rely on the private market must either travel long distances or scour one of the most expensive areas in the country. Like the teaching accommodation, the students' union and indoor sports facilities were designed for fewer people. The main sports ground is spacious enough, but takes 40 minutes to reach.

QUEEN MARY AND WESTFIELD COLLEGE
Mile End Road, London E1 4NS (tel. 0171-975 5511)

Founded1882 Westfield, 1887 Queen Mary, merged 1989
Times ranking: 28 *(1998 ranking: 27)*

Enquiries: Admissions office
Total students: 7,800
Male/female ratio: 56/44
Mature students: 19%
Overseas students: 17%

Main subject areas: arts; engineering; informatics and mathematical sciences; law; medicine; physical and biological sciences; social studies.

Teaching quality ratings
Rated excellent 1993-95: English, geography with environmental studies.
April 1995-97: modern languages 23; drama, dance and cinematics 21; electrical and electronic engineering 21; materials technology 20; general engineering 19.

The merger with St Bartholomew's Hospital and The London Hospital medical schools ushers in a new era for QMW, creating a broadly based institution of 8,000 students. The arts-based Westfield and the scientific Queen Mary came together in 1989, but it has taken time to mould the new college and overcome financial difficulties. Following the sale of Westfield's Hampstead site to King's College, QMW has been pouring money into the Mile End campus. A new Dental and Medical school opens in the year 2000 at Whitechapel. In addition to the library and students' union built in the 1980s, an arts building for 1,000 students opened in 1992 and there is a new building for basic medicine, which caters for pre-clinical students from the two teaching hospitals. Altogether £63 million has been spent on the campus in the last decade, transforming an otherwise uninspiring stretch of the East End. Student numbers are expected to continue to increase for some years. The college, already the fourth largest in London University, is one of the federation's five designated areas for expansion of the sciences. Concern that the absence of a university title put QMW at a disadvantage with prospective students led to talk of a breakaway, but no change is imminent.

Leading subjects include English, geography, aeronautical engineering, Hispanic studies and law, although no subject attracted a top rating in the last research rankings and only two departments out of eight were considered excellent for teaching in the first round of assessments. There is a well-established interest in outer space, with courses in astronomy and astrophysics. Encouragement for interdisciplinary study has continued through the combination of languages, the study of European institutions and a specialism in science or technology. Most degree courses are organised in units to offer maximum flexibility. The majority of students take at least one course in departments other than their own, some arts students even migrating to another college.

The college has expanded its catering and is adding to the 1,000 residential places on campus as part of the post-merger development plan. Another 700 students live a 30-minute tube journey away, and first-years from outside London are guaranteed rooms. There is a students' union building on campus and good sports facilities, although the main sports ground is several miles away in Essex.

ROYAL HOLLOWAY UNIVERSITY OF LONDON
Egham, Surrey TW20 0EX (tel. 01784-434455)

Founded 1849 Bedford College, 1886 Royal Holloway College, merged 1985
Times ranking: 26th equal *(1998 ranking: 30)*

Enquiries: Academic registrar
Total students: 5,300
Male/female ratio: 46/54
Mature students: 22%
Overseas students: 15%

Main subject areas: biochemistry; biology; classics; computer science; drama; economics; electronics; geography; geology; history; management; mathematics; modern languages; music; physics; psychology; social policy; social science; theatre and media arts.

Teaching quality ratings
Rated excellent 1993-95: geology; history.
April 1995-97: drama, dance and cinematics 23; French 21; Italian 21; sociology 21; German 19.

London University's 'campus in the country' occupies 120 acres of woodland between Windsor Castle and Heathrow. Classic Victoriana mixes with less distinguished modern architecture. The Founder's Building, modelled on a French chateau, is one of Britain's most remarkable university buildings. Both partners in the current college were originally for women only, their legacy producing a majority of female arts students. But, as one of the university's five designated centres of expansion for the sciences, the balance is gradually shifting. The college has an upmarket reputation and attracts a high proportion of students from the Home Counties. As a result, the campus can seem empty at weekends.

The top-rated departments are mainly on the arts side, with drama, dance and theatre studies achieving a near-perfect score in the official assessment of teaching quality. Although music and drama are the only starred departments for research, English, Italian, sociology and physics are also strong. History and geology led the way in the teaching assessments, which have produced a string of good results. All 19 departments encourage interdisciplinary work, which is facilitated by the modular course structure with examinations at least at the end of every year. Semesters have been introduced, running from the end of September to April, with a five-week 'examinations term' to follow. An Advanced Skills Programme, covering information technology, communication skills and foreign languages, further encourages breadth of study,.

The merger with Bedford College enabled Royal Holloway to upgrade its facilities with a £24-million building programme, which has since been extended. A new media arts building with TV studio and a well-appointed library have been opened recently. There are also new buildings for the earth sciences, life sciences, mathematics and computing, history and social policy. The students' union has also been given larger, modern premises, which are assured of heavy use given the rural setting.

Like other parts of London University, the college has had financial problems. A proposal to solve them by disposing of part of Thomas Holloway's valuable art collection met with stiff opposition and a challenge in the courts, but the eventual sale of a Turner seascape raised enough (£11 million) to provide for the upkeep of the Founder's Building with its 600 student beds. New halls of residence have brought the number of college places to more than 2,200. Every new student is guaranteed a place and about half of those in their final year can be accommodated, but private housing for the rest is scarce and expensive. Sports facilities are conveniently-placed and improving.

SCHOOL OF ORIENTAL AND AFRICAN STUDIES
Thornaugh Street, Russell Square, London WC1 0XG (tel. 0171 637 2388)

Times ranking: 6 *(not ranked separately in 1998)*

Enquiries: Admissions Office

Total students: 2,500

As the major national centre for the study of subjects relating to Asia and Africa, SOAS is renowned worldwide for having the highest concentration of scholars in these fields. Nationals from over 90 countries make up the student body, although over 80% of undergraduates are British.

Student recruitment generally is on the rise. An increase in postgraduates is expected to help SOAS address its financial deficit as it faces hard times financially, like many of Britain's universities. Numbers of research students continue to grow, attracted by the school's excellent record in teaching assessments, with art and archaeology, and African and Middle Eastern language rating particularly high. Almost two-thirds of those graduating in the last two years achieved firsts or upper second-class degrees.

Students do not have to concentrate exclusively on Oriental and African studies. SOAS students can choose to read degrees in familiar subjects, such as history or geography, but with a different area of emphasis from that in other universities. Nearly all students make use of the unique opportunities available for learning one of the wide range of languages on offer. Students benefit from the exceptional collection of work on Africa and Asia in the School's library and they can also make use of some of the other libraries belonging to the University of London of which SOAS is a part.

The School is located in Bloomsbury, with all departments and academic activities situated on the University's central campus. The West End location is convenient for many of the capital's attractions. SOAS guarantees all first-years accommodation either in Dinwiddy House or the newly completed Robeson House. Ten per-cent of all returning students can also be given a place in residence. Other students can choose to apply to either one of the eight central intercollegiate halls belonging to the University of London or rent privately, although this will inevitably strain their budgets to the full. Although student clubs and societies provide a wide range of sporting, athletic and social activities, the sports ground and home ground for the Schools' teams, is some distance away in Greenford.

UNIVERSITY COLLEGE LONDON
Gower Street, London WC1E 6BT (tel. 0171-380 7365)

Founded 1826
Times ranking: 5 *(1998 ranking: 5)*

Enquiries: Admissions office

Total students: 13,500
Male/female ratio: 50/50
Mature students: 21%
Overseas students: 11%

Main subject areas: full range of disciplines in seven faculties: arts, social and historical sciences; built environment; clinical sciences and medicine; engineering; law; life sciences; mathematical and physical sciences.

Teaching quality ratings
Rated excellent 1993-95: anthropology; architecture; English; geography; geology; history; law.
April 1995-97: history of art 24; German 23; Scandinavian 23; Dutch 22; electrical and electronic engineering 22; linguistics 22; French 21; chemical engineering 20; Italian 20; Iberian languages 19.

UCL, which describes itself as 'a university within a university', claims to be among the top three multi-faculty institutions in England – a position confirmed in *The Times* rankings. Only Oxford and Cambridge outscored the college in an analysis of research funding allowing for subject difference. Its size and breadth of expertise long ago made it one of London's academic powerhouses, with a history of pioneering subjects that have become established features of higher education. Modern languages, geography and the fine arts are examples.

Now boasting 72 departments, the largest college of London University is a thoroughly modern institution, with lucrative links with Japanese companies in particular. UCL incorporates the Slade School of Fine Art and the Institute of Archaeology, and other small, specialist units have been invited to join them. The Institute of Ophthalmology, the Institute of Child Health and the Institute of Neurology have all done so recently. The University College and Middlesex School of Medicine, formed through a merger in 1988, swiftly emerged as a leading medical school soon to be enhanced by the addition of the Royal Free Hospital Medical School. Anatomy, archaeology, several branches of engineering, modern languages and pharmacology are among the top-rated subjects for research. History, anthropology, geography and law have achieved the maximum score for both research and teaching. A growing number of degrees take four years. Science courses and some in the arts are divided into modular units for greater flexibility.

Almost a third of UCL's students are foreign – 4,500 in all – reflecting the college's high standing abroad. Several departments offer first-year students from home or overseas peer tutoring by more experienced colleagues to help them adapt to degree study. The high costs of running a large research-based college in the capital led UCL to consider breaking away from the federal university but that option has been shelved.

The college now houses almost 4,000 students, and expects to add to its residential stock in the next few years. First-years are guaranteed accommodation even if they come from London, and 80 per cent of those who apply to live in during their final year are accepted. The students' union is cramped for the size of college, but the spacious and under-used University of London Union is on the doorstep. Indoor sports facilities, which are also open to the public, are good and conveniently placed, but the 60-acre athletic ground is a coach ride away.

LONDON GUILDHALL UNIVERSITY
133 Whitechapel High Street, London E1 7QA (tel. 0171-320 1000)

University status 1992, formerly City of London Polytechnic, City of London College founded 1848.
Times ranking: 95 *(1998 ranking: 89)*

Enquiries: Admissions office
Total students: 8,900
Male/female ratio: 47/53
Mature students: 50%
Overseas students: 4%

Main subject areas for degrees and diplomas: arts design and manufacture; business; human sciences.

Teaching quality ratings
Rated excellent 1993-95: social policy.
April 1995-97: modern languages 19; media studies 17; sociology 17.

Spilling over from the Square Mile into the East End of London, the new university's academic interests reflect the stark contrasts in its location. Its City traditions are maintained in a range of business-related courses, while a variety of craft subjects cater for the neighbouring community. One in 14 students is taking a further education course, the highest proportion of any university.

The university did not have an easy birth, finding itself unable to adapt its previous title because of possible confusion with City University as well as having to juggle teaching accommodation to cope with long-standing property complications. But initial recruitment difficulties have eased, and London Guildhall is building on its strengths in business and some aspects of social science. The social policy and management degree was rated as excellent by funding council assessors even before the first graduates emerged. History scored well in the last research assessment exercise and new degrees have been established in banking studies, European business studies and insurance studies.

More than half of the students take business subjects, many coming from City firms to join part-time courses at degree level or professional level. The faculty is one of the largest in Britain, taking advantage of its position in the use of guest lecturers from the City to supplement almost 300 full- and part-time academic staff. Although not on the same scale, the silversmithing and jewellery courses are the largest in Britain, while those in furniture restoration and conservation were the first of their kind in Europe. Following the vocational theme that runs through all its courses, the university even offers ground training for civil aviation pilots.

An imaginative twin-track system allows students who know what they want to study to enrol on 'early specialist degrees' while others embark on the modular programme, postponing the choice of single or combined honours until the end of the first year. There is a regular flow of students into the university at this stage, thanks to a well-established credit accumulation scheme.

True to the university's origins in the Metropolitan Evening Classes for Young People of almost 150 years ago, some 40 per cent of the students are on part-time courses and many of the full-timers live at home. As a result, London Guildhall manages with fewer than 500 residential places in three halls of residence. The prospectus acknowledges that finding somewhere to live in the right area at the right price 'can be something of a challenge', but the university insists that it has never had homeless students and the Accommodation Service will help students to rent privately.

London Guildhall has eschewed most of the airs and graces embraced by many of the new universities. It has a provost, rather than a vice-chancellor, for example, and although the numbers have dropped since polytechnic days, 13 per cent of students are still on further education courses. The downside has been the university estate, spread over seven main sites in buildings which students have often found crowded and in poor condition. Some £3.5 million has been spent on refurbishment over the last three years and new purchases are beginning to bring the university together. A recent acquisition provides a home for the Fawcett Library, perhaps the country's most important collection of books on the women's movement.

As in most city centre universities, the main sports facilities are some distance away, although there is a well-equipped fitness centre nearby and discounts are available at a local sports centre. Social life centres on the students' union, which also acts as a focal point for the university.

LOUGHBOROUGH UNIVERSITY
Loughborough, Leicestershire LE11 3TU (tel. 01509-263171)

Founded 1909, royal charter 1966
Times ranking: 26th equal *(1998 ranking: 26)*

Enquiries: Undergraduate admissions office
Total students: 9,300
Male/female ratio: 67/33
Mature students: 14%
Overseas students: 12%

Main subject areas: education and humanities; engineering; science; social sciences and humanities.

Teaching quality ratings
Rated excellent 1993-95: business and management.
April 1995-97: drama 23; mechanical engineering 23; sociology 23; chemical engineering 22; electronic and electrical engineering 22.

Best known for its successes on the sports field, Loughborough has established a solid academic reputation recently, consistently finishing well up *The Times* table and establishing some the best records for teaching ratings. The news is filtering through to schools and colleges: there were an extra 1,000 applicants last year while others were hit by the introduction of tuition fees. A strong portfolio of courses in a limited range of subjects appears to be the secret of its success. There has been concerted development in business and management for example, which have been rated as excellent for teaching.

Loughborough has abandoned its technological title but, with 45 per cent of the undergraduates taking arts or social science subjects, the university is trying to tilt the balance further towards the sciences. Physical education and engineering continue to be the main strengths. Electronic and automotive engineering are also popular and highly regarded by employers. Although no departments achieved the top rating for research, almost a quarter were in the next category.

Most subjects are available either as three-year full-time or four-year sandwich courses. The popular sandwich option, with a year in industry, has helped to give Loughborough's graduates an outstanding employment record. Loughborough's Careers Service has been voted the best overall by the Graduate Recruiters Survey. The university prides itself on a close relationship with industry, which was recognised in 1994 with a Queen's Anniversary Prize. The judges were particularly impressed with the Systems Engineering degree, which was designed, and is taught in partnership, with British Aerospace. It is one of several subjects available as a five-year extended programme leading to a Masters qualification.

Now that merger with Leicester University is no longer an option, Loughborough is pursuing modest growth. The 216-acre campus offers plenty of scope for expansion, despite an active construction programme, which saw the opening of a £6.5-million students' union extension in 1994 and a £3.9-million Business School in 1998. The next stage of development involves an Integrated Engineering Faculty project, bringing together all the engineering departments with their 2,500 students. The vacated space will make room for an information centre and new learning resource centre.

Much of the building has involved halls of residence, adding 1,600 places since the start of the decade, making more than 5,000 in all. As a result, the university continues to house 70 per cent of its students, priority going to first-years and those in their final year. Many of the rooms are connected to the advanced computer network. Private accommodation is in short supply in the small town of Loughborough, a mile from the campus.

The indoor and outdoor sports facilities are some of the best in Britain, and the representative teams have a tradition second to none. There are up to 30 sports scholarships a year, the largest such programme in the university system. Nineteen staff and graduates went to the Olympic Games in Atlanta in 1996 to compete, officiate or conduct research. The union serves as the centre for most students' social activity, although both Leicester and Nottingham are within easy reach.

UNIVERSITY OF LUTON
Park Square, Luton, Bedfordshire LU1 3JU (tel. 01582-489262)

University status 1993, formerly Luton College of Higher Education
Times ranking: 93 *(1998 ranking: 94)*

Enquiries: Admissions officer
Total students: 11,100
Male/female ratio: 48/52
Mature students: 55%
Overseas students: 12%

Main subject areas: applied sciences; business; design and technology; health care and social studies; humanities. Diplomas offered as well as degrees.

Teaching quality ratings
Rated excellent 1993-95: none.
April 1995-98: media studies 22; building 22; linguistics 21; electronic engineering 20; modern languages 20; sociology 18.

Having broken all records for expansion in its quest for promotion from a college of higher education, Luton faced more difficulty than most in adapting to the last government's insistence on a period of consolidation. The institution and its building programme were geared to further growth. But the dash was worth it: Luton was the last English university to be created before additional obstacles were placed in the way of other ambitious colleges. Hundreds of combinations are now available at degree level, most as part of a modular scheme with credit transfer for students with prior experience elsewhere.

After a slow start, in which none of the first dozen departments were considered excellent, Luton has recorded some good scores in teaching assessments. Building and linguistics have led the way, but the university's limited foray into research assessment was not a success. No subject reached the top four categories out of seven. Many are far from traditional. Some are aimed at the latest career opportunities in business and the media, and all students are encouraged to take a job-seeking skills course. Those on the popular media-production degree enjoy access to broadcast-standard video equipment, a five-camera studio and high-quality editing suites. The accent on technology is maintained throughout the university. The £3-million learning resources centre combined library and computerised information services, and has already been enlarged. Students have access to libraries all over the world. A £5-million computer centre opened on the main campus in 1997.

Mature students are encouraged to apply, and there are access courses for students who lack traditional entry qualifications. The open access approach, together with Luton's youth as a university, accounts for its low position in *The Times* table.

The main campus is in the centre of Luton, with a teaching site in Dunstable catering mainly for vocational courses. There is also an attractive management centre at Putteridge Bury, a neo-Elizabethan mansion three miles outside Luton. All have easy access to London, half an hour away by train. The university has been building new residential accommodation, as well as sub-letting property to students to ensure reasonable standards. Now complete, the construction programme involved 1,500 new residential places and all first-years can now be accommodated by the university.

There are restaurants on all the main sites and an active students' union, which now has its own nightclub, the Underground. There is a rigid no-smoking rule throughout most of the university. Membership of the sports association, giving access to facilities on the main campus and at the Luton Regional Sport Centre, cost £15 last year.

UNIVERSITY OF MANCHESTER
Manchester M13 9PL (tel. 0161-275 2077)

Founded 1851, royal charter 1903
Times ranking: 20 *(1998 ranking: 17th equal)*

Enquiries: Admissions office
Total students: 20,900
Male/female ratio: 51/49
Mature students: 11%
Overseas students: 7%

Main subject areas: full range of degree courses in 10 faculties: arts; biological sciences; business administration; dentistry; economics; education; law; medicine; science; theology.

Teaching quality ratings
Rated excellent 1993-95: anthropology; business; chemistry; computer science; geography; geology; law; mechanical engineering; music; social policy.
April 1995-98: drama, dance and cinematics 21; German 21; history of art 21; linguistics 21; materials science 21; sociology 21; aerospace engineering 20; electrical and electronic engineering 20; Iberian languages 20; Middle Eastern and African studies 20; town planning 20; French 19; Italian 19; civil engineering 18; Russian 16.

Always one of the giants of British higher education, with 20 Nobel Prize-winners to its credit, Manchester is emerging from a difficult period which included a lengthy spell without a permanent vice-chancellor. It attracts more applications than any other institution, and a string of good teaching reports has coincided with significant reorganisation of the university to restore a sense of vibrancy. In other times, Manchester might have expected to be even higher in *The Times* rankings. But valuable ground was lost at the start of the decade when it declined to expand too rapidly beyond its already considerable size, in the process sacrificing funding for teaching and research.

Improved research scores have since begun to restore the university's fortunes although Manchester might have hoped for better in the last assessments. Although a third of academics in the exercise reached one of the top two categories, only the relatively small areas of accountancy, metallurgy and theologies were starred. The School of Biological Sciences won the Queen's Anniversary Award in December 1996. Chemistry, geography, social policy and law are among the subjects rated as excellent for teaching.

Manchester remains the model of a traditional university, equally balanced between arts and sciences, with school-leavers still filling most of the undergraduate places, but more than 2,000 postgraduates underlining the emphasis on research. Graduate schools have been introduced to cater more effectively for their needs, while a modular system has been introduced for first degrees. The university's reputation, allied to the continuing popularity of the city among students, ensures that applicants are highly qualified in most disciplines.

The university precinct, not far from the city centre, is shared with UMIST, the teaching hospitals and the headquarters of Manchester Metropolitan University, providing some of the best facilities in Britain. The John Rylands Library is one of the largest in any university, with 3.5 million books, one million manuscript or archival items, and space for more than 2,000 students. The university has eight libraries in all. The Whitworth Art Gallery houses valuable collections, especially of English watercolours, as does the award-winning Manchester Museum. The university also runs the Jodrell Bank Science Centre, the Planetarium and the Arboretum.

First-year students are guaranteed a place in the country's most extensive bank of university accommodation, which is shared with UMIST. Hundreds more places have been added recently making more than 9,000 in all. Owens Park is the biggest student village in Britain, and there are self-catering flats on the main campus, as well as further afield.

Facilities in the two sports centres are excellent and conveniently placed. There is a relatively new students' union building, which has eased previous overcrowding. Manchester students tend to be fiercely loyal both to their university and their adopted city.

UNIVERSITY OF MANCHESTER INSTITUTE OF SCIENCE AND TECHNOLOGY

PO Box 88, Manchester M60 1QD (tel. 0161-200 3311)

Founded 1824, part of Manchester University 1905-93
Times ranking: 24th equal *(1998 ranking: 25)*

Enquiries: Registrar's department
Total students: 7,000
Male/female ratio: 67/33
Mature students: 17%
Overseas students: 20%

Main subject areas: biological and physical sciences; business; engineering and technology; mathematics and computation; social sciences and languages.

Teaching quality ratings
Rated excellent 1993-95: business and management.
April 1995-97: chemical engineering 22; civil engineering 22; modern languages 18.

Now fully independent of Manchester University, UMIST is primarily a research institute concentrating on management and languages, as well as science, technology and engineering. More than a quarter of the students are postgraduates. Until October 1993, UMIST was technically a faculty of Manchester University, albeit one with considerable freedom of action. The new arrangement preserves access to joint facilities such as accommodation, and there is still a great deal of collaboration. The institute is a full partner in the new Manchester Federal School of Business and Management, for example, and its own business and management studies having been rated excellent for teaching and research. UMIST is also near the top of *The Times* business rankings. A purpose-built management school, costing £8 million, opened in 1998. Almost half the academics throughout the institute assessed for the last research rankings reach one of the top two categories. Management and materials and corrosion science were rated as world-beaters.

Much of the development planned over the next few years is designed to strengthen the research base still further. But there will also be more degree courses combining science or technology with a modern language or environmental study. A four-year mathematics degree has been developed and specialist courses, in subjects such as polymeric materials, are planned.

Student numbers are still growing after passing UMIST's target of 6,000 but entry qualifications are still high. New students had an average of 23 UCAS points last year, and requirements were high throughout most of the period of expansion, despite the shortage of well-qualified candidates in UMIST's main subjects. Part of the reason for the institute's success has been the good employment record of its graduates, who were second only to Cambridge as employers' favourites in a recent national survey. A Queen's Award for export achievement and two Anniversary Prizes for innovation have also confirmed its high quality.

Students have access to Europe's largest computer centre and a £4-million library that is one of the most high-tech in Britain. A third of the 600 study places have computer facilities and there is a formal commitment to maintaining book purchasing in line with the increases in students.

All first-years are guaranteed a residential place. Some halls are shared with Manchester University, and a 444-bed hall has been added to cope with rising numbers. The total pool of accommodation grew by 47 per cent in two years. Students have access to Manchester University's sports facilities, as well as a ground of their own. A £2-million sports hall, to be shared with Manchester Metropolitan University, was added recently. Student union facilities were modernised in 1990.

MANCHESTER METROPOLITAN UNIVERSITY
All Saints Building, Oxford Road, Manchester M15 6BH (tel. 0161-247 1035)

University status 1992, formerly Manchester Polytechnic
Times ranking: 71st equal *(1998 ranking: 74th equal)*

Enquiries: Academic division
Total students: 24,600
Male/female ratio: 44/56
Mature students: 30%
Overseas students: 5%

Main subject areas: art and design; community studies and education; clothing design and technology; hotel catering and tourism management; humanities; law; management and business; science and engineering; social sciences. Certificates and diplomas offered as well as degrees.

Teaching quality ratings
Rated excellent 1993-95: mechanical engineering.
April 1995-97: drama 23; modern languages 21; sociology 21; town planning 20.

Since taking in Crewe and Alsager College, the former Manchester Polytechnic has become the largest conventional university in Britain. Only the Open University and the two federations in London and Wales can match its total of around 30,000 students, including part-timers. More than a third of the students are over 21 at entry, and the university prides itself on keeping a balance between the sexes. The 400 courses at degree level and below cover more than 70 subject areas, mostly linked directly with business, industry or the professions.

Among the teaching strengths are mechanical engineering, which received an excellent rating in the funding council's teaching assessment, hotel and catering and retail marketing. Drama managed a near-perfect score in the latest round of assessments. The addition of Crewe and Alsager, 40 miles south of Manchester, has enhanced the university's already substantial reputation. Social sciences and business courses have been ranked among the best in the country. Sports science achieved the best rating for research. Overseas links have expanded rapidly, both in Europe and farther afield. Law courses, for example, are being taught in Hong Kong, with a return of £500,000 for the university over three years.

Although the main campus is in the university area of Manchester, four of the five main faculties are out of the city centre. Those at Didsbury, where a former college campus caters for 3,500 education and community studies students, are the farthest flung of the original university sites. A third of the students come from the Manchester area, easing some of the pressure on accommodation. There are almost 3,000 residential places, mostly reserved for first-years. Three halls of residence are near the central campus, which adjoins Manchester University and UMIST. Three are near the Didsbury campus and one is in Whalley Range, with a further 800 places at Crewe and Alsager. Given the city's huge student population, to help students find a home all three Manchester universities run Manchester Student Homes, a comprehensive accommodation bureau which tries to make competition in the private sector a little less fierce.

The students' union is a well-organised, multi-million pound operation serving all of the seven campuses. The university has two sports centres: on the main site and at Didsbury. Manchester's image as a vibrant, youth-oriented city is a great attraction to would-be students. Though some are daunted by the metropolitan university's size, courses and sites are not necessarily impersonal.

MIDDLESEX UNIVERSITY
White Hart Lane, London N17 8HR (tel. 0181-362 5000)

University status 1992, formerly Middlesex Polytechnic
Times ranking: 85 *(1998 ranking: 82)*

Enquiries: Course enquiries office
Total students: 17,700
Male female ratio: 43/57
Mature students: 46%
Overseas students: 19%

Main subject areas: art and design; business studies and management; education and performing arts; engineering; health, biological and environmental studies; humanities; mathematics; science; social science. Certificate and diploma courses also offered.

Teaching quality ratings
Rated excellent 1993-95: none.
April 1995-97: modern languages 19; sociology 19.

Middlesex has been reassessing its priorities following a year in which it failed to meet its recruitment targets for some courses. But the mixture of community involvement and international outlook will remain. Half of the students come from London, but there is a growing network of partner colleges abroad. Almost 3,000 foreign students take courses at the university, and a high proportion of undergraduates go abroad for part of their course.

The modular degree system offers a wide range of subjects from which to construct a study programme, and all students are encouraged to take a language course. The system also gives students the option of an extra five-week session in July and August, during which they can try out new subjects or add to their credits. Although Middlesex was famous at one time for the largest philosophy department in the country, 90 per cent of students are on vocational courses, with one-fifth at sub-degree or postgraduate level. Hotel and restaurant management is popular, dance performance degrees even more so.

Student numbers doubled in the space of five years, with a teaching campus in Tottenham reopening to cater for 2,000 students. A £3 million learning resources centre opened there in 1998. There are now six in sites dotted around London's North Circular Road, and one in Bedford. They include a country estate at Trent Park, an innovative warehouse conversion at Bounds Green, and a house in Hampstead that was once the home of the ballerina Anna Pavlova. A network of partner colleges adds to the numbers taking Middlesex courses; the university is committed to "blurring the division" between further and higher education.

Middlesex is heavily involved in applied research, and has pioneered a number of degrees, including performance arts. Its engineering courses have achieved high placings in *The Times* rankings and the 43 per cent of academics entered for assessment in the research rankings was among the highest proportions in the new universities. The university won a Queens's Anniversary Prize for its centre developing professional learning in the workplace and other off-campus locations. The active students' union, which staged effective protests against the overcrowding that came with the first wave of expansion, operates on all the main sites, and sports facilities are good. First-years are given priority for the 2,500 residential places, but a third still have to live out.

NAPIER UNIVERSITY
219 Colinton Road, Edinburgh EH14 1DJ (tel. 0131-444 2266)

University status 1992, formerly Napier Polytechnic of Edinburgh
Times ranking: 56 *(1998 ranking: 64)*

Enquiries: Information office (tel. 0131-455 4330)

Total students: 9,200
Male/female ratio: 60/40
Mature students: 38%
Overseas students: 2%

Main subject areas: accountancy; biology; business studies; chemistry; civil, mechanical, electrical and electronic engineering; communication studies; computing; design; economics; film and television; health studies; hotel and catering management; information technology; languages; law; mathematics; physics; surveying. A number of diploma courses also offered.

Teaching quality ratings 1994-97
Rated excellent: none.
Rated highly satisfactory: building; cellular biology; chemistry; civil engineering; hospitality studies; mass communications; mathematics; organismal biology; statistics.
From 1998: European languages 19.

Napier was Scotland's first and largest polytechnic. Now a university of over 11,000 students, of whom 3,000 are part-timers, it aims to develop into an institution that ranks with the best in Britain, although *The Times* table suggests that there is a long way to go. The university was still waiting for its first 'excellent' rating for teaching at the end of 1998 and only four academics reached any of the top three categories in the last research assessment exercise.

A new campus at Craighouse, in the south of Edinburgh, promised to be 'one of the finest in Britain', will help the process. Two new libraries and a £2.5-million refurbishment of the science laboratories have also shown that Napier means business. A £7-million music centre opened in October 1996 while the incorporation of Lothian College of Health Studies and the Scottish Borders College of Nursing has added the largest nursing and midwifery facility north of the border.

The university has its roots as a college of science and technology which merged with a college of commerce, and remains strongly and avowedly vocational. Most courses include a work placement and one result of the close relationship with industry and commerce is consistent success in the employment market for new graduates. Another is a flourishing consultancy business, which ploughs money back into departments. A learning resource centre specialising in distance learning opened in 1997. Particular strengths include a degree in energy and environmental engineering, including the social and political aspects of the subject, a communication degree aimed at marketing, advertising and public relations, and a BA in photography, film and television. Movement between courses of different levels is facilitated by a modular system in all degree subjects and the range of independent study has increased.

The main academic development is in joint honours degrees, with 1999 seeing the introduction of a number of potentially popular combinations, such as languages with tourism management, and accounting with entrepreneurship. Among the innovative multi-level programmes is the Scottish

Churches Open College, offering training for community work through regional study centres to certificate, diploma or degree level

The university, like the polytechnic before it, was named after John Napier, the inventor of logarithms. The tower where he was born still sits among the concrete blocks of the Merchiston site, in the student district of Edinburgh. The five main sites and six teaching outposts are linked by a free university minibus service. Sighthill, a 1960s building, is in the west of the city while Craiglockart, once a military hospital where the war poets Siegfried Sassoon and Wilfred Owen met, is close to the other university buildings.

Napier's new central students' union provides a venue for bands and a night club. There is a student's association bar on all the main sites. The university has just over 1,000 residential places so, with many students living at home, most first years from at least 25 miles outside Edinburgh can be accommodated.

UNIVERSITY OF NEWCASTLE UPON TYNE
Newcastle upon Tyne NE1 7RU (tel. 0191-222 8672)

Founded 1834 (as part of Durham University), royal charter 1963
Times ranking: 19 *(1998 ranking: 19)*

Enquiries: Admissions officer
Total students: 12,600
Male/female ratio: 54/46
Mature students: 20%
Overseas students: 6%

Main subject areas: wide range of disciplines in eight faculties: agriculture; arts; education; engineering; law; medicine; science; social and environmental science.

Teaching quality ratings
Rated excellent 1993-95: architecture; English; geology; social policy.
April 1995-97: linguistics 22; modern languages 22; chemical engineering 21; electrical and electronic engineering 21; town planning 21

Newcastle now vies with its former parent university, Durham, for recognition as the top university in the Northeast. The civic university has a big advantage in terms of size, having grown by almost 50 per cent in the last five years. Recent funding allocations have been favourable and research income has been breaking all records. The university switched recently to a modular semester-based system. Newcastle's residential stock has also been increased. With the University managing around 5,000 places every first-year who wants accommodation can have it. Most of the halls are within easy reach of the city-centre campus where 40 per cent of the full-time students are based.

Originally a medical school, Newcastle has maintained its reputation in that field, as well as in dentistry. It has also long been one of the top centres for agriculture. Particularly highly rated is the architectural studies degree, though engineering and modern languages have also scored well in recent teaching assessments. The fine art degree is one of the few single honours courses in the traditional universities, attracting 15 applicants per place in 1996. Civil engineering is the only starred department for research. But agriculture, computing, education, earth sciences, geography, law and physiology were all considered nationally outstanding. The university switched recently to a modular, semester-based system

The campus itself is spacious and varied, occupying 45 acres close to the main shopping area, Northumbria University and Newcastle United's ground, which is overlooked by one of the halls. The university boasts a theatre, an art gallery and three museums. Newcastle itself has become an increasingly fashionable city among students from the south as well as from the Northeast. It topped a recent student poll based on the quality of nightlife, student services and computer facilities. The city has plenty of social facilities, and is generally welcoming towards students. University sports facilities are excellent, and include a new sports centre, three grounds within the city limits and access to the university's country estate in Northumberland. The students' union is large and lively.

UNIVERSITY OF NORTHUMBRIA AT NEWCASTLE
Ellison Place, Newcastle upon Tyne NE1 8ST (tel. 0191-232 6002)

Royal charter 1992, formerly Newcastle Polytechnic
Times ranking: 62nd equal *(1998 ranking: 60)*

Enquiries: Education liaison officer (tel. 0191-227 4265)
Total students: 15,300
Male/female ratio: 50/50
Mature students: 51%
Overseas students: 7%

Main subject areas: arts, design and humanities; business and management; engineering, science and technology; health, social work and education; social sciences. Wide range of certificate and diploma courses also offered.

Teaching quality ratings
Rated excellent 1993-95: business and management; English; law.
April 1995-97: modern languages 23; drama, dance and cinematics 22; sociology 20.

Already one of the largest of the new universities, Northumbria has now passed its target of 20,000 students, including 10,000 part-timers, with the incorporation of a college of health studies. Numbers increased again in 1997, when traditional terms were replaced by two semesters. The university has benefited from Newcastle's growing reputation as an exciting student city.

Northumbria has also been expanding geographically, both at home and abroad. Two new campuses have been established in recent years for business courses. That in Carlisle is intended to have 800 students before the end of the decade and to act as a link for Cumbrian firms seeking academic expertise. The other domestic development is Longhirst Campus, 15 miles north of Newcastle at Morpeth, which also offers business courses and admitted its first full-time students in 1994. Considerably farther afield, smaller centres have also been established in Kuala Lumpur and Moscow. In Newcastle itself, the university has begun building up a network of feeder colleges to encourage applications from students without traditional qualifications. One result is that almost half the students are over 21 at entry and over half are from the north of England.

The fashion school is perhaps Northumbria's best-known feature, though the school of art is also well regarded. Most degrees are available as sandwich courses, with placements of up to a year in industry. A near-perfect teaching assessment for modern languages and another high score for drama and film studies followed early successes for business studies, law and English. Entry requirements are generally modest, although law (three Bs) and business studies are notable exceptions.

The main campus is in the centre of the city, within sight of Newcastle University. Most of the buildings are sixties glass and concrete, but law is taught in a converted Victorian drill hall used by the Northumberland Hussars. Another site, three miles away, contains the bulk of the 2,000 residential places, for which first-years are given priority. Coach Lane is also acquiring more academic facilities. The first phase of the £40 million expansion plan includes a learning resource centre and sports facilities, as well as teaching space for the university's 1,600 student nurses. The scheme should satisfy those who have complained of overcrowding in recreational and library facilities. A further 500 rooms opened on campus recently, but half of the new intake are assisted in finding private-sector housing.

UNIVERSITY OF NORTH LONDON
166-220 Holloway Road, London N7 8DB (tel. 0171-607 2789)

University status 1992, formerly Polytechnic of North London
Times ranking: 90 *(1998 ranking: 87)*

Enquiries: Course enquiries office
Total students: 11,700
Male/female ratio: 44/56
Mature students: 66%
Overseas students: 18%

Main subject areas: business and management; environmental and social sciences; humanities and teacher education; science, computing and engineering. Certificate and diploma courses also offered.

Teaching quality ratings
Rated excellent 1993-95: English.
April 1995-97: modern languages 20; food science 19; materials technology 19; media studies 17.

North London is shaking off a reputation for student militancy, replacing it with one for spreading higher education into ethnic communities otherwise little seen in the university system. As a polytechnic, it pioneered access courses aimed at the local, ethnically mixed population. Today more than a third of North London's students are Afro-Caribbean. The university has dedicated itself to more of the same, rather than trying to compete with the traditional universities. Its mission statement stresses a commitment to widening educational opportunities and expanding international and business links. A third of new students enter through clearing and barely half are selected on A levels, which average less than three Ds.

Nevertheless, some departments are heavily involved in research as well as teaching and a high proportion of staff for a new university was entered for the last research assessment exercise. Sociology was the most success-ful subject. The analysis, which evened out subject differences, made North London second among the new universities and fifteenth overall for market share of research funds. Sandwich and part-time degrees in electronic engi-neering are highly rated, as are health studies, teacher education and leisure and tourism. About a quarter of the students are on sub-degree or professional courses. Many programmes at all levels are designed for mature students, who account for almost three-quarters of all entrants, the highest proportion in the country. Most degrees are modular and allow credit transfer. Some students feel that the full flexibility of the system is not understood and that it has been under-exploited, but efforts have now been made to explain it more clearly.

The university has been improving its facilities, with a new teaching centre, student services building and student centre all opening recently. Though still crowded and run-down in parts, UNL has been concentrating teaching in the Islington/Holloway area, and is still to complete its building programme. A "millennial tower" is being built to provide a new main entrance and focus for the university, with teaching and exhibition areas. Redevelopment nearby will bring together the environmental and social sciences, with a purpose-built science block following.

Sports facilities are reasonable, if distant for outdoor games. The stu-dents' union is especially active politically. There are only 900 hall places and first-years are guaranteed one if they live 25 miles away and accept a place before clearing begins. The university advises those who miss out on a hall place to arrive well before term starts, such is the scramble for afford-able housing. Fortunately, a high proportion of mature students means that many live at home.

UNIVERSITY OF NOTTINGHAM
University Park, Nottingham NG7 2RD (tel. 01159-515151)

Founded 1881, royal charter 1948
Times ranking: 11 *(1998 ranking: 11)*

Enquiries: Admissions office
Total students: 15,300
Male/female ratio: 49/51
Mature students: 30%
Overseas students: 11%

Main subject areas: wide range of disciplines in seven faculties: agricultural and food sciences; arts; education (mainly postgraduate); engineering; law and social sciences; medicine; science.

Teaching quality ratings
Rated excellent 1993-95: architecture; business and management; chemistry; English; geography; law; manufacturing engineering; music.
April 1995-97: mechanical engineering 24; agriculture 23; civil engineering 22; electrical and electronic engineering 22; German 22; chemical engineering 21; sociology 21; Russian 19; Iberian languages 17; French 16.

Already the occupant of one of the most attractive campuses in Britain, Nottingham is now developing a second main site. The £50 million project is necessary to help meet the burgeoning demand for places which has come with the university's rise up the pecking order of higher education. Consistently rated among the top dozen universities, it is also among the most popular, with at least 14 applications to the place.

The 30-acre campus, a mile from the original one, will house the schools of management and finance, computer science and education. Opening in October 1999, it will also add 750 places to Nottingham's residential stock, 150 of them reserved for postgraduates. The university expects to have 17,000 students by the turn of the century, but the new development is designed to make room for many more if Government policy permits.

Though it sees itself as a 'research-led university', with some 3,500 students taking higher degrees, it has been expanding its undergraduate intake (by more than 30 per cent since the start of the decade) and plans to grow further. Its strength in teaching has not been affected by this expansion, however. Two-thirds of the subjects inspected, including all but three of the 11 subjects covered in the first round of teaching assessments, were considered excellent. Since then, manufacturing engineering has registered a perfect score and agriculture has come close. German followed a high teaching score with a 5-star rating for research. Pharmacy, genetics, food science and Russian were the other top-rated research areas, with another 10 subjects in the next best category. Arts degrees are acquiring a growing reputation with the aid of a £5-million arts centre opened in 1991. There are pockets of excellence, too, in the social sciences: politics is especially popular.

Already the occupant of one of the most attractive campuses in Britain, Nottingham is now developing a second main site. The £50 million project is necessary to help meet the burgeoning demand for places which has come with the university's rise up the pecking order of higher education. Consistently rated among the top dozen universities, it is also among the most popular, with at least 14 applications to the place.

The 30-acre campus, a mile from the original one, will house the schools of management and finance, computer science and education. Opening in October 1999, it will also add 750 places to Nottingham's residential stock, 150 of them reserved for postgraduates. The university expects to have 17,000 students by the turn of the century, but the new development is designed to make room for many more if Government policy permits.

The university has more than 3,000 residential places in halls and self-catering flats. All first-years are guaranteed accommodation if they meet the August 1 deadline and come from outside the Nottingham area. Sports facilities are extremely good and conveniently placed with a 25-metre swimming pool the latest addition. However, they are not cheap by the standards of other universities. There are user charges on top of a £20 membership fee, or a season ticket costs £40. Much of the social life centres on the halls, but the students' union is also well equipped.

NOTTINGHAM TRENT UNIVERSITY
Burton Street, Nottingham NG1 4BU (tel. 01159-418418)

University status 1992, formerly Nottingham (originally Trent) Polytechnic
Times ranking: 69 *(1998 ranking: 73)*

Enquiries: Admissions office
Total students: 20,400
Male/female ratio: 54/46
Mature students: 28%
Overseas students: 3%

Main subject areas: art and design; business and management; economics; education; engineering and computing; environmental studies; humanities; law; science; social sciences. Certificate and diploma courses also offered.

Teaching quality rating
Rated excellent 1993-95: business and management; chemistry.
April 1995-97: sociology 19; modern languages 17.

Nine out of 10 students in the university's annual opinion survey said they would recommend Nottingham Trent to a friend. The survey is part of a systematic attempt to involve students in decision-making: the new university had a student charter before the last Government latched onto the idea.

Nottingham Trent would have preferred a 'city university' title but was obliged to return to its roots with its new name. It set itself the target of challenging its older established rivals in research within five years without compromising the values it championed as a polytechnic. It has remained true to its word, giving opportunities to thousands more students and a quarter of its places to part-timers. The research effort predates university status by several years. The strategy is to focus on interdisciplinary combinations, such as business and engineering and overlaps between the academic world and private enterprise. Undergraduates will benefit both from the funding the university thereby expects to attract and the high-calibre research staff that should follow in its wake.

Although Nottingham Trent's last research ratings were unspectacular, the strategy appears to be working where undergraduates are concerned. Business studies and chemistry received top ratings for their teaching and applications have held up well. The law school is one of Britain's largest, offering postgraduate legal practice courses for both solicitors and barristers among a wide variety of vocational programmes. Fashion courses are another successful area. Courses, which are fully modular and allow credit transfer, include a variety of vocational programmes, such as fashion marketing and communication, as well as more traditional degrees. The university's popularity allowed it to grow by one-third in five years, with another quarter of the student body taking sandwich courses. A £13.8-million 'electronic library' opened at the city site in August 1997. All courses will soon have a computer appreciation component, and all students have the opportunity to learn a language. Nottingham Trent's vocational slant, coupled with its high proportion of sandwich degrees, has produced a good employment record, with the university featuring in the top 10 for both undergraduates and postgraduates going straight into jobs.

The university has two sites. Most faculties are based on the main, city-centre campus. Humanities and science students are five miles away in a former teacher training college at Clifton, with education in a Georgian mansion nearby. A union with student offices, a supermarket and a book-shop opened at Clifton in 1996. Private accommodation is at a premium in the Nottingham area, where one in 10 adults is a full-time student. But the university has been increasing its stock in a six-year programme which has produced 3,600 residential places. First-years are given priority while a new accreditation programme ensures that only approved flats and houses from the private sector are offered through the accommodation office. Sports and social facilities are good on both main sites. The students' union runs its own employment bureau and the growing band of media students has been putting theory into practice on the award-winning Kich FM radio station.

UNIVERSITY OF OXFORD
University offices, Wellington Square, Oxford OX1 2JD (tel. 01865-270000)

Founded 1096
Times ranking: 3 *(1998 ranking: 2)*

Enquiries: Admissions office or individual colleges
Total students: 16,000
Male/female ratio: 59/41
Mature students: 6%
Overseas students: 12%

Main subject areas: full range of disciplines in six faculties: arts; engineering and technology; mathematics; medicine, science; social sciences.

Teaching quality ratings
Rated excellent 1993-95: anthropology; chemistry; computer science; English; geography; geology; history; law; social work.
April 1995-98: general engineering 23; materials technology 23; East and South Asian studies 22; Middle Eastern and African studies 22; modern languages 21.

Oxford is the oldest and probably the most famous university in the English-speaking world. *The Times* table suggests that it is still close to Cambridge in terms of quality, and head and shoulders above the other non-specialist universities. Attempts to distinguish between Britsin's two most prestigious universities are bound to be generalised: it is between the colleges that noticeable differences emerge – and between colleges that prospective students must choose.

The arts faculties have been the envy of other universities for centuries and topped *The Times* subject rankings, while the new Magdalen College science park epitomises a drive to enhance Oxford's reputation in the sciences. The university has also added a management school, which will grow in scale and importance following a £20-million donation from the Syrian businessman, Wafic Said.

The 30 undergraduate colleges continue to teach students in small tutorial groups, with lectures an optional extra which some find only marginally useful. With more then 18,000 students, Oxford is already one of the largest of the traditional universities. It is expected that future growth will focus on postgraduates.

See chapter 9 for information about individual colleges.

OXFORD BROOKES UNIVERSITY
Gipsy Lane Campus, Oxford OX3 0BP (tel. 01865-483040)

University status 1992, formerly Oxford Polytechnic
Times ranking: 53 *(1998 ranking: 51st equal)*

Enquiries: Communications office
Total students: 8,900
Male/female ratio: 44/56
Mature students: 34%
Overseas students: 14%

Main subject areas: architecture; art, biology; business; computing and mathematics; construction and earth sciences; education; engineering; health; hotel management; humanities; languages; law; planning; publishing and music; real estate management; social sciences. Certificates and diplomas available in most areas.

Teaching quality ratings
Rated excellent 1993-95: anthropology, English, geography, law.
April 1995-97: French 22; modern languages 22; media studies 21; sociology 21; German 19.

As one of the top polytechnics, Oxford pioneered the modular degree system that has swept British universities. After 20 years experience, the scheme now offers more than 2,000 modules in its undergraduate programme, which can pair subjects as diverse as history and physical sciences, or catering management and history of art.

Each subject has compulsory modules in the first year and a list of others that are acceptable in the second and third years. Students are encouraged to take some subjects outside their main area of study. Continuous assessment and regular examinations enable undergraduates to predict their final results well in advance. Students are given a printed record of results at the start of each term. They can call a halt at eight modules and collect a Certificate in Higher Education, qualify for a diploma at 16 modules, take an ordinary degree with 20, or an honours degree with a full 24 modules.

The university's location has always attracted students, but it brought problems when it came to finding a name that avoided confusion with an illustrious neighbour. The title, chosen after months of deliberation, celebrates the achievements of John Brookes, who is regarded as a founding father of the institution. With one site fully developed and another stifled by Green Belt restrictions, the chance to acquire the late Robert Maxwell's 15-acre estate at Headington Hill Hall came at an opportune moment. The university had called a temporary halt to expansion to stave off problems of overcrowding. The hall provides much-needed space for a students' union and extra teaching accommodation. There are now three main sites, two practically joined and only a mile from the city centre. Education and business are five miles away at Wheatley, where there is also residential accommodation and students' union facilities. Some health care students are based at Oxford's Radcliffe Hospital, where they benefit from world-class facilities.

As Oxford Brookes has grown, Open University-style learning packages have been introduced to help staff and students cope with larger classes. Most courses make some use of the computing facilities, which have won a national award, and several of the work station rooms are open 24 hours a day.

The university has been among the most successful of the former polytechnics for graduate employment and in the funding council's teaching assessments. There was praise for the breadth of the top-rated law degree, while French and other modern languages have scored well recently. Oxford Brookes entered more of its academics for the last research assessment exercise.

Last year, Oxford Brookes became the first of the new universities to overtake a clutch of traditional rivals in The Times league table. But it retains many of the characteristics of polytechnic days. Almost a third of the students are over 30 on entry, for example, and a higher proportion still are part-timers or on distance learning courses.

With extra places provided recently, there is residential accommodation for more than 2,200 students. First-years are given priority, and three-quarters of those who apply are housed in university-managed rooms. Others are advised to make an early visit to Oxford, where rents are high and flats scarce. Oxford Brookes attracts more independent school pupils than any other new university. An ultra-modern sports centre has satisfied critics of recreational facilities, which are now rated among the best in the new universities.

UNIVERSITY OF PAISLEY
Paisley, Renfrewshire PA1 2BE (tel. 0141-848 3000)

University status 1992, formerly Paisley College
Times ranking: 75th equal *(1998 ranking: 78)*

Enquiries: Admissions office (tel. 0141-848 3698)
Total students: 7,200
Male/female ratio: 50/50
Mature students: 20%
Overseas students: 6%

Main subject areas: business; education; engineering; health and social studies; science and technology. Sub-degree courses are also offered.

Teaching quality ratings 1993-98
Rated excellent: none
Rated highly satisfactory: cellular biology; chemistry; civil engineering; mathematics and statistics; mechanical engineering; organismal biology; psychology; social work; sociology; teacher education.
From 1998: European languages 19

Paisley, only seven miles from Glasgow, is Scotland's largest town. The university now has more than 9,000 students, including the many part-timers, a high proportion coming from the Glasgow area. Student numbers have grown rapidly in recent years, but class sizes still compare favourably with those of rival institutions.Most courses are strongly vocational, with a technological thrust. There are close links with industry and commerce, notably with the computer giant IBM. All students are offered hands-on computer training. Paisley is still waiting for its first excellent rating for teaching, but a majority of subjects assessed so far have been given Scotland's unique highly satisfactory grade.

Courses are flexible. Science and technology students, for example, can choose from 20 interlinked degrees. More than 2,000 students are on the credit accumulation and transfer scheme, which covers 800 subject modules for day or evening classes. First-year science courses are also franchised to three further education colleges in the west of Scotland, with admission to Paisley after a year. Many students are on sandwich degrees.

In 1993, Paisley took in Craigie College, in Ayr, Scotland's smallest college of education. The addition of teacher training for both primary and secondary schools has expanded the university's range of vocational degrees and diplomas. Further courses, in health, nursing, media studies and business and social studies are being introduced on the Craigie campus as the university expands. Research and consultancy is concentrated on 14 specialist units in areas such as alcohol and drug abuse and learning technology. Pure research is not Paisley's forte: fewer than one academic in 10 was entered for the last assessments and the university had no departments in the top three categories.

The main campus covers 20 acres in the middle of Paisley. A third campus at Dumfries opened in 1996 in collaboration with a local college. As yet, there are barely more than 100 students, but there are plans to increase the range of courses available there by opening a new teaching centre. Recent building developments in Paisley have included the modernisation of the library, central computing facilities and chemistry laboratories, and the addition of an interactive video suite. A £7-million Learning Resource Centre opened at Paisley in 1998 and a new Management Centre has been established in the listed 18th-century Craigie House, at Ayr.

There are only 1,000 residential places, with preference given to first-years whose homes are more than 25 miles away. A student village at Thornly Park, two miles from campus, opened in 1996 with 250 beds. The university accommodates two-thirds of first-years wanting a place, but most undergraduates will still have to rely on the relatively cheap private accommodation available locally. The students' association building is a ten-minute walk from the campus. Though not designed to contend with the university's current 7,000-strong student body, it has at least been refurbished recently. Sports facilities, situated on the edge of town, are limited, but the university plans to upgrade them.

UNIVERSITY OF PLYMOUTH
Drake Circus, Plymouth, PL4 8AA (tel. 01752-232158)

University status 1992, formerly Polytechnic South West, originally Plymouth Polytechnic
Times ranking: 64 *(1998 ranking: 68th equal)*

Enquiries: Registry
Total students: 13,600
Male/female ratio: 53/47
Mature students: 35%
Overseas students: 6%

Main subject areas: agriculture, food and land use; arts; business studies; education; human sciences; science; technology.

Teaching quality ratings
Rated excellent 1993-95: environmental science; geography; geology; oceanography.
April 1995-97: sociology 20; materials technology 19; electrical and electronic engineering 18.

The university now has offshoots across much of Devon, despite turning its back on the regional title it adopted as a polytechnic. The choice of 'Plymouth' for the university's name followed the marketing men's creed that applicants identify with cities. But the institution has never had much trouble attracting students in most subjects, even though a high proportion of courses are in science and technology. Some 36,000 students applied in 1996. An arts faculty and education college in Exeter, an agricultural faculty near Newton Abbot and a college of education in Exmouth have all been added in recent years. In addition, the university is responsible for Dartington College of Art, near Totnes, and Falmouth School of Art, and also franchises courses to a dozen further education colleges – a system which won a Queen's Anniversary Prize in 1994. A high-speed telematics network links them all.

A joint programme in international relations with the Royal Naval College, at Dartmouth, is the latest outside venture. Unlike many new universities, 90 per cent of the students are on full-time or sandwich courses, mostly degrees. Engineering is one area of strength, with four-year extended degrees available for those without the normal entry qualifications, and an MEng with an extra year's study open to high-fliers throughout the faculty. A modular course system provides a wide range of options throughout the seven faculties.

Plymouth, one of the most persistent advocates of the right to university status, has a long-standing commitment to research as well as to teaching. The business school, for example, which moved into £6.5-million headquarters in 1994, has an 'aroma room' to aid research in the perfume industry, as well as a range of sophisticated computer hardware for the students. Almost half of the academics were entered for the last research assessment exercise, but no subject was rated in the top three categories. The university is best known for marine studies, and teaching assessments have confirmed that Plymouth offers high quality in these and other sciences.

Facilities – and especially the prospect of securing a residential place – vary considerably between the campuses. More than 1,100 first-years can be housed in Plymouth, but this is still less than half the number arriving. Those from Devon or Cornwall are not normally offered a place. Most first-year students are housed on the former Rolle College campus, in Exmouth, which specialises in education, and at Seale-Hayne, where agriculture, food, land use and tourism are based. Exeter's art students have to rely on private housing, with help from the accommodation office.

All sites benefit from their proximity to the sea and areas of natural beauty. Plymouth, with more than 14,000 students, is inevitably the liveliest, with excellent facilities for watersports. The students' union has a base on each campus. Students' views are taken seriously: library and computing services were upgraded when a survey completed by 45 per cent of the student population showed dissatisfaction in this area.

UNIVERSITY OF PORTSMOUTH
University House, Winston Churchill Avenue, Portsmouth PO1 2UP (tel. 01705-876543)

University status 1992, formerly Portsmouth Polytechnic
Times ranking: 68 *(1997 ranking: 62nd equal)*

Enquiries: Assistant academic registrar (admissions)
Total students: 13,600
Male/female ratio: 582/48
Mature students: 25%
Overseas students: 7%

Main subject areas: business; environment; humanities; science; social sciences; technology. Certificate and diploma courses offered as well as degrees.

Teaching quality ratings
Rated excellent 1993-95: geography.
April 1995-97: French 23; German 21; civil engineering 20; electrical and electronic engineering 20; Italian 20; sociology 20; Iberian languages 18; Russian 18.

Portsmouth only narrowly missed university status before the polytechnics were created, and never gave up the chase. Degree work goes back to the beginning of the century and now three-quarters of students are at this level or above. Postgraduate numbers have been rising steadily. Staffing levels are among the most generous in the new universities and the ultra-modern library one the best. It stocks 500,000 volumes, takes 3,000 journals and has room for 840 readers. Completion rates are also among the best in the sector, while the graduate employment rate is good, especially for a university where a high proportion of students take arts subjects.

Languages are Portsmouth's greatest strength, as teaching and research assessments have shown. The near-perfect score for French was the best in the country, while the research rating for Russian was among the best for any subject in the former polytechnics. Every faculty is involved in research and the 44 per cent of academics entered for assessment was among the most in the new universities. The result was a healthy boost for Portsmouth's finances. One student in five takes a language course, and the facilities rival those of many traditional universities. Some 1,000 Portsmouth students went abroad for part of their course last year. The range of subjects has widened in recent years after mergers with the Solent School of Nursing and the Portsmouth College of Art, Design and Further Education. There are now 3,000 part-time students and more than 11,000 full-timers, of whom one in ten is from overseas, many coming from the Continent.

The main Guildhall campus consists of 26 buildings dotted around the city centre, which are being refurbished and in some cases replaced in an £8 million programme. The business school and information technology are three miles away at Milton, with education and English nearby at

Langstone. Only health studies are off Portsea Island, based at Queen Alexandra Hospital, in Cosham. Two new academic buildings have been put up in the city centre. The aluminium-clad £8.3-million St Michael's Centre opened in June 1996. The Portland Building – eco-friendly, with solar panels, and costing £5.9 million – opened in 1996. A building programme is also underway to add to the stock of residential accommodation. Eleven halls,, some overlooking the sea, already provide 1,778 places, three-quarters of which are reserved for first years. The students' union runs 'secure-a-home' days at the beginning of September to help the remaining new arrivals with house-hunting.

Sports facilities are good, especially for water sports. In addition to the university's own facilities, students may use the city's at half price. The students' union, which operates on both main sites, is lively.

QUEEN'S UNIVERSITY, BELFAST
Belfast BT7 1NN (tel. 01232-245133)

Founded 1845, royal charter 1908
Times ranking: 43 *(1998 ranking: 41)*

Enquiries: Admissions officer
Total students: 13,500
Male/female ratio: 49/51
Mature students: 12%
Overseas students: 11%

Main subject areas: agriculture and food science; arts, economics and social sciences; education; engineering; law; medicine; science; theology.

Teaching quality ratings
Rated excellent 1993-95: English; geology; history; law; music; social work.
April 1995-97: civil engineering 22; chemical engineering 21; Iberian languages 21; mechanical engineering 21; French 20; modern languages 19; sociology 19.

Queen's is generally regarded as Northern Ireland's leading university. It was one of three university colleges for the whole of Ireland in the 19th century, and still draws students from all over the island. However, the numbers coming from mainland Britain declined as the Troubles dragged on. Fewer than three per cent come from 'over the water' now although the number of applications this year has risen by some thirty per cent.

The emphasis is on research, although the university has been boosting its undergraduate numbers recently. An unusually high proportion of undergraduates go on to further study, giving Queen's a good record in the jobs league. Research ratings were variable in the last assessment exercise, with only one area – manufacturing and mechanical engineering – achieving a 5-star grading. Six subjects were placed in the next highest category, but anatomy and dentistry were near the bottom of the scale. Successes in the teaching ratings have come mainly in the arts and engineering. Music and mechanical engineering are highly rated for both teaching and research. English, history, law and social work have all been graded excellent. All courses (apart from medicine) are now modular, and the university has moved to a two-semester year. In February 1999 Queens formed a new partnership with St Mary's College and Stranmilh's College aimed at integrating the three institutions academically.

Applicants are not usually interviewed, but those receiving offers are invited to visit the university. The high proportion of home-based students means that most are familiar with the surroundings already. The majority of students live within a mile of the main campus, which is in turn a mile from the centre of Belfast. The university's 2,200 residential places accommodate almost all first-years, and private sector rents are relatively low. A new library has been built, and students have access to almost 2,000 computer workstations across the university. Last summer saw the refurbishment of a new teaching facility on the main site, paying special attention to proper facilities and access for the disabled.

The university area, among the most attractive in Belfast, is one of the city's main cultural and recreational centres. Queen's runs an arts festival each November, and its cinema is one of the best in the province. The university also has excellent sports facilities within two miles of the campus.

Though Queen's has been criticised for religious imbalance among its staff, it remains firmly committed to an equal opportunities policy. Although nightlife has returned to the city centre, social life is concentrated on the students' union and the surrounding area of Southern Belfast.

UNIVERSITY OF READING
Whiteknights, PO Box 217, Reading RG6 2AH (tel. 01734-875123)

Founded 1892, royal charter 1926
Times ranking: 24th equal *(1998 ranking: 28)*

Enquiries: Registrar
Total students: 9,900
Male/female ratio: 45/55
Mature students: 25%
Overseas students: 15%

Main subject areas: agriculture and food science; education and community studies; letters and social sciences; urban and regional studies.

Teaching quality ratings
Rated excellent 1993-95: environmental studies; geography; geology; mechanical engineering.
April 1995-97: sociology 22; town planning 22; building 21; French 21; German 20; Italian 20; linguistics 19.

Best known for its agricultural courses, which have always attracted large numbers of overseas students, Reading is also strong in subjects as diverse as mechanical engineering (top-rated for teaching), Italian, environmental biology and French. The merger with Bulmershe College in 1989 strengthened education courses and saw film and drama and American studies introduced.

The university's vice-chancellor, Professor Roger Williams, is committed to breaking down the barriers between the arts and sciences. Reading has already taken some steps in this direction, notably in a joint initiative with the Open University to develop standardised course materials to help underqualified students cope with physics degrees. The programme will be used to diagnose the gaps in students' knowledge and help to bring them up to the standard of other undergraduates. The scheme won a prize for innovation in 1992, and Reading was also one of nine institutions chosen to lead a new national project to widen access to physics degrees. The scheme is now set to extend to engineering. A four-year degree in the subject includes an access year for those without the necessary qualifications for the conventional degree. Arts and social science students take three subjects for their first two terms. All degrees are now modular, but possible combinations of degrees are usually limited to subjects within the same faculty.

Reading's high research standards allow it to attract some leading academics. Environmental sciences, construction and plant sciences reached the top rung of the research ladder in 1996. One in five of the academics assessed was in one of the top two categories. Town planning and sociology have achieved the best scores in recent teaching assessments.

The main campus is set in 300 acres of parkland on the outskirts of Reading, but the old college, less than two miles away, has its own facilities. The university has spent more than £60 million on new buildings in the past decade. Meteorology and management were the latest areas to benefit, with agriculture next on the list. The university has 13 halls of residence and access to two others owned by the neighbouring Gyosei International College, a Japanese institution with strong links with the university. With 4,700 places, first-years are guaranteed a place if they are holding Reading as a firm choice by the end of June. Sports facilities are good and have recently been extended; there is a nominal fee for their use. The main students' union is large and has a well-equipped branch at Bulmershe.

THE ROBERT GORDON UNIVERSITY
Schoolhill, Aberdeen AB10 1FR (tel. 01224-262000)

University status 1992, formerly the Robert Gordon Institute of Technology
Times ranking: 59 *(1998 ranking: 58)*

Enquiries: Admission office
Total students: 7,200
Male/female ratio: 49/51
Mature students: 20%
Overseas students: 5%

Main subject areas: applied sciences; architecture; art and surveying; business management; computer and mathematical sciences; electronic and electrical engineering; food and consumer studies; health and social work; librarianship and information studies; mechanical and offshore engineering; nursing; pharmacy; public administration and law. Also linked diplomas.

Teaching quality rating 1994-98
Rated excellent: chemistry; nutrition and dietetics.
Rated highly satisfactory: architecture; business and management; graphic and textile design; mathematics and statistics; mechanical engineering; pharmacy; physiotherapy; physics; radiography; social work.
From 1998: European languages 19.

Early links with the North Sea oil and gas industries exemplify Robert Gordon's commitment to vocational education. All offshore workers must have a certificate from its Survival Centre, and some longer courses are tailored to the industry's needs. Mechanical and offshore engineering is the biggest such course. Other strengths include engineering, pharmacy, business and management, architecture and art and design. Chemistry is top-rated for teaching, but no subject reached the top three of the seven research assessment groups.

Courses are flexible. Membership of credit accumulation and transfer schemes allows easy transfer in and out of the university, which also takes large numbers of students without the standard entrance qualifications. The integration of HNDs with the degree programmes allows students to switch levels with ease, which has helped to widen access further. There are now more than 70 degree courses, and fleeting talk of a merger with Aberdeen University is long forgotten. Students from the two institutions mix easily, and there is a healthy academic rivalry in some areas.

The main city-centre campus adjoins Aberdeen art gallery. As well as six other sites in the city, the university runs an attractive field study centre at Cromarty, in the Highlands. Residential accommodation has long been a problem in the city, but the university is adding places every year. The university currently has 1,500 places in halls of residence, in which first-years are given priority, but there are still not enough to guarantee new students accommodation. Disabled students are well provided for, though. The students' association, based in the city-centre union building, is active. Sports facilities are unremarkable but there is access to some at other institutions.

UNIVERSITY OF ST ANDREWS
College Gate, North Street, St Andrews KY16 9AJ (tel. 01334-476161)

Founded 1411
Times ranking: 10 *(1998 ranking: 10)*

Enquiries: Schools liaison office
Total students: 5,600

Male/female ratio: 46/54
Mature students: 7%
Overseas students: 3%

Main subject areas: arts; divinity; science; medicine.

Teaching quality ratings 1994-97
Rated excellent: cellular biology; chemistry; economics; geography; history; mathematics and statistics; organismal biology; physics; psychology.
Rated highly satisfactory: business and management; computer studies; English; geology; history of art; medicine; philosophy; theology.
From 1998: European languages 22.

St Andrews is the oldest Scottish university and the third oldest in Britain. The town is steeped in history, as well as being the centre of the golfing world. The university is set in the heart of St Andrews, and accounts for about a third of the town's 16,000 inhabitants. There are close relations between town and gown, particularly on the cultural and social side. Many colourful traditions remain. New students acquire third- and fourth-year 'parents' to ease them into university life, and on Raisin Monday give their academic guardians a bottle of wine in return for a Latin receipt, which can be written on anything. Every Sunday, students wearing red gowns process along the pier of St Andrews harbour. Another unusual feature is that all humanities students are awarded an MA rather than a BA.

The preponderance of students from south of the border has earned St Andrews the nickname of Scotland's English university, a trait that will be tested by the introduction of fees, which favours Scottish and Continental students. Scottish numbers have already crept up to almost half the undergraduate total and more than half the postgraduates.

The main buildings date from the 15th and 16th centuries, but sciences are taught at the modern North Haugh site a few streets away. Everything is within walking distance, although bicycles are common. Although small, St Andrews maintains a wide range of courses. The variety of subjects rated excellent for teaching demonstrates quality across the board. Although psychology was the only starred department for research, mathematics, classics, history, philosophy and theology all finished in the next highest group. The university's reputation has always rested primarily on the humanities. It has the largest medieval history department in Britain, for example. But a full range of physical sciences are available, with sophisticated lasers and the largest optical telescope in the United Kingdom. A £4.2-million extension to the Gatty Marine Laboratory will pioneer research into whales, dolphins and seals.

The university has room for two-thirds of its students, so accommodation is no problem for first-years. A new residence of 350 rooms with en-suite facilities has brought the number of places to 3,000. Sports facilities are excellent and there are even two £5,000-bursaries awarded by the Royal and Ancient Club to promising golfers. Academic bursaries are also available to Scottish entrants. Social facilities are sufficient for the size of university.

St Andrews is a tight-knit community much favoured by independent schools and much loved by most of its students but not to everyone's taste.

UNIVERSITY OF SALFORD
Salford M5 4WT (tel. 0161-745-5000)

Founded 1896, Royal charter 1967
Times ranking: 57 *(1998 ranking: 56)*

Enquiries: Admissions office
Total students: 13,700
Male/female ratio: 41/59
Mature students: 38%
Overseas students: 6%

Main subject areas: art and design technology; business management; conservation studies; engineering; environment; healthcare; humanities; languages; media; music and performance; science; social sciences.

Teaching quality ratings
Rated excellent 1993-95: music.
April 1995-97: housing studies 22; drama, dance and cinematics 21; Arabic 20; sociology 20; civil engineering 19; electrical and electronic engineering 16.

A merger with University College Salford, with which there were already close links, provided a second opportunity to forge a new type of higher-education institution as the university celebrated its centenary. Uniquely among the older universities, it now has almost five per cent of its students on further education courses. The main victim of the university cuts of the early 1980s, Salford has bounced back as the prototype decentralised, customer-oriented university. Although not in the top rank of universities, it is generally regarded as stronger now than before the cuts.

Previously a College of Advanced Technology, Salford has retained its technological bias, although growing numbers of social scientists now make up a good third of full-time undergraduates. Over 30 per cent of the students are on sandwich degrees, many going abroad for their placements. A modular course structure is now complete. European studies and engineering are among Salford's specialities, although engineering ratings have been disappointing. The area attracts many of the 1,500 overseas students, but only music of the 11 departments covered in the first rounds of teaching assessment was considered excellent. Consumer studies and health care account for much of the recent growth, with a national centre for prosthetics and orthotics and a high reputation for the treatment of sports injuries.

Fewer than half the academics were entered for the last research assessment exercise, when the built environment was the only subject area to be starred. European studies was also rated as nationally excellent. Nonetheless, the university remains committed to research: it has established six multi-disciplinary research institutes and a graduate school to oversee teaching and research for postgraduate students.

The modern landscaped campus is only two miles from the centre of Manchester and has a mainline railway station. At its centre is a municipal park, a haven of lawns and shrubberies on the banks of the River Irwell. Nine out of 10 first-years are offered one of the 2,700 places in mostly purpose-built accommodation close enough to walk or cycle to lectures. Private rents are relatively low, although the size of Manchester's student population creates some problems. The students' union has plenty of facilities and sports enthusiasts are well catered for with two sports halls, pitches nearby, a new swimming pool and an outdoor pursuits officer for other activities.

UNIVERSITY OF SHEFFIELD
Sheffield S10 2TN (tel. 01142-222000)

Founded 1828, royal charter 1905
Times ranking: 13 *(1998 ranking: 12)*

Enquiries: Undergraduate admissions office
Total students: 21,000
Male/female ratio: 51/49
Mature students: 19%
Overseas students: 8%

Main subject areas: full range of disciplines in eight faculties: architectural studies; arts; educational studies (postgraduate); engineering; law; medicine; pure science; social sciences.

Teaching quality ratings
Rated excellent 1993-95: architecture; English; geography; history; law; mechanical engineering; music; social work; sociology.
April 1995-97: Russian 24; town and country planning 23; East and South Asian studies 22; linguistics 22; materials technology 22; chemical engineering 21; civil engineering 21; French 21; Iberian languages 21; German 20.

Sheffield has been enjoying one of its most successful periods, climbing The Times rankings with consistently good ratings for teaching and research. A good showing followed in the research rankings. Since then nine departments have secured the top rating in the first rounds of teaching assessment and all of those inspected since have registered at least 20 points out of 24. Russian achieved the maximum score to add to its Grade 5 for research. Four out of 10 academics assessed for research were in the top two categories. Electrical and electronic engineering, materials science, archaeology, information management and theology were all considered internationally excellent. The results made Sheffield the top-placed provincial university in the comparison of research funding which allowed for subject differences.

The university has always enjoyed one of the highest ratios of applications to places – more than 10:1 recently – and began its latest phase of expansion before most of the traditional universities. New degrees include journalism studies, East Asian studies and electronic engineering with a modern language. Over 200 undergraduate courses have been moulded into a modular system, and semesters have been introduced. The university also offers courses in a network of further education colleges, mainly but not exclusively in the north of England. There are plans for a university college in the Dearne Valley, 12 miles north of Sheffield. Medicine has attracted most of the recent investment in bricks and mortar. A £12-million programme is extending teaching facilities for pre-clinical students and the School of Nursing and Midwifery.

First-years are virtually certain of one of some 8,000 residential places, which are within walking distance of the main university precinct, itself less than a mile from the city centre. Few, if any, places are available in clearing, but those who take this route are offered temporary housing until a hall place comes free. Most departments are in the same area, on the affluent side of the city. The students' union, which was extended recently, is well equipped and run; it even has its own pub near the halls. The union's long-established student reception service ensures that new arrivals feel at home, visiting those in private accommodation as well as hall-dwellers. Sports facilities are excellent, the World Student Games, having transformed the city's amenities, complement the already impressive range run by the university. Students invariably like Sheffield. It is said that a quarter stay in the city after graduation.

SHEFFIELD HALLAM UNIVERSITY
Pond Street, Sheffield S1 1WB (tel. 01142-720911)

University status 1992, formerly Sheffield Polytechnic
Times ranking: 65th equal *(1997 ranking: 57)*

Enquiries: Student administration office
Total students: 18,600
Male/female ratio: 56/44
Mature students: 36%
Overseas students: 3%

Main subject areas: business, urban and regional studies; computing; construction; cultural studies; education; engineering; financial studies; health and community studies; information technology; law; leisure and food management; management science; science. Certificate and diploma courses also offered.

Teaching quality ratings
Rated excellent 1993-95: English
April 1995-97: materials technology 22; sociology 22; building 21; mechanical engineering 21; history of art 20; communication studies 19; modern languages 19; civil engineering 18; electrical and electronic engineering 18.

The new university has been undergoing a £51-million transformation designed to alter its image and cater for an even bigger student population as well as to revitalise the city centre. It once considered moving to a less central development area, but will now keep its main site in the heart of Sheffield. The slump in the property market put the university's full centralisation plan on hold, but other development work is continuing apace: new buildings for engineering and information technology have been completed; an atrium provides social space for students and staff; and an innovative library development, the Adsetts Centre, has now opened. For the moment, some students will continue to be based in buildings near the main site, although the Sheffield Business School now has its own city-centre headquarters. There is free transport between the three main sites. Sheffield Hallam now has over 22,000 students, including part-timers, making it one of the largest of the new universities. It was one of the first three polytechnics to be established, and can trace its origins in art and design back to the 1840s.

Business and industry are closely involved in developing the 400 courses, most of which are applied rather than theoretical. There is also growing strength in applied research, which provides more income than most of the new universities can command. Only English was rated as excellent in the first eight teaching assessments, but building, sociology and materials technology have scored well recently. Business and management is by far the biggest of the 12 schools.

More than a third of the students are over 21 on entry. That many live at home gives first-years looking for accommodation a better chance of securing a place from Sheffield Hallam's expanding housing stock, but only 30 per cent can be housed at present. For those who have to fend for themselves in the private sector, rents are relatively low. The university's sports facilities are limited, but those built for the World Students Games are on the doorstep. The students' union is purpose-built, and the new developments have provided more catering and recreational space.

SOUTH BANK UNIVERSITY
103 Borough Road, London SE1 0AA (tel. 0171-815 6109)

University status 1992, formerly South Bank Polytechnic
Times ranking: 79 *(1998 ranking: 80th equal)*

Enquiries: Admissions office
Total students: 14,100
Male/female ratio: 55/45
Mature students: 56%
Overseas students: 11%

Main subject areas: business; built environment; education; engineering; health; science; social sciences. A wide range of certificate and diploma courses also offered.

Teaching quality ratings
Rated excellent 1993-95: none.
April 1995-97: modern languages 22; town planning 22; electrical and electronic engineering 19; sociology 19; chemical engineering 18; land and property management 18; mechanical engineering 17.

South Bank has styled itself 'the university without ivory towers'. The new university's links with the local community are such that 70 per cent of students are from the area, many coming from south London's wide range of ethnic groups. Of more than 19,000 students, a third are part-time, and half the undergraduates are on sandwich courses. The latest of a series of access initiatives gave local mature students the chance to upgrade their maths at a summer school which attracted almost 300 applicants.

South Bank has stayed closer than most of the new universities to the technological and vocational brief given to the original polytechnics. Engineering is second only to business in terms of size. The design students regularly rake in national prizes and modern languages and town planning have scored well in teaching assessments. Social policy recorded the best of several creditable results in the last research assessment exercise, boosting the university's income to the extent that an authoritative analysis which allowed for differences in subject mix places South Bank top of the new universities and eleventh overall. Unusual features include the Centre for Explosion and Fire Research and the National Bakery School. Diploma and degree courses run in parallel, so that students can move up or down if another level of study is found to suit them better than their original choice. All courses are modular and credit transfer allows prior learning, in or out of formal education, to count towards a degree.

The main campus is in Southwark, not far from the riverside arts complex. The university has bought an adjacent derelict site, which wil be developed for teaching accommodation as soon as funds allow. A purpose-built site three miles away houses the faculty of the built environment. Academic facilities include a new library, which is one of the most technologically advanced in the country and houses over 300,000 volumes as well as CD-Roms and videos. All students have access to language courses, mainly through programmed tapes in a manned self-service language laboratory.

Sporting prowess is a particular source of pride. Greg Searle was a South Bank student when he won an Olympic rowing gold medal in 1992. Facilities include two gymnasia and a large sports ground in nearby Dulwich. Students' union facilities have recently been expanded and include one of London's biggest student venues (The Void). The university has doubled its stock of accommodation recently, but only overseas students and first-years living 50 miles from London are guaranteed one of the 1,200 places. More local first-years are given priority for the rest. The usual London housing problems apply for those who have to fend for themselves (including 50 per cent of first-year students).

UNIVERSITY OF SOUTHAMPTON
Highfield, Southampton SO9 5NH (tel. 01703-595000)

Founded 1862, royal charter 1952
Times ranking: 22 *(1998 ranking: 21)*

Enquiries: Assistant registrar (admissions)
Total students: 13,000
Male/female ratio: 53/47
Mature students: 13%
Overseas students: 7%

Main subject areas: wide range of disciplines in eight faculties: arts; education; engineering and applied science; law; mathematical studies, medicine, health and biological sciences; science; social sciences.

Teaching quality ratings
Rated excellent 1993-95: chemistry; computer science; English; geography; geology; music; oceanography; social work.
April 1995-97: sociology 21; modern languages 18.

Having improved its position in the funding councils' latest rankings, Southampton now claims to be among the top research universities. It is in the top five for the proportion of income derived from research. Although it is one of the few traditional universities with a department at the wrong end of the seven-point research scale, the 13 departments in the top two categories more than compensate. Nutrition and electrical and electronic engineering were considered internationally excellent. Eight of the first dozen departments inspected were rated excellent for teaching, demonstrating the university's all-round strength. More recent assessments have continued the trend.

Southampton recently added a new dimension by taking in La Sainte Union College's teacher training and arts degrees to create Southampton New College. The new campus has a regional focus, offering opportunities for students from backgrounds that are thin on the ground at traditional universities. The university had already added Winchester School of Art, where well-established European links will complement the university's own continental outlook. Winchester, which increased the student population by 1,000 students, even has an outpost in Barcelona for a fashion degree. The student traffic flows both ways, with 1,200 overseas students from 100 different countries. The interdisciplinary British Studies programme is a particular draw for those from abroad.

The university opened a docklands campus on the city's revitalised waterfront in 1996. The Southampton Oceanography Centre, a joint project with the Natural Environmental Research Council costing £49 million, is said to be Europe's finest. In the same year, the Avenue campus opened near the main Highfield campus to house all the arts departments. The university is defensive about the contrast between these developments and the more ambitious relocation plans it had earlier in the decade, but they nevertheless ease the pressure on teaching space. Recent developments include new buildings for synthetic chemistry, electronics and computer science, a commercial services centre and a graduate centre for social sciences.

Among Southampton's diverse strengths are chemistry, geography, computer science and music all of which are highly rated for teaching and research. Medicine offers clinical training even in the first two years, allowing fourth-year students to specialise.

First-year students who make Southampton their top choice are guaranteed one of the 4,000 places in mixed residences, provided their home is outside the city boundaries. Those who use the university as their 'insurance' choice may have to wait four weeks. Most of the halls and self-catering flats are within walking distance of the campus, and one was designed specifically for disabled students.

If you meet the sometimes exacting entrance requirements, the process of securing a place should go smoothly. An independent schools' survey rated Southampton admissions (in common with only Oxford and Cambridge) one of the top university admissions services for two years in succession.

The students' union has all the facilities expected at a large university and the athletics union is one of the highest in Britain, with 80 clubs. The university has launched its own employment service for students for part-time jobs during vacations and term-time.

STAFFORDSHIRE UNIVERSITY
College Road, Stoke-on-Trent ST4 2DE (tel. 01782-294000)

University status 1992, formerly Staffordshire (originally North Staffs) Polytechnic
Times ranking: 83rd equal *(1998 ranking: 88)*

Enquiries: Academic registrar
Total students: 12,700
Male/female ratio: 57/43
Mature students: 34%
Overseas students: 4%

Main subject areas: applied science; business and management; ceramics; computing; design; economics; electrical and electronic engineering; fine art; geography; history of art; humanities; law; mathematics; health and nursing; mechanical and computer-aided engineering; politics; psychology; science; sports. Diplomas also offered.

Teaching quality ratings
Rated excellent 1993-95: none.
April 1995-97: history of art and design 21; modern languages 21; electrical and electronic engineering 20; materials technology 17; sociology 17.

The new university has been expanding on two sites, the headquarters in Stoke and the other in Stafford. A massive rationalisation programme, designed to cope with rapid and continuing growth, saw two-thirds of Staffordshire's staff move offices. The rural Stafford site , inherited from a 1960s teacher training college, features the purpose-built Octagon Centre, in which lecture theatres, offices and walkways surround a huge concourse containing more than 800 advanced computer workstations.The business school, which includes a degree in business enterprise, straddles the two sites in a deliberate attempt to foster links with the private sector. A new law building opened in Stoke in 1995.

Engineering and computing, which is one of the largest such departments in the UK, were the polytechnic's traditional strengths, but arts and social science courses have seen the greatest new growth. None of the first 11 departments to be assessed was rated excellent for teaching, though history of art and modern languages subsequently racked up good scores. Extensive language laboratories are open to all students and are heavily used.

There are special incentives for local school and college leavers in the form of the Priority Applications at Stafford Scheme for school and college leavers from Staffordshire, Shropshire and Cheshire. This gives the under-21s resident in the county a guaranteed place if they meet the minimum requirements of a course. Mature students are guaranteed at least an interview if they join one of the range of access courses. The policy is working: more than a third of the students are from the local area.

Good sports facilities, coaches and courses have been attracting growing numbers of top sportsmen and women, including three who have won medals at the World Student Games, the Commonwealth Games and Olympics. Stoke is much better provided for than Stafford. Expansion has placed a strain on student union facilities on all sites.

Hundreds of residential places have been added since a much-publicised accommodation shortage in 1990. The university now has 2,000 self-catering places, most of them reserved for first-years. Further building is planned, and private rents are also lower than in most other student areas.

UNIVERSITY OF STIRLING
Stirling FK9 4LA (tel. 01786-473171)

Royal charter 1967
Times ranking: 33rd equal *(1997 ranking: 36th equal)*

Enquiries: Student recruitment officer
Total students: 6,300
Male/female ratio: 50/50
Mature students: 25%
Overseas students: 10%

Main subject areas: accountancy; biological and environmental sciences; business and management; computer science and mathematics; economics; education; English; film and media studies; nursing and midwifery; marketing; modern languages; philosophy; political studies;

psychology; religious studies; sociology.

Teaching quality ratings 1993-98
Rated excellent: economics; English; environmental science;
psychology; sociology; theology.
Rated highly satisfactory: business and management; cellular biology; finance and accounting; French; history; mass communications; mathematics and statistics; organismal biology; philosophy; politics; social
work; teacher education.
From 1998: European languages 20.

One of the most beautiful campuses in Britain features low-level, modern
buildings in a loch-side setting beneath the Ochil Hills. Stirling Castle dominates the campus and is used for office accommodation. Even after a 20
per cent expansion over four years, the university will still be among the
smallest in Britain and likely to remain so. It also has probably the most
popular chancellor. Spurning the usual dignitaries, the university choose
Dame Diana Rigg for its top post. The actress follows such luminaries as
Lord Robbins, Sir Monty Finnieston and Lord Balfour of Burleigh.

Although highly rated in some research fields – the world-renowned
Institute of Aquaculture pre-eminently – the university concentrates on
teaching rather than research. Social work was the only starred subject in
the last research assessment. Excellent teaching ratings for economics,
sociology, theology and English show Stirling's strength in the arts and
social sciences. Only environmental science has redressed the subject balance so far. The university has taken over three nursing colleges at Forth
Valley, Falkirk, at Inverness and at the Western Isles based at Stornaway,
with a total of 1,300 extra students.

Stirling was the British pioneer of the semester system, now growing in
popularity in other universities. The academic year is divided into two 15-
week terms, with short mid-semester breaks. Successful completion of six
semesters will bring a general degree, eight an honours degree. Since 1993,
the university's modular scheme has been credit-based, allowing transfers
between courses and institutions. The emphasis on breadth of study is such
that there are no barriers to movement between faculties. Undergraduates can
switch the whole direction of their studies as they progress. Each student has
an academic adviser to help plan a programme of courses. International
exchanges are popular, with students going to the USA, Japan, Canada and
Sweden each year.

Film and media studies is particularly popular, and the Scottish Centre
for Japanese Studies, which offers the language with a range of other subjects,
is beginning to break new ground. Business and management courses are
also well regarded.

First-years are guaranteed one of the 2,000 residential places on campus. Another 1,000 places are available in self-catering flats in Stirling
itself. These are usually filled by second, third and fourth-years. Students'
union and social facilities are more than adequate for a small university,

while sports enthusiasts have access to a competition-size pool and the Scottish National Tennis Centre.

UNIVERSITY OF STRATHCLYDE
Richmond Street, Glasgow G1 1XQ (tel. 0141-552 4400)

Founded 1796, royal charter 1964
Times ranking: 45 *(1998 ranking: 42)*

Enquiries: Schools and colleges liaison service
Total students: 14,500
Male/female ratio: 50/50
Mature students: 30%
Overseas students: 10%

Main subject areas: arts and social science; business; education; engineering; science.

Teaching quality ratings 1993-99
Rated excellent: architecture; business and management; chemistry; electrical and electronic engineering; geography; mechanical engineering; pharmacy; physics; politics.
Rated highly satisfactory: cellular biology; civil engineering; computer studies; English; history; hospitality studies; law; mathematics and statistics; social work; sociology; teacher education.
From 1998: European languages 22; chemical engineering 20; planning and landscape 19.

Even as Anderson's Institution in the 19th century, Strathclyde concentrated on 'useful learning'. Some Glaswegians still refer to it as 'the tech'. But if the nickname does less than justice to the current portfolio of courses, the university has never shrunk from its technological and vocational emphasis. Strathclyde aims to offer courses that are both innovatory and relevant to industry and commerce – hence civil engineering with European studies, or mathematics with languages. One of the most popular courses is the five-year BA in international business and modern languages, which combines three business subjects with two languages and offers a year in an overseas business school.

Traditional science degrees have continued to prosper, however, with a series of top ratings for teaching from the funding council. Although only immunology won the coveted 5-star rating for research, six other areas reached the next category, allowing Strathclyde to place itself third in Scotland for research, behind Edinburgh and St Andrews. The business school is one of the largest in Europe, and has achieved high positions in our subject rankings for undergraduate courses. Its European focus is matched elsewhere in the university, which has encouraged all departments to adapt their courses to the needs of the single market. Strathclyde runs a credit-based modular degree system, which has proved especially attractive to mature students. They now account for 30 per cent of the student population, and have a special group to look after their interests.

In 1993, Strathclyde merged with Jordanhill College of Education, the UK's largest teacher training institution. The merger gave the university both a second campus on the west side of the city and the opportunity to open a faculty of education. Jordanhill occupies a 67-acre parkland site with views of the Clyde estuary. There are now well over 16,000 students including part-timers, but 56,000 including the growing number of continuing education students taking short courses or distance-learning programmes.

The main John Anderson campus is in the centre of Glasgow, behind George Square and near Queen Street station. Apart from the Edwardian headquarters, the buildings are mostly modern. The latest is the Health Sciences Building opened in 1998, bringing together pharmacy, physiology and immunology.

The university is losing its image as a 'nine-to-five' institution thanks to a student village on campus, complete with pub. The large union building attracts students from all over Glasgow to its ten floors. The sports facilities are also good and the quality of careers advice made Strathclyde the first university to win a Charter Mark. First-years are given priority in the allocation of 2,000 residential places on or near the main campus and are guaranteed a room if home is over 25 miles away. There are also three halls of residence on the Jordanhill campus, where the pressure on accommodation is lighter than in the city centre. Half the first-years find private accommodation, although they have priority for the campus rooms.

UNIVERSITY OF SUNDERLAND
Langham Tower, Ryhope Road, Sunderland SR2 7EE (tel. 0191-515 3000)

University status 1992, formerly Sunderland Polytechnic
Times ranking: 91 *(1998 ranking: 93)*

Enquiries: Admissions officer
Total students: 11,500
Male/female ratio: 51/49
Mature students: 35%
Overseas students: 10%

Main subject areas: art; business; communications; computing information systems; design; education.

Teaching quality ratings
Rated excellent 1993-95: none.
April 1995-97: media studies 22; sociology 21; mechanical engineering 19; Iberian languages 18; French 17; German 17.

Britain's newest city (upgraded by the Queen in 1993) also has one of the country's newest university campuses. Designed for 8,000 students by the end of the decade, St Peter's Campus, by the banks of the Wear, will eventually accommodate half of Sunderland's eight schools. The business and computing schools have already moved into the 24-acre site, which also contains library and student union facilities. The first stage of St Peter's, completed in September 1995, won the Best New University Buildings in Britain award. The second stage added 500 computers in the School of Computing and Information Systems. The main campus and a third site in one of Sunderland's suburbs are within walking distance.

The university doubled in size in four years, and has taken advantage of urban regeneration programmes to expand its facilities to match. On the opposite bank of the river to St Peter's, 1,000 residential places have been completed, supplementing another new student village at the Chester Road campus. Other facilities had already been improved. A well-appointed science complex opened on the original city-centre site in 1993. Language laboratories have been upgraded, and specialist research centres have been opened for ecology and Japanese studies.

Sunderland has lost Dr Anne Wright, once Britain's only female vice-chancellor, to the University for Industry, which is to have its headquarters in the city after a successful pilot there, but she has given the university a higher profile and forged a productive partnership with the city. She is aiming to double the proportion of students coming from the local area, which has little tradition of participation in higher education. A pioneering access scheme offers places to people without A-levels provided that they are able to reach required levels of literacy, numeracy and other basic skills at local colleges.

Developments have been planned with an eye to history, for example incorporating a working heritage centre for the glass industry at the heart of the new campus, which is built around a 7th-century abbey described as one of Europe's first universities. The glass and ceramics design degree carries on a Sunderland tradition, while the courses in automotive design and manufacture serve the region's new industrial base. The large pharmacy department is another strength.

The university expects to satisfy 85 per cent of first-years requiring accommodation, although the new building programme has barely done more than keep pace with expansion in student numbers. There are now more than 2,500 beds available, 250 of them in a new hall of residence reserved for postgraduates. First-years are given priority in the allocation of places, most of which are within walking distance of lectures. Sunderland makes a special effort to cater for disabled students, 700 of whom were at the university last year. A new course to help dyslexics was added in 1997. Sports facilities have been improved recently with a bigger swimming pool and fitness rooms, and the students' union has expanded, opening its own nightclub. Sunderland itself is not the liveliest student centre, but Newcastle is within easy reach.

UNIVERSITY OF SURREY
Guildford, Surrey GU2 5XH (tel. 01483-300800)

Founded 1891, royal charter 1966
Times ranking: 30 *(1997 ranking: 39th equal)*

Enquiries: Undergraduate admissions officer
Total students: 7,300
Male/female ratio: 48/52
Mature students: 24%
Overseas students: 21%

Main subject areas: biological sciences; chemical, civil and environmental engineering; education; electronic engineering; health and medical sciences; human sciences; information technology and mathematics; language and international studies; management; mechanical and materials engineering; performing arts; physical sciences.

Teaching quality ratings
Rated excellent 1993-95: business and management; music.
April 1995-97: electrical and electronic engineering 23; civil engineering 22; sociology 21; chemical engineering 18; modern languages 18.

Surrey has remained true to the technological legacy of its institutional predecessor, Battersea Polytechnic Institute. Even some of the arts courses carry a BSc and are highly vocational. It's a subject bias which has helped the university to a regular spot at or near the top of the graduate employment league, as well as to a healthy research income. Arts courses have been growing nonetheless.

Surrey hit the headlines a few years back when it awarded a first-class degree to a 13-year-old, the youngest graduate of modern times. But its real priorities are work experience and language competence. Most degrees last four years, one (or two half-years) of which is spent in work placements, often abroad. Student numbers have reached 11,000 after several years of growth almost entirely through full-time programmes. This expansion has been well-managed, and the relatively new area of business studies was the first to win top-rating for teaching from the funding council. All students are encouraged to enrol for a course at the new European language centre, and new engineering degrees have a language component. With more than 1,000 work stations, the use of computers is also common to all Surrey's courses. Electrical and electronic engineering was the only starred department in the last research assessment exercise and has since recorded a near-perfect score for teaching. Sociology and toxicology were considered nationally excellent for research with sociology also registering a good score for teaching.

The compact campus is a ten-minute walk from the centre of Guildford. Most of the buildings date from the late 1960s, when the university was developing. The campus includes two lakes, playing fields and residential accommodation. A neighbouring 70-acre site houses the Surrey Research

Park, which is attracting tenant companies rapidly. Successes in technology transfer contracts abroad and, in particular, in attracting overseas students won the university a Queen's Award for Export Achievement. The university has been strengthening its research effort, for example with an extension in 1997 to a centre for satellite engineering research. The Queen's Anniversary Prize for Satellite Engineering was awarded to the centre in February 1997. A university company, Surrey Satellite Technology Ltd, is Britain's only company to launch micro-satellites.

Some 3,000 campus residential places, plus another 350 in a university development not far away, enable Surrey to offer accommodation to all first-years and many finalists. The service is welcome: Guildford is an extremely expensive area for renting in the private sector. Sports and social facilities on campus are good. The proximity of London, little more than half an hour away by train, is an attraction to many students, but can also make the university less lively at weekends.

UNIVERSITY OF SUSSEX
Falmer, Brighton BN1 9RH (tel. 01273-678416)

Royal charter 1961
Times ranking: 38th equal *(1998 ranking: 35)*

Enquiries: Undergraduate admissions
Total students: 9,000
Male/female ratio: 50/50
Mature students: 32%
Overseas students: 20%

Main subject areas: African and Asian studies; biological sciences; chemistry; cultural and community studies; engineering; English and American studies; environmental science; European sciences; mathematics and computing; physics; social sciences.

Teaching quality ratings
Rated excellent 1993-95: anthropology; English; music.
April 1995-97: sociology 24; French 22; linguistics 22; electrical and electronic engineering 21; history of art 20; modern languages 17.

Its heyday as the most fashionable campus in Britain may have been a quarter of a century ago, but Sussex's all-round academic reputation has seldom been higher. Applications have been rising steadily, and there are plans for considerable expansion, particularly in part-time courses and off-campus programmes. The interdisciplinary approach, which has always been Sussex's trademark, is being re-examined to see whether this 1960s concept needs adaptation for the 21st century. The university has hopes of becoming more creative in the combinations it offers to students, although breadth of study is already taken for granted. Potential applicants have long had the choice of a conventional prospectus or a computerised version to mull over the options. Sussex claimed to be the first university to use the floppy disk format, which is in keeping with its desire to make full use of the latest educational technology.

A commitment to taking candidates with no family tradition of higher education partly explains a relatively high proportion of mature students and lower average entry grades than in most of the leading universities. However, a transformation in the fortunes of Sussex graduates in the labour market, high library spending and a good research record have ensured high placings in *The Times* tables. The university recently surveyed its graduates five years after leaving Sussex and found an enviable employment record. Proof that research matches this enviable record was supplied in 1996 when Sir Harry Kroto, from the Chemistry Department, won the Nobel Prize for Chemistry – Sussex's third Nobel Prize. Although only history of art achieved the top score for research, half the academics assessed were in the next category of nationally excellent. Established favourites such as American studies are still highly rated and popular with students. Sociology registered the maximum score for teaching quality, with French and linguistics also doing well.

Sussex offers a year abroad in many subjects, and one student in five takes advantage of the facility, either in Europe or North America. Some courses offer joint qualifications with European universities. For those who stay behind, the university has added hundreds more residential places in recent years, and can now guarantee accommodation to first-years who accept a place by the end of June. Overseas students, who represent 17 per cent of the university population when Europeans are included, are the other priority group in the allocation of places, which are self-catering. The aim is to house all students for two years of their courses by the end of the decade, although many enjoy a spell in Brighton itself. A high proportion of the students are from the London area, where many return at the weekends, leaving the campus quiet at times. Sports facilities are good, and the active students' union has most of the usual amenities although not its own building. Though students find the cost of living high and have a tradition of criticising the university, few would choose to go elsewhere.

UNIVERSITY OF TEESSIDE
Borough Road, Middlesbrough, Cleveland TS1 3BA (tel. 01642-218121)

University status 1992, formerly Teesside Polytechnic
Times ranking: 87th equal *(1998 ranking: 80th equal)*

Enquiries: Admissions office
Total students: 8,000
Male/female ratio: 55/45
Mature students: 33%
Overseas students: 6%

Main subject areas: business and management; computing and mathematics; design; health; humanities; international studies; law; science and technology; social sciences. Certificates and diplomas also offered.

Teaching quality ratings
Rated excellent 1993-95: computer science.
April 1995-97: electrical and electronic engineering 21; civil engineering 19; sociology 19; chemical engineering 17.

Teesside has dubbed itself the 'Opportunity University', stressing its open access policies and consumer-oriented approach. Although never one of the more fashionable polytechnics, the new university now has more than 13,000 students, a quarter of them on part-time courses. Expansion will now resume with the change of Government policy. Good use has been made of links with multinationals with bases in the area. Computing and design are strong, and electrical and electronic engineering showed up particularly well in teaching assessments. The research record is less impressive, with almost 90 per cent of the academics assessed relegated to one of the bottom two categories.

The university is based mainly in Middlesbrough, with an outpost, used mostly for postgraduate or short courses, five miles away at the foot of the Cleveland Hills. Some £20 million has been spent on the town-centre site in recent years. A state-of-the-art Open Learning Centre opened in 1995, and the main library was replaced at a cost of £11 million two years later. An innovation centre is the latest addition, incorporating virtual reality facilities, computer laboratories and an array of high technology. Other building has increased the university's residential stock, although it still only has room for three-quarters of the first-year students requiring accommodation. Priority is given to new students in the allocation of the 1,050 hall places and the university's 400 more places in privately-owned flats and houses. A high proportion of mature students, many of whom live at home, eases the pressure on the housing market.

Teesside is using its new facilities to provide degrees in subjects such as interactive entertainment systems and virtual reality. It also offers an Individual Programme of Study Scheme, which allows students to take combinations outside the usual range of courses. The idea is to tailor a qualification to personal needs, as long as at least half of the final award is from Teesside courses

True to its traditions, the new university has almost a quarter of its students on sub-degree courses. It also runs extended degrees in engineering for those with arts qualifications who want to switch. Some courses are franchised to further education colleges in the region, helping to swell participation in an area where few could take advantage of higher education in the past. Almost all courses are now within the modular system of credit accumulation. There are now 3,500 health students based mainly in hospitals around Teesside. There are plans for an £8 million centre to bring them together on the campus.

Sports facilities at Teesside are improving although many require membership, which costs £15 a year, bringing with it discounts at some local venues. The lively students' union, which claims to sell some of the cheapest beer in the country, is the centre of social life for most undergraduates. It boasts a 1,000 capacity nightclub, The Zoo, which opens until 2am.

THAMES VALLEY UNIVERSITY
St Mary's Road, Ealing, London W5 5RF (tel. 0181-579 5000)

University status 1992, formerly West London Polytechnic
Times ranking: 94 *(1998 ranking: 74th equal)*

Enquiries: Guidance centre, 18-22 Bond St., London W5 5AA
Total students: 15,400
Male/female ratio: 38/62
Mature students: 55%
Overseas students: 20%

Main subject areas: American and European studies; business; communications; history; information management and computing; languages; law; leisure and tourism; management and accountancy; media and music; nursing and health; politics; sociology. Certificates and diplomas also offered.

Teaching quality ratings
Rated excellent 1993-95: none.
April 1995-97: linguistics 22; sociology 22; modern languages 18; American studies 15.

A disastrous year for Thames Valley saw the publication of a highly critical report on academic standards, the subsequent resignation of the university's high-profile vice-chancellor and the collapse of applications for places. An action plan put together by Sir William Taylor, who once performed a similar role in less challenging circumstances at Huddersfield University, should put TVU back on a firm academic and financial footing,but a full recovery will take time. Action to trim a multi-million pound deficit will include the pruning of some courses.

Although most of the data used to compile the Times league table predates the university's recent difficulties, it has also slipped dramatically in our rankings. An unusually low score for graduate destinations was the main factor behind a 20-place drop in the table, leaving it third from bottom. TVU's policy of open access is a handicap in a ranking which takes account of entry standards, but low scores in other areas have masked an improvement in teaching quality assessments.

The split-site university will maintain the unconventional approach which has become its hallmark, however. It describes itself as "student-driven" and takes a higher proportion of sub-degree students than any of its rivals. Yet it was one of the few new university with a top-rated department in the last research assessments, which saw most areas given low scores. A meteoric rise in the early years of the decade saw the new university achieve its present status only a year after becoming a polytechnic. The breakthrough came when Ealing and Thames Valley colleges agreed to merge, producing an institution of sufficient size to become a polytechnic at the most opportune moment.The downside of such rapid expansion became obvious when administrative problems led to some students being passed with inadequate marks. Although the new Quality Assurance Agency cleared the university of deliberate "dumbing down", a full report in 1998 found a number of serious shortcomings in academic and administrative procedures.

TVU London, as the university likes to be known, occupies town-centre sites in Ealing and Slough, which are linked by a free bus service. Health-care courses are run in Ealing, Slough and Reading, while the London College of Music and Media, whose students have access to the Ealing Studios, further widens the scope of the university. The university is eager to expand its Ealing base, which was built for far fewer students and has been suffering from overcrowding. Limited construction projects have eased the problem and several buildings have been refurbished. A £2.2-million law building was followed by a high-tech learning resource centre. A prize-winning equivalent designed by Sir Richard Rogers has opened in Slough.

Courses are fully modular, and the majority of the 27,000 students are part-timers. Almost half are from London or Berkshire, a trend further encouraged through the designation of East Berkshire College as an associate college. The move towards an electronic university already sees students issued with bar codes that set out timetables and give access to the library.

The students' union operates on both sites, and has been fully refurbished in Ealing and Slough. Sports facilities leave something to be desired, although the Slough multi-gym is impressive. TVU has no residential accommodation though it does have an accommodation service which helps place students in private housing (though in an area which tends to be expensive).

UNIVERSITY OF ULSTER
Coleraine, County Londonderry BT52 1SA (tel. 01265-44141)

Royal charter 1984, formerly the New University of Ulster and Ulster Polytechnic (merged 1984)
Times ranking: 54th equal *(1998 ranking: 54)*

Enquiries: Admissions officer
Total students: 16,300
Male/female ratio: 52/48
Mature students: 25%
Overseas students: 12%

Main subject areas: art and design; business and management; education; humanities; informatics; science and technology; social and health sciences. A wide range of certificate and diploma courses also offered.

Teaching quality ratings
Rated excellent 1993-95: environmental studies; music; social policy.

April 1995-97: American studies 22; land management 21; media studies 21; electrical and electronic engineering 20; French 20; civil engineering 19; German 19; Iberian languages 18; sociology 17.

Ulster's charter is unique in stipulating that there should be courses below degree level, but that did not stop Ulster briefly catching Queen's, Belfast, in *The Times* rankings. Although the gap has since reopened, community consciousness has done the university's reputation no harm in Ireland. Almost 40 per cent of the students come from blue-collar backgrounds, more than twice the UK average, while the student profile also mirrors the religious balance of the province, from which 80 per cent of students are drawn. Nearly a third of the university's students are part-time, a proportion that has been growing steadily and now includes more than 2,500 on degree courses alone. Mature students are strongly represented and well catered for, with the facilities of a nursery and three playgroups in the university. The corporate plan stresses both continuing commitment to such diversity as well as some significant change. The academic year is divided into two semesters and all courses are modular and permit credit transfer. The main sites in and near Belfast have never been busier, and the expanded Magee College in Londonderry attracts students from both sides of the border. The original university at Coleraine is more traditional, following the campus style of the 1960s.

Although research is not the university's principal strength, Ulster was chosen as the site of a prestigious new Centre for Conflict Resolution, formed in collaboration with the Tokyo-based United Nations University. A 5-star rating for biomedical science led a mixed set of results in the last research assessments. American studies has achieved the best score for teaching quality.

High technology brings the university together for teaching purposes, but the sites are 80 miles apart at the farthest point, and very different in character. Jordanstown, seven miles out of Belfast, has the most students, Coleraine still has an isolated feel, and Magee, for many years the poor relation confined to adult education, is now a thriving centre. Some courses offer lectures on more than one campus, but for the most part students are based on a single site throughout their university life.

The Derry campus has been the scene of considerable recent development. New residential accommodation, a sports hall and a teaching block with computer laboratories, have all gone up recently. The university is still hoping to open a "Peaceline" campus bridging the two communities in Belfast, but finance has been the inevitable stumbling block so far.

The university has more than 1,150 residential places including many controlled by a students' housing association. A high proportion of students live at home, which eases pressure on the rooms: the university houses less than half of the first-years requiring accommodation. The sporting and students' union facilities naturally vary between sites, with Jordanstown having the main sports centre and Belfast the biggest student building.

UNIVERSITY OF WALES
Cathays Park, Cardiff CF1 3NS (tel. 01222-382656)

Founded 1893

Enquiries: To individual colleges
Total students: 33,750
Male/female ratio: 55/45

The university, which celebrated its centenary in 1993, is second only to London, its federal counterpart, in terms of full-time student numbers, with more than 45,000 students including part-timers. Like London, it is surrendering more power to its colleges. At the same time, however, inter-collegiate links have been increasing, especially in research. The Higher Education Funding Council for Wales had to squeeze budgets for 1998, but has increased research funding by £2 million, including a number of collaborative projects involving all six colleges. A new structure was introduced in 1996, bringing the university colleges in Cardiff and Newport into the fold. However, they are not on a par with the existing member institutions.

Not listed separately:
University of Wales College of Medicine, Heath Park, Cardiff CF4 4XN (tel. 01222-747747). Founded 1931. Full-time students: 850 (BMedSci, BSc, BDS, BN). Based at the University Hospital of Wales, two miles from the centre of Cardiff.

UNIVERSITY OF WALES, ABERYSTWYTH
PO Box 2, Aberystwyth, Ceredigion SY23 2AX (tel. 01970-622021)

Founded 1872
Times ranking: 48 *(1998 ranking: 48)*

Enquiries: Admissions officer
Total students: 7,200
Male/female ratio: 50/50
Mature students: 18%
Overseas students: 11%

Main subject areas: accounting and finance; biological sciences; computer science; economics; education; English; European languages; geography and earth sciences; information and library studies; law; mathematics; media studies; physics; politics; Welsh.

Teaching quality ratings 1993-97
Rated excellent: accounting and finance; earth studies; economics; English; environmental science; geography; information and library studies; politics; Welsh.

Although the oldest of the Welsh university colleges – 125-years-old in 1997 – Aberystwyth has long prided itself on a modern outlook. The college's move to modular degrees, completed in 1993, was the culmination of a long-standing policy of flexibility in undergraduate programmes. Both vocational and academic courses benefit from the same arrangement.

In spite of its rural surroundings, 'Aber' is as keen as its big city rivals to tailor courses to the needs of business and industry. It was among the recipients of a £1-million grant from the last government to promote business awareness among staff and students, and is working closely with the Welsh Medium Enterprise Agency to promote self-employment among Welsh speakers. The collaboration resulted in a new degree course in Welsh and accountancy. The college also received £1.2 million to spend on information technology and an extension to the library, which is the National Library of Wales.

Nevertheless, financial pressures felt throughout the University of Wales have forced Aberystwyth to make cuts recently. Biological sciences, geology and continuing education have all lost staff. More positively, a new school of Management and Business has been established and a Community University of Rural Wales is taking higher education to people who previously have been starved of opportunities.

Merger with the Welsh Agricultural College produced a new Institute of Rural Studies in 1997, allowing Aber to claim the widest range of land-related studies in the UK. The institute shares the Llanbadarn campus with information and library studies and a further education college. Teaching ratings have been impressive, especially in the arts and social sciences. Although no subject managed a 5-star rating for research, applied mathematics held onto its Grade 5 score, where it was joined by politics and Celtic studies. Mathematics and science courses accept general studies as full A or AS levels as long as applicants have passed two other subjects. Some 35 entrance scholarships are available (with a closing date in mid-December) worth £600 a year.

An attractive seaside location does the college no harm when the applications season comes around. Aberystwyth is always heavily oversubscribed even though student numbers have increased considerably in recent years and have now exceeded the college's target. Almost a third of the students are Welsh. Student accommodation is being increased accordingly. An ambitious student village has been built next to the campus, adding another 1,000 beds so that more than 3,100 places are now available. First-years are guaranteed accommodation.

Sports facilities are good, and the students' union is the focus of social life. A new arts centre, built with the aid of £2.5 million from the National Lottery, is due to open in 1999. Aberystwyth itself is small and travel to other parts of Wales and to England slow, so applicants should be sure that they will be happy to spend three years or more in a tight-knit, remote community. Most are: 95 per cent of first-year students responding to the university's annual survey said they would choose Aberystwyth if they had their choice again.

UNIVERSITY OF WALES, BANGOR
Bangor, Gwynedd LL57 2DG (tel. 01248-351151)

Founded 1884
Times ranking: 51 *(1998 ranking: 46)*

Enquiries: Registrar
Total students: 6,400
Male/female ratio: 41/59
Mature students: 33%
Overseas students: 11%

Main subject areas: accountancy and banking; arts; biological and environmental sciences; education; electrical and electronic engineering; health studies; languages; mathematics and computing; pure and applied sciences; social sciences; sports sciences.

Teaching quality ratings 1993-97
Rated excellent: biology; chemistry; forestry; music; ocean sciences; psychology; Russian; theology; Welsh.

Bangor emerged from major restructuring in the late 1980s as a leaner, fitter institution although students still make up a third of the local population. Departments such as philosophy and physics closed to enable the college to develop strengths in a range of different subjects. The result has been one of the best records in Britain in teaching assessments, with half of the subjects inspected rated excellent. There are still 270 degrees to choose from. Ten new degrees opened in 1998, including biology with a European dimension and English with film studies. A range of £1,000-scholarships, offsetting the introduction of fees for some students, helped attract more than 7,000 applications in 1997.

Bangor merged with a teacher training college, Coleg Normal, in August 1996. The university has already achieved its aim to expand from 5,250 students to 7,000 by the end of the decade, launching new courses in popular disciplines. There were 1,300 applications for 80 places on a new sport, health and physical education degree. Other initiatives have seen the health-studies faculty, which includes nursing, offer a new course in radiography. And the highly-rated agriculture, forestry and biology departments have come together in an Institute of Environmental Studies. Longer-established favourites include a unique course in agroforestry, a four-year electronic engineering degree and psychology.

Based at the water's edge, little more than a stone's throw from Snowdonia, Bangor is one of the university's centres for Welsh-medium teaching. It also offers a single honours degree in the subject. More than 10 per cent of the students speak Welsh and several departments now offer tuition in the language. One of the seven halls of residence is also Welsh-speaking. The regional role has been strengthened with the establishment of a Community University of North Wales, allowing students to take diploma courses, or start some degrees, in further education colleges.

Bangor has more than 2,300 residential places on four sites. The college guarantees to house all first-years who are invited to sample the facilities, with or without their parents, during the summer vacation. Twenty-five per cent of accommodation is reserved for second- and third-years. Private housing is in short supply, but not expensive, for those who choose to live away from the university. The students' union is spacious for the size of institution, and incorporates a separate Welsh union. Sports facilities are also good, especially for outdoor pursuits and watersports. The university is the focus of social and cultural life in the small town (officially a city) of Bangor.

CARDIFF UNIVERSITY OF WALES
PO Box 68, Cardiff CF1 3XA (tel. 01222-874000)

Royal charter 1988, formerly University College (founded 1883) and University of Wales Institute of Science and Technology (founded 1866), merged 1988
Times ranking: 35 *(1998 ranking: 34)*

Enquiries: Admissions officer
Total students: 14,400
Male/female ratio: 46/54
Mature students: 16%
Overseas students: 16%

Main subject areas: business studies and law; health and life sciences; humanities and social studies; engineering and environmental design; physical sciences.

Teaching quality ratings 1993-97
Rated excellent: accounting and finance; anatomy and physiology; archaeology; architecture; biochemistry; biology; chemistry; civil engineering; dentistry; education; environmental engineering; English language; electrical and electronic engineering; maritime studies; mechanical engineering; medicine; optometry; pharmacy; philosophy; psychology; town planning.

Cardiff has established itself as the frontrunner in Welsh higher education after a period of financial instability. Not only is it the university's largest college by far, it also won pride of place in both *The Times* rankings and the last research assessment exercise. With 21 subjects covered by "excellent" assessments for teaching, Cardiff claims the best record in Britain, while one analysis placed Cardiff in the top 10 in the country for research. Only city and regional planning managed a 5-star rating for research but almost half the academic staff entered for assessment were placed in one of the top two categories. Psychology and mechanical engineering have excellent ratings for teaching and research. More than half of all subjects are now rated as excellent for teaching, and Cardiff registered a 41 per cent increase in research funding in 1997-8. Many of the 350 degree schemes already feature a common first year, and the introduction of a fully modular structure with two semesters will make degrees even more flexible. Cardiff now has more than 14,000 students with an average of three Bs at A level and is planning for more by the end of the century.

The university is hoping for a new academic and residential complex in Cardiff Bay to complement its city-centre site, having already opened an impressive new physics and computer science complex. Recently, however, it has been concentrating on improving and expanding its residential stock. More than £17 million has been spent on accommodation, and extra hall places have provided the university with more than 4,800 beds. It can house 40 per cent of students and all first-years are guaranteed a place. After that many students find flats in the north of the city.

The university enjoys a central location in the Welsh capital, forming a significant part of the civic complex around Cathays Park. The acquisition of the former headquarters of Glamorgan council will allow the social sciences the luxury of a 'superschool' for 1,000 students. Library services are provided through ten specialist libraries close to the relevant departments. Some computer links are open 24 hours a day.

The students' union has some of the best facilities in Britain including seven bars, and sports enthusiasts are equally well provided for, especially since the opening of a £1.5-million sports hall. Cardiff pioneered offering part-time employment for students through the Unistaff scheme, which provides essential back-up services for the university. Little more than a third of the students are Welsh, and many come from overseas.

UNIVERSITY OF WALES, LAMPETER
Lampeter, Ceredigion SA48 7ED (tel. 01570-422351)

Founded 1822, part of University of Wales since 1971
Times ranking: 58 *(1998 ranking: 55)*

Enquiries: Assistant registrar
Total students: 1,600
Male/female ratio: 50/50
Mature students: 26%
Overseas students: 6%

Main subject areas: ancient Greek; ancient history; archaeology; classics; English; geography; history; informatics; Islamic studies; medieval studies; modern languages; philosophy; religious studies; theology; Victorian studies; Welsh studies; women's studies.

Teaching quality ratings
Rated excellent: archaeology; classics and ancient history.

In the whole of England and Wales, only Oxford and Cambridge were awarding degrees before Lampeter. Yet only Buckingham University is smaller today. Based on an ancient castle site and modelled on an Oxford college, St David's College was established mainly to train young people for the Anglican ministry. The full title has receded into the small print recently, as the college has preferred to stress its membership of the University of Wales. There have been significant changes in the last few years – notably the introduction of information studies – and there are now 300 combinations available from the college's joint honours programme. But there is no immediate aim to go beyond 1,600 students, itself almost double the numbers taken a few years ago.

Lampeter will remain an arts-dominated haven in rural Wales. Even informatics leads to a BA, and the Bachelor of Divinity is the only other undergraduate award. The college is best known for languages and theology, the top-rated research department. But students are opting increasingly for joint honours, incorporating broad courses such as Victorian studies. Modular degrees have been introduced over three years. The BA degree, taken by most undergraduates, is still divided into two parts, with the first year designed to ensure breadth of study. Students are encouraged to try a new language, such as Arabic, Greek or Welsh. Part two normally takes a further two years, although languages or philosophy take three.

Though the majority of students are English, most departments offer the option of tuition in Welsh. Lampeter is deep in Welsh-speaking West Wales, and both the college and the students' union have strong bilingual policies. Although only four hours from London and two from Cardiff, Lampeter's isolation would be a problem for the unprepared. The town has only 4,000 inhabitants, and the nearest station is at Carmarthen, more than 20 miles away. A high proportion of students run cars.

Compensations include guaranteed accommodation on the college's doorstep and an escape from the overcrowding experienced on many campuses. The college trades on its small and friendly character. There is even a "walk you home" service when the bar shuts, although the crime rate is among the lowest in Britain. Two-thirds of students live in hall, where rents are lower than at most universities. A crêche, funded by the National Lottery, opened in December 1996.There is a purpose-built students' union, which is the centre of social life at the college. The sports hall is modern and there are outdoor pitches close at hand.

UNIVERSITY OF WALES, SWANSEA
Singleton Park, Swansea SA2 8PP (tel. 01792-295784)

Royal charter 1920
Times ranking: 46 *(1998 ranking: 43)*

Enquiries: Schools liaison office
Total students: 8,700
Male/female ratio: 46/54
Mature students: 19%
Overseas students: 7%

Main subject areas: arts and business; economics; engineering; health; law; science; social sciences.

Teaching quality ratings 1993-97
Rated excellent: biosciences; chemical engineering; civil engineering; classics and ancient history; computer science; electrical and electronic engineering; geography; German; history; Italian; materials engineering; physics; psychology; Spanish.

Phased expansion over several years has exceeded Swansea's target of 10,000 students, including part-timers, but the university (no longer a mere college) is still stretched financially. As part of the development plan, a wide variety of new courses has been introduced, many with a language component but staffing levels have had to be reduced. A fully modular course system is now in place. Swansea takes its European interests seriously, having over 90 links with Continental institutions. Science students, as well as those on arts courses, are being encouraged to undertake some of their studies abroad. A number of inter-faculty courses combine languages with subjects such as management and engineering. The new law school also offers options in European and international law, as well as the British legal system. Swansea counts European management science and modern languages among its strengths although all branches of engineering are highly rated. Civil engineering and metallurgy and materials were the top-scoring departments in the latest research assessment, while the overall performance was mixed. Computer science and history started a succession of excellent ratings for teaching. German,too has high scores for both teaching and research.

For all of the concentration on international activities, Swansea has not forgotten its local responsibilities. In 1993 it opened a University of the Valleys, offering part-time courses for mature students in an area hard hit by pit closures and the decline of the steel industry. Franchised courses are being introduced in local further education colleges and a compact with schools in mid-Glamorgan encourages students in areas of economic disadvantage to aspire to higher education.

The immediate locality is far from depressing, however. A coastal position two miles from the centre of Swansea offers ready access to excellent beaches on the Gower Peninsula, and the campus itself occupies an attractive parkland site. Apart from Singleton Abbey, the neo-Gothic mansion which houses the administration, most of the buildings are modern. A new Museum of Egyptology opened in 1997.

Some 3,000 students live in college rooms, and all first-years from outside the area are guaranteed accommodation. Half of the halls are on campus, the rest 30-minutes' walk away in a well-equipped student village. Both the students' union and sports facilities are good. Swansea has a good record in competitive sport, particularly rugby, and offers scholarships to outstanding sportsmen and women. The university makes a particular effort to cater for disabled students. There are facilities for the blind, deaf and wheelchair-bound.

UNIVERSITY OF WARWICK
Coventry CV4 7AL (tel. 01203-523523)

Royal charter 1964
Times ranking: 7 *(1998 ranking: 6)*

Enquiries: Academic registrar
Total students: 11,600
Male/female ratio: 52/48
Mature students: 10%
Overseas students: 9%

Main subject areas: arts; education; science; social studies in 29 departments.

Teaching quality ratings
Rated excellent 1993-95: business and management; computer science; English; history; law.
April 1995-97: drama and cinematics 24; sociology 24; German 23; media studies 23; French 21; history of art 21; Italian 21.

Now the most successful of the first wave of new universities, Warwick was derided by some in its early years for its close links with business and industry. Few are critical today. Tony Blair described the university as "at the cutting edge of what has to happen in the future". Both research and teaching are highly rated by the Funding Council. The university was the first to see two subjects – theatre studies and sociology – register maximum points for teaching, while three areas were top-rated for research. Teacher training courses are the latest to be lauded. Ofsted gave high ratings to the primary training programmes, which cater for undergraduates as well as graduates.

The overall standard of the 29 departments has also brought Warwick a top European award, and the science park, one of the first in Britain, is among the most successful. Warwick's Arts Centre – the second largest arts complex in the UK – has won £3 million of National Lottery money.

While other universities have tried to cover the whole range of academic disciplines, Warwick has pursued a selective policy. Without the expense of undergraduate medicine, dentistry or veterinary science to bear, the university has invested shrewdly, especially in business, science and engineering. However, the university does regret the absence of medicine and has launched a joint bid with Leicester University to base a school in Coventry.

Warwick built up its numbers in science and engineering when other universities were struggling to fill their places. The business school has also been growing rapidly, with a new £1-million wing added recently and further expansion planned. Some £35 million was spent on buildings and facilities during 1996, and the projects are now bearing fruit. An extension to the students' union, designed to attract members who did not use the existing facilities, opened in 1998. The humanities and chemistry buildings have been refurbished and a new computer science building is in the pipeline.

Though Warwick has been increasing undergraduate admissions by 5 per cent a year, it still sees itself primarily as a research university. As a result, the emphasis has been on building up postgraduate courses, taking 6 per cent more students each year for higher degrees and adding residential places to match. Pure maths, computer science and history are the top-rated research subjects but almost half of the staff assessed for research were in the top two categories. Such is the demand for places that many departments tend to stick to their offers which averaged 26 UCAS points last year. There is no sign of entry becoming any easier this year. There is now a separate postgraduate school, although all students still mix on the 720-acre campus three miles south of Coventry.

There are more than 5,000 residential places on campus, almost 2,000 of which have en-suite facilities. First-years (except those who got places through clearing) are guaranteed accommodation, and about half of those in their final year also live in, although restrictions on cars put some off. Sports and students' union facilities are both good. Union facilities were revamped in 1997.

UNIVERSITY OF WESTMINSTER
309 Regent Street, London W1R 8AL (tel. 0171-911 5000)

Founded 1838, university status 1992, formerly Polytechnic of Central London
Times ranking: 61 *(1998 ranking: 70)*

Enquiries: Central student administration unit
Total students: 19,700
Male/female ratio: 48/52
Mature students: 43%
Overseas students: 7%

Main subject areas: biosciences; business and management; computing; design; electronics; environment; languages and communication; law; mathematics; social studies. Certificate and diploma courses also offered.

Teaching quality ratings
Rated excellent 1993-95: none.
April 1995-97: East and South Asian studies 23; French 23; electrical and electronic engineering 21; civil engineering 20; German 20; linguistics 20; Iberian languages 18; Italian 19; Russian 18; sociology 18.

Westminster has been undertaking the biggest university construction project in Europe after reaping the benefits of its highly publicised success in the 1992 research assessments, when five academics from the Centre of Communication and Information Studies became the first members of a new university to secure a top rating. They repeated the feat in 1996, but missed out on the coveted new 5-star rating. Even in polytechnic days, research was given a high priority, and their achievement boosted Westminster's reputation immeasurably. The degree in media studies was already popular.

However, teaching, both on full and part-time courses, will continue to be the university's bread and butter. The main base, in the heart of London's West End, provides an ideal catchment for part-time students, who account for almost half of the 19,000 places. Only the Open University has a higher proportion of part-timers, and the balance enabled Westminster to avoid the full effects of the last government's squeeze on higher education.

Language teaching is one of the main strengths, with courses available from the most basic level to postgraduate. The School of Communications claims to teach the largest number of languages (28) in any British university. Chinese and French recorded near-perfect scores for teaching. Although none of the nine subjects covered in the first assessments was considered excellent, recent scores have shown real improvement. Engineering – highly rated in polytechnic days – has been shown to be strong. The university was also one of the pioneers of the Enterprise in Higher Education initiative, which weaves work-related skills into degree programmes.

What was Britain's oldest polytechnic occupies three sites in central London and one in Harrow, in the northern suburbs, where major development has taken place. Academic blocks, 468 residential places and a new sports hall have all been included in a £33-million programme. A high-tech information resources centre is already open, and by the end of the century the former higher education college campus will take 7,500 students. That will enable the university to consolidate on four sites. Design, media studies and the Harrow Business School are already in their new surroundings, and £10 million has gone into the refurbishment of Westminster's historic West End base. For the moment, accommodation remains a problem, with the university housing only 35 per cent of the first-years requiring places. More halls opened in 1997 but, although they are given priority in the allocation of places, at least half of all new students have to rely on expensive private accommodation. There are good outdoor sports facilities at Chiswick, in West London, although Harrow students inevitably find them distant.

UNIVERSITY OF THE WEST OF ENGLAND, BRISTOL

Coldharbour Lane, Frenchay, Bristol BS16 1QY (tel. 01179-656261)

University status 1992, formerly Bristol Polytechnic

Times ranking: 63rd equal *(1998 ranking: 59)*

Enquiries: Admissions officer
Total students: 18,400
Male/female ratio: 51/49
Mature students: 20%
Overseas students: 2%

Main subject areas: applied sciences; art, media and design; built environment; business and management; computer studies; economics and social science; education; engineering; health and social care; humanities, languages and European studies; mathematics; More than 5,000 students are taking certificate or diploma courses.

Teaching quality ratings
Rated excellent 1993-95: business and management; English; law.
April 1995-97: sociology and social policy 23; town and country planning 23; land and property management 22; media studies 22; building 21; modern languages 21

One of the top new universities in *The Times* table, the University of the West of England (UWE) chose a regional title from more than 100 suggestions in order to reflect the institution's ambitions. The university has forged close links with business and industry in the region and is the biggest in the Southwest with 1,000 academics and more than 300 degree programmes.

A high ratio of applications-to-places confirms the university's standing in a wide range of subjects. UWE has the best records of all the new universities in the teaching quality assessments, with sociology and town planning close to maximum points. A strong vocational bias, which the new university is committed to retaining, has also helped the institution to the top employment rating in previous years' tables. UWE was also among the top new universities in the last Research Assessment Exercise, achieving one of the sector's best scores for media studies. The business school is among the biggest in Britain, with 3,000 students on a wide range of courses. Law, like business rated excellent for teaching, received a commendation from the Legal Practice Course Board. Links with local colleges encourage entry from the region. The entrance system credits vocational qualifications and practical experience equally with traditional examination results.

There are five sites in Bristol itself, mainly around the north of the city, with regional centres in Bath, Swindon and Gloucester. Only Bower Ashton, which houses art and design, is in the south. The main campus at Frenchay, close to Bristol Parkway station, also houses England's Higher Education Funding Council. The university has more than 3,200 residential places and guarantees accommodation to first-years who meet certain criteria. Others have to fend for themselves in a relatively expensive housing market. There are complaints that Frenchay is isolated, but sports facilities are reasonable and the students' union well organised.

UNIVERSITY OF WOLVERHAMPTON
Wulfruna Street, Wolverhampton WV1 1SB
(tel. 01902-321000)

University status 1992, formerly Wolverhampton Polytechnic
Times ranking: 77 *(1998 ranking: 90)*

Enquiries: Admissions office
Total students: 15,500
Male/female ratio: 45/55

Mature students: 28%
Overseas students: 8%

Main subject areas: applied sciences; art and design; built environment; business and management; computing and information technology; education; engineering; European studies; health sciences; humanities; languages; legal studies; nursing and midwifery; social sciences. Certificate and diploma courses also offered.

Teaching quality ratings
Rated excellent 1993-95: none.
April 1995-97: Russian 22; American studies 21; linguistics 21; general engineering 20; Iberian languages 20; sociology 20; drama, dance and cinematics 19; French 19; German 17.

Wolverhampton is one of the biggest universities in the UK. It pioneered the 'high street higher education shop', bringing in thousands of students who might otherwise never have continued their education. The shop is part of the university's open-door policy to widen access to higher education across the west Midlands. There are big outreach programmes, taking university courses into the workplace. Half of the students come from the region.

Business courses were highly rated while Wolverhampton was still a polytechnic, particularly for an innovative one-year BA in Business Enterprise (BABE), designed mainly for mature students with diploma qualifications and potential for further progress. The area is still the university's largest, but recent assessments have been average. Inspectors were critical of Wolverhampton's franchising operation, which is increasing the number of students the university can take by running the first year of some degrees at further education colleges. Hotel, tourism and licensed retail management were found to be patchy, although procedures have been tightened up since. A more direct form of expansion has come with the opening of a campus in Telford, given a separate identity as The University in Shropshire. Business, computer-aided product design, computing and teacher training courses are being offered, appropriately in an enterprise zone, to serve a county without its own university.

The new base gives the university five campuses, linked by a free bus service. In addition to that in Telford, there are two in Wolverhampton, one in Walsall for teacher education, and one in Dudley for humanities and social sciences. The original site adjoins the Wolves ground and boasts three pubs. There are now more than 25,000 students, including part-timers. 3,000 took a work placement last year. The university plans to increase its student intake by around 6 per cent a year. Wolverhampton takes its responsibilities seriously. It was the first university to be registered under the British Standard for the quality of its provision; it gained a Charter Mark in 1994 and has been an Investor in People since 1996.

Accommodation is still limited, although the university now has more than 2,400 residential places. Virtually all first-year students who live more than

50 miles away will be offered accommodation and there is a guarantee of a place for new students from overseas. Many students live at home, and private rents in Wolverhampton are among the cheapest in the country. Social and sporting facilities vary considerably between sites, the best being in Wolverhampton.

UNIVERSITY OF YORK
Heslington, York YO1 5DD (tel. 01904-433533)

Royal charter 1962
Times ranking: 12 *(1998 ranking: 9)*

Enquiries: Undergraduate admissions office
Total students: 6,700
Male/female ratio: 50/50
Mature students: 12%
Overseas students: 10%

Main subject areas: 31 departments covering arts; economics; engineering; mathematics; philosophy; politics; science; social science.

Teaching quality ratings
Rated excellent 1993-95: architecture; computer science; English; history; music; social policy; social work.
April 1995-97: modern languages 22; Iberian languages 20

York is another university to have demonstrated both in successive *Times* rankings and the last research assessment exercise that youth is no bar to academic excellence. Its successes have continued with the teaching assessments, which have brought York more top ratings than any university of its size. York was second in *The Times* teaching rankings with all but one of the first eight subjects assessed rated excellent. There has been no slackening of the pace under the new system.

Like Warwick, the only one of York's contemporaries to rate as highly in our table, York has chosen its subjects carefully and has no plans for dramatic growth. But if there is no medicine, dentistry, veterinary science or law for example, the available subjects are offered in a range of unusual combinations. Many courses include a language component, and all students are actively encouraged to use the free language tuition. They can now add a York Award to their degree to demonstrate proficiency in job-orientated areas such as language and IT skills, community activities and voluntary work.

Still one of the smaller universities, York has no plans to expand its student population significantly. There have been at least ten applications for each place at York throughout the last ten years. Few universities have such high average entry requirements. Unlike many universities, York's main growth over the past decade has been in science and technology, balancing an initial bias towards the arts and social sciences. York received a Queen's Anniversary Prize in 1997 for work in computer science. Most of the top-rated courses are still in the established areas but economics, social policy and the new history of art degree are also among the strengths.

Since 1990 York has begun reviewing its courses every three years. Its first external 'academic audit' was generally complimentary about quality assurance procedures, and found students satisfied with the tuition arrangements. Computer science, which already had an excellent rating for teaching, reached the 5-star grade for research, as did psychology. Almost half the academics assessed for research were placed in the top two categories.

Every student has a "supervisor" responsible for their academic and personal welfare. A number of 24-hour terminal rooms are available for access to the university's computer network. With two newspapers, television and radio stations, as well as several magazines, students should be well informed on campus issues.

The seven colleges mix academic and social roles. All first-years are guaranteed a residential place on the lakeside campus, two miles from the centre of York, where two-thirds of all the university's students can be accommodated. Over the next four years all students' rooms will be fitted with telephones. Only archaeology and history of art are located off campus. They share a medieval building in the centre of the city.

Social life is based mainly in the colleges with no separate students' union building. Sports facilities are patchy: 40 acres of playing fields on campus (including an all-weather area added in 1996), some indoor facilities, but no university swimming pool.

11
UNIVERSITY CITIES

O ne glance at their glossy prospectuses shows that universities today are well aware that prospective students look almost as carefully at their future surroundings as at their chosen courses. Those set in rolling countryside or a lively city flaunt their advantages. The lecture room and library are only part of the story, and students are not going to achieve peak performance if they are tied for three years to a place they do not like. These pages offer a brief guide to the main student centres. All have at least two universities.

Fashions change quickly among students, and a popular city can soon lose its attraction. London, for example, used to be a magnet for students, but some of the capital's universities have struggled to fill their places recently because of the high cost of living. Manchester, by contrast, with its full-time student community of 40,000, has become a particular draw while Newcastle is also challenging for the position of the student's favourite city.

ABERDEEN

Population: 201,000
Student population: 16,500

University of Aberdeen
Distance from city centre: One mile.

The Robert Gordon University
Distance from city centre: Main campuses in the city centre; others two miles away.

Scotland's third largest city may suffer from foul weather, but Aberdeen is anything but bleak. The influx of moneyed oil workers during the 1980s gave the city an enviable selection of pubs, clubs and restaurants, but also put pressure on the stock of private accommodation. The situation has improved in recent years, but accommodation is still scarce and prices correspondingly high.

Social life tends to be focused on the students' unions, especially the older university's excellent facilities, to which all students have access. Nonetheless, the city has a vibrant social scene, and the Exhibition Centre is the most northerly stop on the tour circuit for many touring bands. The city's streets are safe and the locals friendly. For students who find

Aberdeen's atmosphere a little bland, communications to Edinburgh and Glasgow are good by both bus and train. The city is close to spectacular countryside and excellent beaches, as well as being a bustling social and commercial centre. Two theatres and three cinema complexes supplement the usual mix of pubs and clubs.

BELFAST

Population: 279,000
Student population: 18,000-plus

Queen's University Belfast
Distance from city centre: One mile.

University of Ulster
Of the university's 15,000 students only about 850 are based in Belfast, but many of those who study at Jordanstown live in the city. Plans for a new Belfast campus are still being considered.

The magnificent view from the Divis Mountain, looking down over green-domed civic buildings to Belfast Lough, is one which will surprise any student accustomed to images of Belfast as a battle-scarred mess of bombs and bullets. While the effects of the Troubles still intrude into students' lives, students will find that Belfast's inhabitants are very friendly and welcoming.

Indeed a student union representative stressed the danger of over-emphasising the Troubles, given that many students remain quite oblivious to goings on, wrapped as they are in the blanket of university life. Student life concentrates around Queen's campus in the south of the city. One offshoot of this is that this area, with its migrant population, has the highest incidence of burglary and car theft in the city. But the area is popular and is home to a wealth of restaurants, theatres and shops. Student bars tend to be particularly lively on Thursday nights, after which many students go home for the weekend. This weekly exodus can leave the campuses a little deserted, though this is less of a problem now that the number of overseas students has increased. Though social life may be concentrated in the campus area, Belfast does not lack for pubs and clubs. Music ranges from big-name concerts at Queen's union and King's Hall to impromptu folk music sessions which spring up in the city's pubs. The University of Ulster's Belfast based union has a resident DJ from Cream performing at the Art College, among a variety of other live acts.

As the cultural as well as political capital of Northern Ireland, Belfast is better endowed than most student cities with theatres and cinemas. Each November, Queens hosts an international arts festival to which all are welcome. Sports enthusiasts are not so well served.

BIRMINGHAM

Population: 938,000
Student population: 44,000

Aston University
Distance from city centre: The modern campus is a ten-minute walk.

Birmingham University
Distance from city centre: The red-brick campus is two miles south.

University of Central England in Birmingham
Distance from city centre: Nine sites. The main site is at Perry Barr, three miles north of the city centre.

To the casual observer, Birmingham may appear an unlovely sprawl of tarmac and concrete, albeit one which has been cleaned up over recent years. But beneath the grime, Birmingham has much to offer its 44,000 students, and the further 30,000 living in nearby Coventry and Wolverhampton.

Although considered not as lively or prosperous as some other cities of its size, Birmingham is currently undergoing something of a face-lift using the International Convention Centre and the National Exhibition Centre to draw thousands of visitors to the city. In the mean time, Birmingham is nonetheless well-equipped with cinemas, theatres, clubs, live music venues, restaurants and adequate shopping. Rag Marlut and the market area is especially popular with students. But if it lacks a clearly defined city centre, it has escaped the exorbitant prices of more cosmopolitan Manchester and London.

Birmingham Rep, Sadler's Wells, Symphony Hall and D'Oyly Carte ensure that top-class culture is available regularly. For those with more pop tastes, Birmingham NEC sees to it that the big-name acts do not miss the Second City. Sports enthusiasts can choose from Premiership football, test and county cricket, major tennis tournaments and indoor athletics.

The distance between the universities' sites mean that each is surrounded by its own student areas, and that students from different institutions are more likely to meet at city-centre pubs and nightclubs than at each others' student unions. Tension between 'posh' students and locals is a problem in some areas, while women may find the city centre's maze of subways unnerving, there are now fewer than there were, and following the G8 summit there are many more CCTV cameras which make the centre feel much safer.

BRIGHTON

Population: 138,000
Student population: 16,000

University of Brighton
Distance from city centre: One site in Eastbourne and three in Brighton.

University of Sussex
Distance from city centre: About four miles.

With more than 50 nightclubs and a pub for every night of the year, Brighton affords endless possibilities for entertainment to students who can stand the pace – and the cost of living in one of England's most diverse towns. With Brighton's diversity comes tolerance towards all types of people. In a town where students make up such a high proportion of the population, it makes good business sense for clubs and pubs to welcome them with open arms, and generous concessions. The variety of nightlife in the town centre means that Brighton's student unions are less well used than those at other universities although with a pint at almost half the price as in a club, the bars are still popular. Campus bars also benefit from their easy accessibility, compared with those in the centre. The overwhelming majority of Brighton students come from the London area, contributing to the town's reputation as 'London by the sea': the similarity to the capital city manifests itself not only in Brighton's variety and vitality, helped too by the large number of international students, but also in high prices and a somewhat slavish trendiness. Relaxed places, such as the North Lanes, do exist, however, if you know where to look.

Like many other seaside towns, Brighton offers a wide selection of off-season accommodation, although the quality can be suspect. For those who can afford it, the shopping is first-rate and, especially in The Lanes, trendy to boot.

BRISTOL

Population: 372,000
Student population: 30,000

University of Bristol
Distance from city centre: Pleasant Victorian campus spread throughout the city centre.

University of the West of England at Bristol
Distance from city centre: Of the four modern campuses, Redland (two miles away) is closest to the city centre.

Pretty, pricey and perennially popular among Sloanes, Bristol is described by students as being exactly the right size for a university city: large enough to be lively, but not so large as to be daunting.The city, which perches on hills overlooking the Severn estuary, is generally welcoming to students and offers a good deal of student-orientated entertainment. Clubs range from UWE's Friday night 'Fried' to the variety of Whiteladies Road, where there are plenty of student nights. While many students from the former polytechnic (colloquially known as UWE) and locals come to gigs in the older university's union, pubs in the town tend to be more segregated.

The range of shops in the city – everything from High Street standards to designer boutiques like Red or Dead – reflects its inhabitants' spending power. Part-time work is not too hard to come by, though temping agencies are swamped in the summer.

When looking for accommodation, students – especially those at Bristol University – tend to gravitate towards Clifton, Cotham and Redland, none of which is cheap. UWE students get a better deal by house-hunting near their main campus.

CAMBRIDGE

Population: 107,000
Student population: 23,000

Anglia (soon to be the University of Eastern England)
Distance from city centre: Modern campus about ten-minutes' walk from the city centre. Other campuses in Chelmsford and Brentwood.

Cambridge University
Distance from city centre: Ancient buildings forming the city centre.

The gulf between old and new universities is nowhere wider than in Cambridge: for students at Anglia, finding accommodation is a major headache; for those at Cambridge it is rarely even an issue. Nonetheless, the two universities' students do mix, and those at Anglia enjoy access to a wide range of discos, gigs and so forth. This is fortunate, for the range of events held outside the university is limited: Cambridge has a small town's choice of nightclubs and two gigging venues, which have played host to the likes of Suede over the past few years, but little else. In a town so dominated by students, town and gown relations are generally good: both sides can unite behind the common cause of hating tourists.

The atmosphere in a small city of such beauty can feel cloistered or even stifling, especially to those from larger and livelier places, but London is within easy reach. The city centre is pedestrianised and a very pleasant place to shop, with a wide variety of high street names to choose from.

CARDIFF

Population: 277,000
Student population: 25,000 plus

University of Glamorgan
Distance from city centre: The university campus is in a rural location about ten miles north of Cardiff, though many students live in and around the city.

Cardiff University of Wales
Distance from city centre: Modern and grandiose Victorian buildings all round the city centre.

University of Wales, College of Medicine
Distance from city centre: Based at the University Hospital of Wales, about two miles from the city centre.

Welsh pride in their capital city can be intense, but then there is much to be proud of in Cardiff, a smallish but prosperous and sometimes attractive city, which seems a million miles away from the dejected relics of south Wales' mining industry to the north.

The university's buildings are dotted around the city's civic centre, a dignified and open area dominated by gleaming white buildings. Cardiff has all the cultural and commercial facilities one would expect in a small capital city, and sports facilities are particularly good.

Those unlikely to score a try at the new National Stadium will at least be able to attend big rock concerts: many famous names have performed there. The city's good public transport system gives students access to the beautiful Brecon Beacons, an ideal location for walking or mountaineering.

Cardiff's student union building is one of the best in the UK, with its own recently refurbished nightclub, restaurants and a massive mock-Tudor bar. The university has its own employment agency, Unistaff, which finds students work within the university.

The city is well-supplied with theatres and cinemas, as well as its own opera company. The choice of shops is as extensive as you would imagine in a capital city. Cardiff has recently been cited as the best value city in the world by the British Tourist Authority. Communications are good for the many English students wanting a weekend at home.

COVENTRY

Population: 306,000
Student population: 20,000

Coventry University
Distance from city centre: Purpose-built campus in the city centre.

University of Warwick
Distance from city centre: Modern landscaped campus about five miles from the city centre.

Razed by the Luftwaffe during the war, Coventry rose from the ruins like a concrete phoenix. But if the city lacks any noticeable beauty, it makes up for its dowdy looks with good communications and low prices.

The paths of students from the two universities rarely cross. Students at Warwick tend to stay on campus, and prefer the less grim ambiences of Kenilworth and Leamington Spa to Coventry when looking for accommodation off-campus. The former polytechnic's students, on the other hand, revel in their city-centre location and make copious use of the city's pubs, clubs and sports facilities, as well as their own sports centre and students' union.

The city has good shopping centres and the locals are, for the most part, welcoming to students. However, those hoping to relax with a can of beer amidst Coventry's pre-fab splendour should beware: public drinking outdoors has been illegal in the city centre since 1988.

Entertainment is more plentiful than the city's image suggests, and Birmingham is on the doorstep for special events. Earlsdon and Whitton Ash are the main student areas for accommodation and rent is affordable.

EDINBURGH

Population: 500,000
Student population: 50,000

University of Edinburgh
Distance from city centre: Mixture of old and new buildings scattered around the city centre, with three main concentrations. Science and Engineering campus is two miles south of centre.

Heriot-Watt University
Distance from city centre: Green-belt campus seven miles away.

Napier University
Distance from city centre: Mainly modern buildings, most about two and a half miles west of the city centre.

Edinburgh, one of the most elegant cities in Europe, feels every bit a capital, albeit one where the pace of life is less frenzied than in London. The hills on which the city is built add to the grace of its tall, grey-stone buildings, but also emphasise bitterly cold winds.

Though students at Heriot-Watt tend to stay on their parkland campus, all three universities have access to each others' student union facilities. Few students will be able to resist the lure of the enviable selection of pubs and bars in the compact city centre. While 1 am is the norm for closing time, many bars are open until 3am and for those who choose, 24 hour drinking is still possible. The range of nightclubs is wide, although students tend to eschew the big glitzy clubs and concentrate on the rapidly changing range of smaller clubs.

Students make up a good proportion of Edinburgh's population with three higher education colleges swelling the numbers. They are generally welcomed in the cosmopolitan capital. Areas such as Marchmont and, for the better off, New Town (Britain's most beautiful housing estate) are the most popular for accommodation. The city is by no means cheap, however, whether for shopping, entertainment or renting a flat.

GLASGOW

Population: 654,000
Student population: 46,000

University of Glasgow
Distance from city centre: Compact campus in West End district of Glasgow, about three miles from the city centre.

Glasgow Caledonian University
Distance from city centre: Modern campus near the city centre.

University of Strathclyde
Distance from city centre: Main campus in the centre. Another campus

to the west.

One of Britain's largest and liveliest cities, Glasgow is probably Scotland's cultural capital, even if Edinburgh is the civic centre. Scotland's opera, ballet and national orchestra are based in the city, which also boasts a profusion of art galleries and theatres. Eight cinema complexes should be enough for the most demanding film buffs.

It is not just the climate which can be described, like the local rock band, as Wet Wet Wet. Glaswegians are famously fond of their pubs, though the city's reputation as 'home of the head-butt, land of the lagered-up' is something of an exaggeration. Generally, students find the locals very friendly.

The city's club scene rivals those of London and Manchester, with an excellent range of clubs, which are up-to-date without being as pretentious as some of their southern counterparts. In particular, Glasgow University Union's nightclub attracts over 2,000 students every weekend and is the most popular venue in the West End. Live music fans will also find an exhaustive range of venues in the city, from the cavernous SECC, to the popular Barrowlands and the improbably named King Tut's Wah-Wah Hut. Many bands also perform at the second of Glasgow University's Unions, the Queen Margaret Union.

The three universities are within easy reach of each other and many students live in the attractive West End of the city, though the area's desirability has led to an increase in prices over recent years. Road and rail links are good for week-ends away.

HULL

Population: 253,000
Student population: 20,000

University of Hull
Distance from city centre: Modern campus three miles north.

University of Lincolnshire and Humberside
Distance from city centre: Several sites within six miles of the centre, plus others in Grimsby and Lincoln.

Though chic shopping centres now crowd the harbours in Philip Larkin's adopted city, Hull's heritage as a commercial port extends into the present day. The ever-growing number of students at the city's two universities find Hull a reasonably lively city with a lower-than-average cost of living which recently made national headlines.

The city centre, where students can experience mild hostility from locals, particularly on weekend evenings, has no shortage of pubs. The nightlife is easily on a par with the larger northern cities, with at least one student event taking place every night of the week. There are a number of nationally acclaimed live music venues such as the Adelphi Club, which helped launch the career of Hull's most famous export, The Beautiful

South.The older university's student union is becoming an increasingly regular stop on the itinerary of indie bands.

Communications by road and rail are adequate, considering the city's isolated location. The city has its own telephone network and 10p buys an unlimited local call.

The former Humberside university's venture into Lincolnshire has eased the pressure on accommodation, which was already cheap, and is now plentiful. The two universities' location as immediate neighbours has always meant that their students frequent the same areas creating what has been described by one student as a tight-knit, bohemian village feeling. Students take full advantage of Hull's proximity to the continent, with Amsterdam the favoured destination. Celebrating its 700th Anniversary this year, Hull is intent on dispelling the ghost of its collapsed industries, and is reinventing itself as a young, exciting and forward thinking city for the 21st Century.

LEEDS

Population: 717,000
Student population: 35,000

University of Leeds
Distance from city centre: Compact redbrick campus a mile away.

Leeds Metropolitan University
Distance from city centre: High-rise campus near the city centre. Beckett Park campus three miles away.

There is something for everyone in Leeds. The northern city has a dazzling array of clubs, including Nato, the Warehouse and Back to Basics, rated among the best in the country. And they stay open late. For shopping Leeds is unrivalled in the north of England with everything from high street shops, to Kirkgate Market and the only Harvey Nichols outside London.

The two universities huddle together in the city centre, and there is much interchange between their student unions: the older university's bar is one of the largest in Europe, with 96 beer pumps. Students who live out also tend to live in the same area, making a compact student enclave. Property rental prices are low, helped by the fact that the city is one of the few with a surplus of accommodation.

Students say that the cost of living is generally low, especially considering how friendly and lively the city is. Three theatres including the new £12 million West Yorkshire Playhouse, three cinema complexes and various independent cinemas offer reasonable provision for culture vultures, while sports enthusiasts will find plenty to watch and a good range of facilities for participation. The Yorkshire Dales, the Pennines, the North York Moors and the Vale of York on the city's doorstep allow ample opportunity for a peaceful escape should you be in need.

LEICESTER

Population: 272,000
Student population: 24,000

De Montfort University
Distance from city centre: One campus in the city centre, one at Scraptoft and a new campus in Milton Keynes.

Leicester University
Distance from city centre: Modern campus about one mile away.

When you think of Leicester, if you ever think of Leicester, your conception will probably be of a drab, dull Midlands town. While the city's architecture is unlikely to dazzle, Leicester is rich in green spaces and rejoices in its designation as Britain's first 'environment city'. Students find the city ideally sized: neither dauntingly large nor tediously small.

Student social life tends to be concentrated in the universities' good student unions (which have reciprocal arrangements), though the city centre is welcoming and friendly. The city has two main venues, the De Montfort and Granby Halls. They attract many touring rock bands. There are also many clubs to choose from.

Life in the city is cheap, and the fresh food market, reputedly the largest in England if not in Europe, helps student grants to stretch that little bit further. Eating out is easy, as there are more curry houses in Leicester than in Madras. The older university offers employment to students in, for example, halls of residence kitchens.

Leicester's central location means that it is conveniently placed for students from all over England. Accommodation is still not too hard to find and is reasonably priced. This is despite an influx of students in recent years.

LIVERPOOL

Population: 510,000
Student population: 34,000

University of Liverpool
Distance from city centre: Modern campus a few minutes' walk away.

Liverpool John Moores University
Distance from city centre: Sites all round the city centre, most situated between Liverpool's two cathedrals.

Liverpudlian pride is fierce, and can infect the many students who make the city their home. Crime rates may not be as high as many fear and the economy seems to be improving, indeed students insist that Liverpool is lively and Scousers generally friendly.

Ever-anxious to outdo Manchester, Liverpool claims to have the highest ratio of clubs to people in Britain. Sports enthusiasts will not need to be told of the city's passion for football, but other games are available as well. Five theatres and as many cinemas are available for those who prefer the arts.

Both universities are centrally located, near the two cathedrals which dominate the city's skyline. The compact city centre offers good shopping, and the renovated Albert Docks provide a magnificent home to up-market shopping centres and the renowned Northern Tate. Clubs and pubs in the city are ever busier.

Students tend to live and socialise around the reasonably central Smithdown Road area, where cheap rents contribute to the generally low cost of living in the city although the Kensington area is also popular. However, for those who need part-time work Liverpool is not ideal.

LONDON

Population: 6.7 million
Student population: 188,000

Twelve separate universities. The University of London is a loose affiliation of 40 colleges and other institutions. The other universities, with the exception of City University and Brunel, are all former poly-technics, upgraded in 1992.

Whether you are interested in parks or pubs, theatres or cinemas, shopping or sightseeing, museums or art galleries, dancing non-stop throughout the weekend or eating every cuisine under the sun, London can meet your requirements. The city will also present you with a fairly hefty bill for most of the above, and for travel between them. That said, the diligent hunter will find bargains, but the temptation to spend is omnipresent.

Whatever bargains can be found elsewhere, accommodation will be a major expense for every student: even if rents away from the smart areas of the city centre are slightly less astronomical, travel to and from college can easily eat away any savings made although recent efforts by ULU (the students union) mean most students can get thirty per-cent off bus and tube fares. The capital city's hectic pace can overwhelm as easily as it excites, and loneliness can be a problem in a city where you might be living miles away from your college. Nevertheless, London is justly renowned as one of the most exciting cities in the world and, for those who can strike a balance between making the most of life and avoiding spending their way to bankruptcy, it is the ideal place to be a student.

MANCHESTER

Population: 2.5 million
Student population: 60,000

University of Manchester
Distance from city centre: City-centre campus.

University of Manchester Institute of Science and Technology
Distance from city centre: City-centre campus.

Manchester Metropolitan University
Distance from city centre: Five city-centre campuses, plus one each
at Crewe and Alsager.

University of Salford
Distance from city centre: Campus in Salford, one mile from the city
centre.

The late 1980s saw 'Madchester' fêted as the epicentre of a musical and
cultural youthquake. The hype always stayed one step ahead of the reality,
however, and the scene's Altamont came when Uzi automatic rifles became
fashion accessories in nightclubs such as the Hacienda. But the city
remains probably the most fashionable in Britain for prospective students.

The city's club scene has diversified and survived. Clubs like Home and
the Paradise Factory have taken over from the Hacienda as the places to go.
The city centre is awash with theatres, museums, galleries and a choice of
music venues which range from the brand new Bridgewater Hall, to the Nyrex
arena which seats some 15,000. Female students in Manchester feel no more,
or less, safe than in any other big city. Male students, however, are the favoured
targets of an increasing number of muggings, both in the city centre and in
some of Manchester's less savoury suburbs such as Moss Side. It is largely for
safety reasons that students tend to live out in student-dominated enclaves,
like Fallowfield. These habits mirror the compact nature of the city-centre
university precinct, which holds three of Greater Manchester's four universities.

All that said, Manchester is still a great place for student life, as shown
by the fact that at least 30,000 students from outside the city choose to
study there. The centre is lively and rebuilding has begun on the multi-million pound project to create a new shopping and leisure quarter following
the 1996 IRA bombing. Sports fans are well provided for, and will get more
facilities as preparations continue for the Commonwealth Games in 2002.

NEWCASTLE

Population: 283,000

Student population: 28,500

University of Newcastle upon Tyne
Distance from city centre: Redbrick campus in the city centre.

University of Northumbria at Newcastle
Distance from city centre: Two main campuses in the city centre;
another three miles from the centre; others outside Newcastle, 15
miles away at Longhirst and 55 miles away in Carlisle.

Vying with Manchester as the most fashionable student city, Newcastle headed a recent poll for top university location, its vibrant nightlife an instant attraction for the young. The city's cultural legacy to the nation may include Viz,Alan Shearer and that infamous student tipple, Newcastle Brown Ale, but you should not allow this to put you off the capital of the northeast. Students enjoy living in the centre of a busy city with the best pubs and shopping facilities and one of the lowest costs of living in the north. Theatres, from the Playhouse to the Theatre Royal, and music venues, such as Riverside and the Telewest arena are also very popular. Burglaries are a problem even in the popular student areas such as Fenham. and Newcastle is not as tough as it may seem to those whose only experience of the city is derived from Jimmy Nail's pugilistic portrayal of Spender.

Shopping facilities are extensive. In addition to the usual medley of high-street names, department stores, markets and street stalls, Newcastle's near-by Gateshead Metro Centre is the biggest shopping and leisure complex in Europe. Pubs in the city centre are cheap and generally welcoming to students, though those around the Bigg Market tend to be very local-orientated at weekends. Clubs in the city are fairly traditional, though student nights are popular. The recently redeveloped Quayside Area has become a popular student haunt.

Don't expect to be able to get into the football ground, but Sunderland is not too far away for the game's devotees. Sir John Hall is gradually ensuring that other top-class sport is also available, and there is always Durham cricket in the summer.

Northumberland and the coast are easily accessible for those who wish to engage in quieter pursuits. Students benefit from the cheap Metro system which runs to the airport, city centre, train station and the coast.

NOTTINGHAM

Population: 262,000
Student population: 33,000

University of Nottingham
Distance from city centre: Attractive, landscaped campus about four miles from the city centre.

Nottingham Trent University
Distance from city centre: One city-centre campus; two more about four miles from the centre.

Home, ironically, to both Boots the Chemist and John Player the fag makers, Nottingham is probably still most famous for the legendary Robin Hood, whose redistribution of income policy would no doubt be welcomed by the city's 21,000 students.

The distance between the two universities means that their students tend to move in their own orbits, and live out in different areas: Lenton is favoured by students at the older university; Forest Fields by those at Nottingham Trent.

What Nottingham lacks in rock venues it makes up for in clubs. The accolade 'best clubbing city in the Midlands' may sound like damning with faint praise, but Nottingham is well provided for. The prices at some clubs may keep students at arm's length, but there are plenty of student nights. The locals are generally friendly to students. Indeed, many students choose to settle here after graduation.

The city is well-known for having the highest proportion of women in Britain. Although the crime figures suggest it is not quite as homely as it makes out, Nottingham is safe enough for those who are sensible. Accommodation takes some finding, but is not exorbitantly priced.

OXFORD

Population: 99,000
Student population: 25,000

Oxford University
Distance from city centre: Colleges throughout the city centre.

Oxford Brookes University
Distance from city centre: Two campuses in Headington, about two miles from the city centre; another campus in Wheatley, about six miles from the centre.

The screaming tyres of joyriders and angry shouts of rioters a few years ago shocked those who foolishly imagined Oxford a city of nothing more than dreaming spires and dilapidated dons. Oxford's small-scale riots grabbed attention just because they seemed so out of character. The city is ancient, though congested both with people and vehicles,and while you may well curse the constant influx of knap-sacked tourists who increase these numbers many inhabitants depend on the university-tourism industry for their livelihood.

The city is beautiful, if expensive for students: though prices are nearly as high as those in London, Oxford students do not receive the same weighted grant as their metropolitan counterparts. High costs are probably one reason why student social life tends to be concentrated in college bars and the Brookes' student union. The city centre is, however, blessed with plenty of pubs in which students can experience for themselves the Inspector Morse lifestyle.

Contact between students from the two universities is minimal, though probably greatest in the cosmopolitan Cowley Road area of the city, where many students, especially from the new university, find overpriced slum property in which to live. This area is also rich in cheap shops, restaurants and pubs which are slightly less oppressively Brideshead than those in the city centre. The city's clubs range from the dire to the indifferent but at least London is close by.

SHEFFIELD

Population: 503,000
Student population: 36,000

University of Sheffield
Distance from city centre: Redbrick buildings, most about three quarters of a mile west of the city centre.

Sheffield Hallam University
Distance from city centre: Five sites: one in the city centre; three between one and three miles from the centre; one seven miles away.

Sheffield, now equipped with a modern Supertram system, has long been one of the most popular cities with students, a significant proportion of whom choose to settle there after graduation. The city is situated on the edge of the Peak District, whose hills spill into Sheffield, adding to its charm but concentrating pollution in the city-centre basin.

With the exception of the Broomhill district, Sheffield lacks the student enclaves which can make students in some other cities feel part of a tight-knit, and perhaps even isolated, student community. In Sheffield, students live in many parts of the city and integrate well into the local community. Rents are generally reasonable and the cost of living lower than in many University towns.

Though the former capital of Britain's cutlery manufacturing industry does bear some of the hallmarks of industrial decay the rejuvenation of the industrial wasteland with new bars, cafés, restaurants and cinemas has put Sheffield on the map as an up and coming city. The 1991 World Student Games left the city with some of the best sports facilities in the country. Despite long-term unemployment the new Centretainment complex and the other proposed developments for the city centre mean that the service industry is providing more and more part-time work for residents and students.

Not over-endowed with cultural venues, the city relies heavily on the Crucible Theatre (when it is not hosting the World Snooker Championships) and the City Hall though Sheffield is home to the biggest independent cinema outside London, the Showroom. Club life is improving with numerous clubs such as the Republic really taking off, and the Arena is big enough to capture the big names of pop. More recently the National Centre for Popular Music has opened, and this helps to pull new life into the city.